PRINCIPLES OF WRITING

PRINCIPLES
OF
WRITING

JOHN HALVERSON
Princeton University

MASON COOLEY
Columbia University

THE MACMILLAN COMPANY
NEW YORK
COLLIER–MACMILLAN LIMITED
LONDON

Acknowledgment is made to the publishers and authors who granted permission to reprint excerpts from the following copyrighted works:

An American Dilemma by Gunnar Myrdal. Copyright © 1944, 1962 by Harper & Row, Publishers, Incorporated, and reprinted with their permission.

"The Function of Criticism" from *Selected Essays: 1917–1932*, "Lines for Cuscuscaraway and Mirza Murad Ali Beg" from *Collected Poems 1909–1962* by T. S. Eliot. Reprinted by permission of Harcourt, Brace & World, Inc., New York, and Faber and Faber Ltd., London.

"September Undergraduate" from *Saturday Review Education Supplement* (September 15, 1962). Reprinted by permission.

The Sun Also Rises [Fiesta] by Ernest Hemingway. Reprinted by permission of Charles Scribner's Sons, New York, Jonathan Cape Limited, London, and the executors of the Ernest Hemingway estate.

Twelve Million Black Voices by Richard Wright. Reprinted by permission of The Viking Press, New York, and Ernest Benn Ltd., London.

Two Cheers for Democracy by E. M. Forster. "Shooting an Elephant" and "Politics and the English Language" from *Shooting an Elephant and Other Stories*, "Marrackech" from *Such, Such Were the Joys* by George Orwell. Reprinted by permission of Harcourt, Brace & World, Inc.

Third Printing, 1966

Library of Congress catalog card number: 65-15187

THE MACMILLAN COMPANY, New York
COLLIER–MACMILLAN CANADA, LTD., Toronto, Ontario

PRINTED IN THE UNITED STATES OF AMERICA

FOR
PHIL S. GRANT

PREFACE

THIS book presupposes no special background or training on the part of the reader, but it is directed mainly to those who are in college or who have completed a college education; it is meant for people who read and who have a serious interest in writing. The book begins with comparatively elementary aspects of rhetoric and progresses quickly to more advanced matters. Anyone who is uninterested in generalizations about language and rhetoric may want to skip the first chapter; anyone who cannot benefit from a discussion of grammar and usage may skip the second chapter. The rest of the book should be read in sequence.

A few of the numerous quotations in the book have been altered slightly for the sake of appearance (minor abridgments without marks of ellipsis, occasional capitalization of letters, for example), but in no case has the meaning or style been distorted.

For their kind suggestions we wish to thank Mr. Scott Burton, Miss Ann Cooley, Dr. Allan Cox, Mr. J. G. Case, and Professor Lynn Altenbernd.

J. H.
M. C.

CONTENTS

ix

PART FOUR:
ORGANIZATION AND DEVELOPMENT

PART ONE

INTRODUCTION

1

RHETORIC
AND LANGUAGE

W HEN a good political journalist like Richard Rovere sets out
to persuade his readers that the antics of a Senator are dangerous, he does so with the experienced writer's feeling for forceful
language, accurate logic, and significant evidence; he also has a good
idea of his particular audience's expectations, what needs to be explained and defended, and what can be taken for granted. If he
succeeds in convincing his readers of peril in the Senate, then his
essay becomes a proper subject for rhetorical study. Again, if a
literary critic like Edmund Wilson manages to make dull memoirs
of the Civil War fascinating to the general reader, he has rhetorical
lessons to teach. We want to find out how he does it. That is what
rhetoric is. It studies the ways good writers use language persuasively,
and then formulates generalizations about these methods.

The Aims of Rhetorical Study

Obviously, rhetoric must be concerned with many aspects of language. Since persuasive language must be idiomatic, accurate, structurally coherent, and psychologically effective, rhetoric is concerned
with grammar and usage, vocabulary, logic, and at least a rudimentary
theory of the psychological effects of language. Generalizations about
these matters have to be presented with some system; it is even
desirable to offer some rules. But they will not have the reliability of
scientific laws. When a chemist combines nitric acid with hydro-
sulfuric acid, a certain result is guaranteed. The writer does not have
such assurance; he must be content with approximations and rules
of thumb, for the effects of his statements are never altogether cal-
culable. A writer is a man speaking to other men, not a laboratory
technician manipulating inanimate matter, and human beings are

3

notoriously more perverse than chemicals, particularly when appealed to for comprehension and assent. The successful writer must have a "feel" for his work, something beyond the mechanical application of rhetorical precepts. Nevertheless, there is a fund of practical knowledge about writing, which, if not indispensable for every writer, can be of great value to most.

Part of this knowledge concerns the avoidance of common mistakes in writing. Handbooks on writing often approach their subject negatively, telling the writer what to avoid and how to correct errors; such advice is useful, and this book has plenty of it, but it is less than half the problem. More important is the study of positive means for gaining assent. The prizefighter who learns only *not* to lead with his right and *not* to let his guard down may avoid mortal injury, but he is not likely to be on the fastest road to fame and fortune; no one has ever learned to write well just by avoiding errors. Prose that is no more than correct amounts to very little—hence our emphasis on positive ways for the writer to achieve the effects he wants, or should want. For a small example, though we dutifully warn the writer away from participles that dangle, we also show what participial phrases are *good* for. Moreover, we try to explain how things work, and when—to give reasons for the rules and suggestions put forward. If the explanations seem labored in some places and incomplete in others, we hope at least to persuade the reader that rhetorical canons are not entirely arbitrary.

Good rhetoric is purposive. In well-written prose there is a positive reason behind every choice of words, syntactical structures, and modes of argument. And every choice takes place in a unique rhetorical situation. Thus the kind of sweeping advice represented by the familiar handbook rubric to "vary your sentence structure" is hollow. Mere aimless variation has no guarantee of being either pleasing or effective. It is rather like telling a housepainter to vary his colors: the result may be fascinating, but you may not want to live with it. The writer should know what choices he has and why one choice is to be preferred to another. He should be aware of what he is doing and why he is doing it.

Though instruction and example are helpful, a knowledge of rhetorical theory by no means ensures rhetorical skill. That comes from practice and experiment. A knowledge of rhetoric makes practice more fruitful by increasing the writer's alertness to the possibilities of language and by enlarging his capacity for intelligent self-criticism. "Born writers" no doubt exist, but they are the happy few; most of us acquire whatever competence we have by study and practice. Many distinguished writers, as a matter of discipline, devote a regular portion of their day to writing, whether or not the Muse is present. The example is instructive: the good writer practices his craft; he writes as much and as often as he can. We can do no more than urge the necessity for practice and provide exercises and suggestions for composition at the end of the book.

Though we urge moderation and prudence, we do not mean to discourage experiment, for trying out new things is essential to any writer's development. But until the writer is sure of himself, his experiments are best treated as experiments, and not offered as finished achievements. The temptation to show off new skills is as hard to resist in composition as anywhere else. A writer who suddenly discovers metaphor may run wild, sowing figures of speech broadcast. Such enthusiasm is valuable, but not necessarily a matter for public display.

Writing well also involves more than learning a craft. Since writing is about something, since words refer to things and ideas, the writer's accomplishments are inevitably restricted by his knowledge and taste. Anyone who can read and has a willing mind can make good use of the basic principles of predication, say, or of denotation. But the effective use of allusion, on the other hand, depends on the writer's sophistication, as does his sense of the appropriateness of any rhetorical device. Good literary judgment is hardly to be acquired from a book such as this, or indeed from any one book; it is something that forms gradually with education, experience, and maturity. The more youthful the writer, the more he will need the advice of the experienced—usually professional teachers.

Continual attention to the way one is writing is most important for the relatively unpracticed writer, but eventually this awareness becomes only semiconscious. The experienced writer does not ordinarily weigh every word and phrase. We do not suppose that C. S. Lewis ever sat down to the typewriter, saying to himself, "Paratactic sentence structure is what is wanted here," or that A. M. Schlesinger, Jr., ever thinks, "I will now begin this paragraph with a topic sentence in the form of a terse, balanced epigram." They may have, for all we know, but it is not likely. For experienced writers, style becomes a habit requiring little conscious thought; it is a relatively natural and easy form of expression, secondary, as it should be, to the ideas to be communicated. Yet in revising, even the most accomplished writers usually give careful thought to style. They may not count stresses to check the rhythm of their prose (though Flaubert did), for in such matters instinct and taste guide them unconsciously; but they, and their editors, pay close attention to diction, sentence structure, and logical organization. Awareness, then, of the possibilities of style is valuable at every level of skill in writing.

Writer and Reader

In this book we make two fundamental assumptions about language: that it is meant to communicate and that it is meant to persuade. The content, the meaning to be communicated, is of first and absolute importance, but is not in itself a part of the study of rhetoric, which takes for granted a substance to work with. Unfortunately, many unpracticed writers and even a few experienced ones seem to think that rhetoric is a substitute for thought, that fancy language can compensate for feeble content. This is wishful thinking, surely. Is any intelligent reader really misled by a pleasing style to think a silly writer a profound one or an ignorant writer an informed one? Without thought and substance, the most glittering style soon becomes tedious.

Language meant to communicate must be clear: communication cannot succeed when words and sentences are misunderstood or not understood at all. The first purpose of rhetoric, then, is to ensure clarity. Ideally, the reader should understand at first reading and with reasonable certitude just what the writer is saying. English is, however, a complicated and tricky language, and the ideal of immediate comprehension can seldom be more than approximated. But just because the language *is* replete with potential ambiguities, there is all the more need to work for clarity: exact vocabulary, clear sentence structure, valid logic. Clarity is not, however, to be confused with simplicity; good prose does not aim at the style of the primer or at mathematical bareness. Neither can convey the tone, attitude, and background of suggestion that are as vital to prose as its denotative meaning.

The devices of rhetoric are meant to reinforce meaning and illuminate it, not disguise it. Those who think of the art of writing as a decorative process, like flower arranging, seriously misunderstand the nature of that art, and their own writing may suffer from the indiscriminate strewing of rhetorical rosebuds. Pretentious or highly decorated prose focuses the reader's attention on the *way* something is said, distracting him from *what* is said.

The second purpose of language is, in its broadest sense, persuasion. Any effort to communicate implies an attempt to persuade. The intent is obvious in argumentative writing; it is less apparent in exposition and narrative. Yet even the driest, most impersonal scientific report attempts to convince the reader of its accuracy and objectivity; the most subjective "self-expression" has the implicit intention of convincing the reader of its authenticity and significance; even description and narrative aim at getting the reader to accept the author's view of events.

If the writer is to be persuasive, he must consider his prospective audience. When he knows his readers, as does, say, the geologist writing for fellow geologists or the president of a university preparing a memorandum for the trustees, he must keep in mind their potential reactions. When a more general and indistinct audience is addressed, it is harder to decide what will be convincing. But the writer can at least be guided by what he knows of most people's likes and dislikes, including his own. In the long run, rationality, honesty, and temperance—ideals with a real life, after all—are persuasive. The writer who regularly flouts reason and distorts his material invites suspicion and discredit. It is surely safe to generalize further that most people are repelled by conceit, spite, and wishy-washiness; that most people respect modesty, generosity, and strong conviction; and that no one likes to be bored or to be treated as an inferior or to be ordered about.

To get readers to modify their opinions or to think about issues they would rather avoid is a great challenge. If the writer is to meet it, he must at least be taken seriously; he does not have to be solemn or portentous, but he must be listened to with respect. He should give the impression of authority and integrity—which is not much more than saying that he should know what he is writing about, and write about it honestly. He, in turn, must respect his audience, treating his readers as his peers.

Much of what we have just been saying comes down to an admonition to observe elementary standards of civilized behavior. The purely practical side of it comes down to this: don't alienate the reader. It is hard enough even to communicate to a reader who has been offended, much less persuade him.

Consideration for the audience need not, and should not, involve moral compromise. But diplomatic language and diplomatic silence are not vices. The word *underdeveloped* applied to certain nations is more agreeable and indeed more accurate than *backward*. Furthermore, because an honest opinion is honestly held, it does not follow that it must always be announced, in season and out. Neither virtue nor prudence requires you to tell your host that he is a bore, or your opponent in an argument that he is an ignoramus. One is not compromised by silence in such cases. Yet sometimes straightforward denunciation is hardly avoidable. Not everyone deserves respect, and misplaced deference is contemptible. But if a direct attack must be made, it should at least be relevant to the issue at hand, and free of personal malice.

Which Language?

We do not plan to comment on every kind of language to be read or heard. Dialects, argot, experimental writing, the language of fiction and poetry—none of these are of immediate concern. Our subject is rather one part of a nebulous linguistic area called "standard English." The term defies precise definition, but refers approximately to the language written and spoken by most educated Americans and Englishmen. Within this immense totality, we are particularly concerned with a small but various segment, namely, good written English. This we take to be the language of writers of recognized achievement, that is, writers who are awarded prizes for their writing, who have won widespread and authoritative praise, who, at the very least, have been thought good enough to be included in college readers of model prose. Among these writers are men of great literary stature such as Thoreau, Emerson, Arnold, Ruskin, and E. M. Forster, accomplished journalists (Richard Rovere, for example), critics (Edmund Wilson, C. S. Lewis), historians (G. M. Trevelyan, Arthur Schlesinger, Jr.), scientists (Sir Arthur Eddington, George Gamow), philosophers (R. G. Collingwood), public men (Roosevelt, Kennedy). Theirs is the kind of writing you might expect to see in such publications as the *New Yorker*, the *Atlantic Monthly*, the New York *Times, Encounter,* the *Observer, Scientific American, Foreign Affairs,* the *New York Review of Books,* and most of the established literary and political journals.

To approach the standard from the other end, it does not include the kind of writing characteristic of the sensational press, the learned journals, or the avant-garde literary magazines. It does not include the *Reader's Digest* blandness of a Norman Vincent Peale or the vigorous vulgarity of a Westbrook Pegler; it does not include the ponderous prose of a John Dewey, the crankiness of an Ezra Pound, or the "oriental magnificence" of an F. R. Leavis. For whatever the popular success of the first group and however great the achievements of the second, the style of all is outside what we take to be "good written English." Also excluded are certain styles of acknowledged brilliance but of so intensely personal, even idiosyncratic, a nature as to be uninstructive for most writers. In an imitator the exclamatory eloquence of D. H. Lawrence can be catastrophic; the dense metaphorical texture of Wallace Stevens' prose will not serve as a practical model for other writers.

Despite such exclusions, a very wide range of styles remains, and there is ample room for disagreement about their merits. No one style or writer is the perfect model, and we do not regard every distinguished author as a sacred cow; the best writers sometimes write badly. You may for good reasons dislike the style of some of the excerpts we quote approvingly; nevertheless, the style is probably worth discussing. Whether a particular writer happens to appeal to us or not, we are almost certain to be able to learn from him. The way a dedicated and talented writer uses language always repays study, because he opens up to us possibilities in the art of writing that would probably never have occurred to us by ourselves. Even if we finally reject his style, he widens our awareness of the range of stylistic alternatives available within good written English.

As the foregoing remarks suggest, this rhetoric is based on how good writers do *in fact* write English, not on how we might happen to think they *ought* to have written it. Thus we are brought to the brink of a pleasant controversy, still bubbling, particularly in academic circles, about "conservative" and "liberal" attitudes toward language. The teaching of English was once a stern but tranquil business of inculcating The Rules; there were such things as good grammar and bad grammar; usage was correct or incorrect. But then the linguists came along to point out some uncomfortably plain truths about the Emperor's clothes. The rules of grammar are not, after all, sent down from heaven; they are generalizations about linguistic practice, accurate or inaccurate, but hardly good or bad. Furthermore, spoken language is obviously prior to the written language derived from it, and therefore more essential. Some prescriptive grammarians still cry "Anarchy!" at the linguists, and some linguists still sneer "Tyranny!" at the grammarians. But by now the argument has become relatively sensible and civilized.

The conservative argues, rightly we think, that the inevitable changes language undergoes demand a certain resistance if a bond is to be maintained between the past and the present. How many people can now read Hamilton, Jefferson, or John Adams easily? And if *The Federalist* is a hard book to many, the plays of Shakespeare are a closed book to more. Besides, there is nothing inherently desirable about linguistic change in itself. The conservative also argues reasonably that if language is frequently illogical in practice, it does not follow that we should endorse or cultivate that illogicality. If in general practice English is muddled and crude, it does not follow that it should be. Prescriptive grammar becomes, then, an ideal —a statement of what the grammarian thinks would make language logical, precise, and elegant; it need not be an accurate description of general practice. On the other hand, conservatism has the unfortunate tendency to maintain the *status quo* for its own sake, or even worse, to assume that the *status quo* of two generations ago still obtains. The result can be a loss of the sense of reality. Consider an example from Fowler's masterfully instructive and entertaining *Modern English Usage*. After demonstrating the logic of the distinction between *shall* and *will*, *should* and *would* in the first person, he prefaces his illustrations with the characteristically diffident observation that "the *wills & woulds* in the following examples are wrong" —this followed by almost fifty perfectly idiomatic and unambiguous examples of *will* and *would* culled, as he says, from "newspapers of the better sort." *Something* is wrong, certainly: the undaunted conservative is sometimes to be found defending the barricades long after the battle is over.

Some liberal linguists in their first revolutionary fervor seemed inclined to reject all previous rhetorical canons. Now, though a few minor intransigents remain, most linguists admit the desirability of clarity and even sometimes beauty. But they rightly insist on linguistic realism: grammatical rules and rhetorical precepts must be based on the facts of usage, not imposed arbitrarily from without. This admirable realism, however, is sometimes at odds with a second basic tenet: the priority of the spoken language. The initial successes of descriptive linguistics were based on analysis of language as spoken; the written language was often regarded with suspicion and sometimes contempt. There has been, then, a natural tendency to make the facts of spoken usage the standard for the written word. But in fact, most people modify their language when they turn from speaking to writing. For instance, many people, including the most learned, do not in conversation maintain the case distinctions of pronouns. Even professors of English can be heard saying shamelessly, "I don't know who he's talking about." Why not, then, take the same liberties in writing? The question implies the misconception that spoken language, because prior to written language, is therefore superior. If anything, the opposite is nearer the truth. The words of Jefferson remain a living influence not because they were spoken but because they were written. The spoken word is ephemeral; books endure. And the conventions of writing are not identical with those of speech. English, unlike Chinese, has never had a fully developed separate literary language divorced from common speech, but written English is consistently more discriminating about grammar and diction than spoken English. Very often the man who says, "I don't know who he's talking about" will *write*, "I don't know *whom* he is talking about." The man who says, "Smith is full of baloney," will probably *write*, "Professor Smith is mistaken."

In the face of such plain facts, the linguist sometimes invokes the invidious term *prestige language*, meaning a set of linguistic conventions associated with persons and classes of high social position. In England, for instance, one dialect with its variants is identified with the aristocracy, good family, public school, and an Oxford or Cambridge education—"upper-class speech," in short. All that is meant, then, by "good" English is the English of a prestige group. But whatever may be the situation in Great Britain, this view does not fit the facts of American English. If a particular set of linguistic conventions has prestige it is, more often than not, because of its intrinsic merits, not because of the writer's elevated social position. What do Mark Twain, Henry James, Isaac Asimov, James Baldwin, T. S. Eliot, and Richard Wright have in common besides their literary abilities?

Good writers know that the spoken language is the life-giving source of the written language and that it is therefore perilous to stray far from speech. They also know that they are the inheritors of a long tradition of written language equally vital. If they disregard many of the rituals of prescriptive grammar, they also reject the carelessness and license of the spoken language. Between the Tower of Ivory and the Tower of Babel, the writers of recognized excellence have long pursued their own course. It is they whom we try to follow in this book.

Individual Style

Most writers, if they write steadily over a period of years, evolve an individual style that suits their own personalities and aims. A few writers form a style as personal as their signatures, so identifiable that it can easily be parodied; thus Henry James and Ernest Hemingway, representing extremes of involuted complexity and bare terseness, are probably our most parodied modern authors. But writers of such individuality are rare. Most good writers of nonfiction achieve a degree of individuality in their prose, but it is unobtrusive. Their writing has some personal coloring, but they share the main characteristics of their style with many other writers. When a style suits the writer and his subject, there is no reason why it should be markedly different from someone else's.

The beginning writer should not be overanxious about developing a personal style, for style grows slowly, naturally, and to a great extent, unconsciously. If he strains after a strikingly individual mode of expression, the result will probably be eccentricity or affectation. If he goes to the other extreme and tries to duplicate completely the style of an admired author, almost invariably the ring of falseness will be heard. Nevertheless, as an exercise, it can be helpful to imitate the style of others. The imitation of model prose is an ancient and useful exercise, but it is useful because it can help the writer to get the feel of various stylistic possibilities, not because it can teach him to write like Cicero or Carlyle. It is a good deal more useful to study an admired style closely and adapt the results of analysis to one's own prose, using one's own words and ideas. This procedure can open up wide ranges of rhetorical alternatives that can be consciously selected and rationally used. Much of this book is devoted to such analysis, illustrating the purposes and effects of a variety of rhetorical forms available to any writer.

Personal style emerges from choices based on the writer's sensibility, judgment, and purpose. He gradually finds certain syntactical patterns, certain types of vocabulary, certain modes of organizing and unfolding his thought that are congenial to him. His particular combination of choices will produce his particular style. Since there is great variation within the category of good English prose, such handbook imperatives as "Avoid the passive voice" or "Prefer words of Anglo-Saxon origin to words of Latin origin" can stifle the development of individuality in a writer who accepts them uncritically. What these imperatives really mean is, "If you want to write in a *certain style,* then avoid the passive voice and Latinate words." There is an excellent hard, straightforward style to which these two particular recommendations are relevant. There is also a dignified and formal style, quite successful in experienced hands, for which such advice is quite beside the point. An effective and satisfying individual style develops naturally from study and practice, not from the mechanical application of arbitrary rules, and not from the self-conscious cultivation of idiosyncrasy.

2

GRAMMAR, AND ITS PROBLEMS

SOME knowledge of grammatical structure being necessary for an understanding of rhetoric, we present here a minimal sketch, neither thorough nor rigorous, of English grammar. We assume the reader is a native speaker of English and has at least some acquaintance, even if vague, with traditional grammatical terms. Such terms (*subject, object, verb*, etc.) are at best not easy to define precisely; in so brief a presentation as follows, it is nearly impossible to do so. Nevertheless, enough information will be given to enable the reader to follow the rhetorical discussion. In addition to our necessarily simplified definitions, a number of illustrations are given to remind the reader of what he probably already knows.

We shall also comment on familiar problems and bugbears of usage (pronoun case, the split infinitive, dangling modifiers, and the like) associated with particular constructions and parts of speech. Feelings run high in this area. There is hardly anyone professionally involved in writing who does not have some hobby-horse of usage to ride: here, an editor who cannot abide the expression "I would like"; there, a teacher who bridles at "the reason is because." We cannot hope that our recommendations in these matters will satisfy everyone; here and there a hobby-horse will get scratched. But our observations, it might be remembered, are based on the practice of respectable writers, with some support from sweet reason.

Of primary grammatical importance is the *function* of words and word groups: how they work in a sentence, what they do in context. What they may be in isolation or in the abstract is of little importance to our ultimate purpose, which is to explain effective means of expression and communication.

Parts of Speech

The parts of speech are traditionally defined semantically, that is, according to what they refer to in the real world: "a noun is the name

of a person, place, or thing," "a verb names an action or state," etc.
Such definitions have seen good service for generations and are still
useful. But they are seldom really definitive. In the sentence "The
penalty for murder is hanging," the words *murder* and *hanging* may
surely be taken to indicate actions or states, but neither is a verb.
Semantic definitions also encourage a disregard for the context in
which a word is used, and out of context it is often impossible to say
what part of speech a particular word is. The word *back*, for instance,
obviously works very differently in "scratch my back," "back the car
out," "go back," and "back street." Or take a less obvious example,
tree. A noun? Not in the sentence "Old Blue will tree the possum."
Still, *tree* usually is a noun, and semantic definitions are not without
practical value.

It is also useful to define the parts of speech morphologically, that
is, according to their form and alteration of form; thus adverbs usually
end in *-ly*; nouns usually form their plural by adding *-s*. Another
method of definition uses word frames; for example, any word that
will fit idiomatically into the frame "The _____ house" is an
adjective.

None of these approaches, however, tells us much about the
function of words in a sentence. Let us illustrate what we mean by
function from an aphorism of Thoreau's:

The mass of men lead lives of quiet desperation.

How do the words work here? The broadest and most fundamental
function is the assertion made by the whole sentence. There is a
subject—what Thoreau is talking about: "The mass of men"; and
there is a predicate—what he is saying *about* that subject: that they
"lead lives of quiet desperation." Within this larger framework of
"complete" subject and predicate (the framework of nearly all sentences in relatively formal writing), each individual word has its own
function. Thus *mass* is the "simple" subject; *The* modifies it; *of* connects *mass* and *men*; *lives* is the object of the verb; *quiet* modifies
desperation. We can speak, then, of such functional categories as
subject, object, verb, modifier, and connective. These categories indicate the syntactical relationship the words in a statement have to
one another. Furthermore, certain groups of words function like
single words. The prepositional phrase *of men* is a modifier of *mass*;
of quiet desperation modifies *lives*.

The parts of speech are traditionally named noun, pronoun, verb,
adjective, adverb, conjunction, preposition, and interjection. On the

basis of similar function, nouns and pronouns are sometimes grouped together as "substantives," adjectives and adverbs as "modifiers," and conjunctions and prepositions as "connectives."

The following are brief preliminary definitions of the most important grammatical terms used. They will be more fully explained further on, but this list may serve as a convenient reference.

> *Substantives* (*nouns* and *pronouns*) function as subject, object, appositive, predicate nominative.
>
> *Verbs* head or constitute the predication made of a subject (the predication is whatever is asserted of the subject).
>
> *Adjectives* modify (describe, identify, qualify) substantives.
>
> *Adverbs* modify verbs and other modifiers.
>
> *Conjunctions* join together constructions having the same function, and connect subordinate clauses to other constructions.
>
> *Prepositions* connect a substantive object to another word.
>
> *Interjections* ("Oh!" "Heavens!" "Alas!") are exclamations that have no important syntactical relationship to other words in the sentence.
>
> A *clause* is a grammatically complete group of words containing a subject and predicate. (By "grammatically complete" we mean that such words as prepositions, conjunctions, and transitive verbs that require further words to complete their sense are so completed.)
>
> A *subordinate* (*dependent, relative*) *clause* is a clause used as a part of speech.
>
> An *independent clause* is a clause not so used.
>
> A *phrase* is a group of words without subject and predicate functioning as a unit and as a part of speech.
>
> A *sentence* contains at least one independent clause and is grammatically complete.
>
> An *elliptical clause* consists of a subordinating conjunction followed by a construction in which a subject and a form of the verb *be* may be understood but are not expressed: "While sitting in the theater, I smelled smoke" (= "While I *was* sitting . . ."): "When in doubt, punt" (= "When *you are* in doubt . . .").

Substantives: Nouns

A substantive is any word that functions as the subject of a clause, as the object of a verb, verbal, or preposition, as an appositive, or as a predicate nominative.

Of all *branches* of *education*, the *science* of *gauging people* and *events* by their relative *importance* defies *study* most insolently. [HENRY ADAMS]

All the italicized words are substantives: *branches* because it is object of the preposition *of*, *education* because it is the object of the second *of*, *gauging* because it is the object of the third *of*. The preposition obviously requires another word or other words to complete its meaning. To say, "Of all—," and then break off is to elicit the immediate question, "Of all *what?*" The answer to the question, the completion of the sense, is the object of the preposition. Similarly *people* answers the question "gauging what?" and is the object of the verbal; *study* is for the same reason the object of the verb *defies*. *Science* is the simple subject of the sentence, and *importance* is the object of the preposition *by*.

A foolish *consistency* is the *hobgoblin* of little *minds*. . . . [EMERSON]

Here *consistency* is the subject of the sentence, *minds* the object of the preposition *of*; *hobgoblin* is a predicate nominative, that is, a word that renames the subject after a linking verb.

Roger *Taney*, the Chief *Justice*, announced the court's *decision*.

The appositive (*Justice* here), like the predicate nominative, renames another substantive; the difference is, of course, that this renaming is in a contiguous phrase rather than in the predicate. *Roger Taney* is the subject of the sentence; *decision* is the object of the verb.

Substantives: Pronouns

All the preceding examples are nouns. Pronouns are simply substitutes for nouns. The chief classes of pronouns are as follows:

PERSONAL:		First person	Second person	Third person		
	Nominative	I	you	he	she	it
Singular	*Possessive*	my, mine	your, yours	his	her, hers	its
	Objective	me	you	him	her	it
	Nom.	we	you		they	
Plural	*Poss.*	our, ours	your, yours		their, theirs	
	Obj.	us	you		them	

RELATIVE:

Singular	*Nom.*	who, which, that
and	*Poss.*	whose, [of which], —
Plural	*Obj.*	whom, which, that

INTERROGATIVE: who, whose, whom; which; what.

INDEFINITE: whoever, whosever, whomever; someone; anyone; one; etc.

Pronouns function in a sentence as nouns do:

He announced *it* in 1857.

He is the subject, *it* the object of the verb. The important semantic difference between nouns and pronouns is that the pronouns mean practically nothing until we know what nouns they are substituting for. The above sentence conveys no real information unless it is preceded by some such sentence as "Roger Taney announced the court's decision," where *Roger Taney* and *decision* tell us what *He* and *it* refer to; the nouns are the *antecedents* of the pronouns.

Pronoun Reference

Pronoun reference is a common writing problem, not because of any inherent grammatical complexity, but because of inattentiveness to the elementary rule of common sense that in context the antecedent of any pronoun should be clear. To the extent that the antecedent is not clear, communication breaks down. Such a sentence as the following is both obscure and exasperating:

He left the sculpture in a filthy storeroom; it was disgraceful.

There is no way of telling whether *it* refers to the sculpture, the storeroom, or the act of leaving the sculpture. Occasionally, ambiguous pronoun reference is ludicrous:

If the baby doesn't thrive on milk, boil it.

The necessity of using the same form of the pronoun for more than one antecedent sometimes produces mild panic in a writer. If he writes, for example,

Lieutenant Jones told the general he was sorry he had wrecked the plane,

he may wonder whether the pronouns are sufficiently clear, and perhaps, to ensure clarity, resort to the unattractive expedient of adding the antecedent in parentheses:

Lieutenant Jones told the general he was sorry he (Jones) had wrecked the plane.

But probably in most contexts the reader would already have been told which person had wrecked the plane and would understand the original sentence without difficulty. When there is genuine ambiguity, a better solution is to abridge the sentence to eliminate the doubtful pronoun.

> He hoped to see him when *he* came to the club

may be abridged:

> He hoped to see him at the club.

Similarly, our first example,

Lieutenant Jones told the general he was sorry he had wrecked the plane,

may be abridged:

Lieutenant Jones told the General he was sorry to have wrecked the plane.

Or better yet:

> Lieutenant Jones apologized to the General for wrecking the plane.

The most frequent problem of pronoun reference is an indistinctness resulting from excessive use of *it, this, that,* and *which* to refer not to single antecedent nouns but to whole phrases and clauses or merely implied ideas. "Broad reference"—the use of a pronoun to refer to a phrase, clause, sentence, or group of sentences—is common in the best writers; there is nothing intrinsically reprehensible about it. But it does become a vice when used too frequently, for it leads to vagueness. Broad reference is particularly deplorable and self-defeating when, as often happens, it is a symptom of fuzzy thought. Even in so brief an example as the following, it is easy to feel the fog gathering more thickly with each recurrence of *this,* even though each instance of *this* may be meaningful. The writer is proposing a college course in advertising analysis.

The class would study advertising generally. In addition to *this,* the teacher would conduct a small section in the actual experience of the advertising techniques. *This* would consist of having the students take some of the tests that motivational research workers use in their probing. *This* would enable the students to see how they work and how effective they can be.

Not only is *this* vague, but the twice-repeated *they* in the last sentence is ambiguous. Any propensity to overuse the broad reference should be promptly suppressed. One way to do so is by making certain that there is a single preceding noun (or series of nouns) that may be substituted for the pronoun. A second way is to revise the sentence to eliminate the pronoun altogether. For example:

Pinwhistle turned out to be a hopelessly incompetent mayor, but he had been chosen by the party leaders themselves; *this* was why they were particularly embarrassed. Now they wanted him out of office, *which* greatly surprised Pinwhistle.

The italicized pronouns with their broad reference can easily be omitted by reconstructing the sentences:

Pinwhistle turned out to be a hopelessly incompetent mayor, and since the party leaders themselves had chosen him, they were particularly embarrassed. To his great surprise, they now wanted him out of office.

The use of the pronoun *they* with only an inferential antecedent is colloquial and seldom appears in more formal prose:

In Texas, *they* grow a lot of cattle.
I wonder if *they* will get to the moon this year.
They have a special office in Washington to deal with crank letters.

Impersonal constructions are usually to be preferred: "Many cattle are raised," "I wonder if a man will be placed on the moon," "There is a special office." This usage is not the same as that in the expression "They say . . ." which is a generally acceptable idiom.

Pronoun Case: Who, Whom

The pronouns *he, she, they,* and *who* are the only substantives that still have a special form for the objective case. Keeping the cases of the personal pronouns straight is not a great problem for most writers. Once in a while a writer (and rather often a speaker), overlooking syntax, says "between George and *I*" or "There has been some talk about you and *I*." The pronoun, being the second object of the preposition, should logically be in the objective form *me*. A similar confusion sometimes occurs when the personal pronoun is used (or seems to be used) as an attributive modifier: "The award was presented to *we* girls." In more careful usage, the pronoun here would always be *us*.

The relative pronoun *who* can be troublesome. As the name suggests, it is used only in relative clauses. Its case is determined by its function *within* the clause. The objective form *whom* appears to be dying out of speech, but is still carefully preserved in formal writing.

In 1857, Roger Taney, *who* was then Chief Justice, wrote the Dred Scott decision.

Who is in the nominative case because it is the subject of the subordinate clause.

Taney, *whom* Seward denounced, denied collusion with the Democrats.

Whom is in the objective case because it is the object of the verb of the subordinate clause, *denounced*. Similarly:

> Taney, by *whom* the decision was written, was a Democrat.
> Taney, *whom* Seward planned to denounce, bided his time.

The first *whom* is in the objective case because it is the object of the preposition *by*; the second *whom* is the object of the infinitive *to denounce*.

Doubtful instances may be resolved easily by considering what the form of the personal pronoun would be in an equivalent independent clause. Thus:

> *He* was then Chief Justice.
> Seward denounced *him*.
> The decision was written by *him*.
> Seward planned to denounce *him*.

And in somewhat more complicated structures:

> Thompson was the man *who/whom* the Chairman thought was the best choice for the position. ("The Chairman thought *he* was the best choice"—hence *who* is right.)

> Thompson was the man *who/whom* the Chairman thought to be the best choice for the position. ("The Chairman thought *him* to be the best choice"—hence *whom* is right.)

That

As a relative pronoun *that* may be substituted, within certain limits of idiom, for *who, whom,* and *which*. The pronoun is used only in restrictive adjective clauses (clauses necessary to identify the word they modify—see p. 283). Thus we can say,

> The person *that* I came with has disappeared,

as well as

> The person *whom* I came with . . .

but not

> Miss Armbruster, *that* I came with, has disappeared.

We can say,

> The judge *that* wrote the decision was Roger Taney,

but not

> Roger Taney, *that* wrote the decision, was Chief Justice.

We must say,

> Roger Taney, *who* wrote the decision . . .
> Miss Armbruster, *whom* I came with . . .

The idea, still heard occasionally, that the relative pronoun *that* should not be used to refer to persons should be disregarded as a fiction.

Which

The pronoun *which* is always neuter but may refer to persons when its antecedent is a collective noun regarded as a unit: "The committee *which* was appointed by the President . . ."; "The team, *which* was in good spirits . . ."

Whose, of Which

The possessive case of the relative pronoun, because a form of *who*, has in the past been used to refer only to persons, not things. The neuter equivalent is *of which*.

Nash, *whose* mansion is now for sale, was a famous figure in the eighteenth century.

Nash's mansion, the chimneys *of which* have crumbled, is now for sale.

But the tendency in modern English to place relative pronouns at the beginning of relative clauses has led to increasing use of *whose* to refer to things as well as persons.

[Frank Lloyd Wright's] circular tower creates an exhibition room *whose* dimensions in no way can be modified to suit the needs of a particular showing. [LEWIS MUMFORD]

This is a generally acceptable form, though the most formal prose still prefers the *of which* construction.

Agreement of Pronoun and Antecedent

The pronoun should agree with its antecedent in number and gender.

This rule is obvious enough except when *everyone, everybody,* or *each* is the antecedent. In colloquial English, plural pronouns are often used to refer to these words:

> Everyone left when *they* were asked to.
> Each of them recognized *their* duty.

Formal written English requires a singular pronoun:

> Everyone left when *he* was asked to.
> Each of them recognized *his* duty.

When strict adherence to the principle produces a silly-sounding result—

> When the fire started, everyone rushed to the exits, but he couldn't get out—

the sentence is best revised to eliminate the problem altogether ("—but no one could get out").

Verbs

A succinct yet accurate definition of the verb is very difficult; and we assume that the reader knows a verb—at least in a general way—when he sees one. Examples:

> The President *relieved* the general of his command.
> Many *were startled* by the news.
> The general *is* now a business executive.
> No one *knows* what the future *will bring.*

The predication of a sentence—whatever is asserted of the subject of the sentence—is headed by a verb; the rest of the predication depends in some way on the verb. Often the verb by itself constitutes the entire predication ("He *fled,*" "Mary *was weeping,*" "No solution to this problem *has been found*").

The distinctive morphological features of most verbs are, first, that they can be altered to indicate time (I *go,* I *have gone,* I *went,* I *had gone,* I *shall go,* I *shall have gone*) and, second, that they have the ending *-s* in the third person singular, present indicative (*I go,* but *he goes; you know,* but *she knows*). Verbs are usefully classified as transitive, intransitive, and linking verbs. If, in its sentence, a verb has an object, it is transitive; if it does not have an object, it is intransitive. The same verb may be transitive in one sentence and intransitive in another.

He *is shooting* grouse today. (The verb is transitive because it has an object, *grouse*.)

He *is shooting* well today. (The verb is intransitive because there is no object.)

I *read* a French novel last night. (Transitive)

I *read* all night. (Intransitive)

The linking verbs (chiefly, *be, become, seem, appear, look, feel*) join their subject to a construction that either describes or renames the subject, that is, to a predicate adjective or predicate nominative.

He seems tall.	He seems a fool.
He looks tall.	He looks a fool.
He feels tall.	He feels a fool.
He is tall.	He is a fool.

The left-hand set consists of linking verbs with predicate adjectives, the right-hand set of linking verbs with predicate nominatives.

Transitive verbs are in either the *active voice* or the *passive voice*. In the active voice the subject of the verb is the agent of the action expressed by the verb; in the passive voice the subject is the recipient of the action. The form of the passive voice is distinctive, consisting of the appropriate form of the verb *be* plus the past participle of the verb that carries the meaning:

He is watched.	He has been watched.
He is being watched.	He had been watched.
He was watched.	He will be watched.
He was being watched.	He will have been watched.

The active voice is converted to the passive by making the object in the active sentence the subject in the passive, and the subject of the active sentence the object of the preposition *by* in the passive. This perhaps baffling pronouncement may be clarified by following the arrows in the diagram:

Active: The news startled many.

Passive: Many were startled by the news.

(On voice, see further pp. 92–96.)

Sequence of Tenses

For native speakers only one problem of tense sequence seems to occur with any frequency, and that arises with the use of the infinitive. An explanation of the matter would be too complicated to be profitable here. The following sequences are correct and may, perhaps, serve as a useful paradigm:

I am sorry [now] to have missed you [some time before].
I was sorry [some time before now] to miss you [at that same time].
I was sorry [some time before now] to have missed you [even earlier].
I should like to have seen you.
I should have liked to see you.

The form "I should have liked to have seen you" is usually not considered good usage.[1]

Agreement of Subject and Verb

The subject of a verb determines whether the verb is to be singular or plural. The words *each, either,* and *neither* as subjects take singular verbs:

Each of the representatives in Congress *has his* [not *have their*] constituents to consider.

Either of the two men who have applied for the job *is* [not *are*] willing to start now.

Neither of the men *is* willing to start now.

The writer should not be misled by the intervention of plural nouns between a singular subject and verb. In such a sentence as "The over-all atmosphere of the scenes are heavy and stagnant," the writer inattentively takes *scenes* as the subject rather than the singular *atmosphere.*

When a compound subject is joined by the correlative conjunctions *either . . . or, neither . . . nor, not only . . . but, not . . . but,*

1 However, when such excellent writers as Muriel Spark and Iris Murdoch can write, respectively, "He would have liked to have disappointed her more than this," and "He would have liked to have gone over to Demoyte's house," perhaps we should be more cautious of generalizing about the subject. Those interested in pursuing it further should begin with James Thurber's "Ladies' and Gentlemen's Guide to Modern English Usage."

the verb usually agrees with the nearer of the subjects (this is a general rule sometimes violated by good writers):

> Neither the defendant nor his *lawyers are* present.
> Neither the lawyers nor the *defendant is* present.
> Either the comedian or the *jugglers are* on next.
> Either the jugglers or the *comedian is* on next.

The same rule holds for two subjects joined simply by *or:*

> I don't know whether the comedian or the *jugglers are* on next.
> I don't know whether the jugglers or the *comedian is* on next.

A verb that has as its subject any of the relative pronouns *who, which, that* (since they have the same form in the singular and plural) agrees with the antecedent of the pronoun:

> The *snow* that *falls* today will be gone tomorrow.

> The *snows* that *fall* today will be gone tomorrow.

> Only one of the *lawyers* who *are* representing Jones is here.

> Morgan, the only *one* of the lawyers who *is* willing to take the case, is in the hospital.

The verb in a relative clause also agrees in person with the antecedent of the relative pronoun:

> Even *I*, who *am* in favor of his proposal, was disturbed by his presentation.

> *You*, who *are* responsible for the accident, must go to court.

> The bill is being sent to *Jones*, who *is* responsible.

The relative construction with *me* as antecedent, though technically correct, sounds odd and is not much used:

> The question was put to *me*, who *am* supposed to be an authority on the matter.

> Jones has no reason to speak ill of *me*, who *am* his faithful friend.

There is, of course, never a subject (except in sentences such as this one, where it is italicized or put in quotation marks) and has nothing to do with agreement.

> There is nothing to be done. (*is* agrees with *nothing*)
> There are a few solutions to the problem. (*are* agrees with *solutions*)

When *there is/are* precedes a compound subject, the verb usually agrees with the nearest subject.

There is a fine painting by Vermeer, two excellent Rembrandts, and a Dali in the collection.

There was a policeman and two plainclothesmen present.

The plural would also be common in the second example; in the first sentence *There are* would not sound quite idiomatic because of the distance of the other subjects from the verb.

Collective nouns, in American usage, tend to be treated predominately as singular (contrary to British usage).

> A committee *was* appointed by the President.
> The team *is* ready for the trip.
> The planning commission *is* in session now.

If the idea of plurality is necessary, the collective noun is often changed rather than used as plural. We usually say, "The committee members are quarreling with one another," rather than, "The committee are quarreling with one another." On the other hand, a collective noun modified by an *of*-phrase with a plural object tends to be treated as plural:

> A team of experts *are* in the area now.
> A mob of students *were* milling about.
> One group of Senators *remain* obdurate.

The singular verb would be idiomatic in each example also; and if the verb precedes the subject, the singular is usually preferred:

> There *is* a team of experts in the area now.
> There *was* a mob of students milling about.
> There *remains* one group of obdurate Senators.

More than is probably best considered as an adjective group not affecting agreement:

> There *is* more than one way to skin a cat; in fact, there *are* more than two ways.

None, though etymologically meaning "no *one*," is indifferently singular or plural, the plural probably being more common:

> None of the lawyers are present.
> None of the lawyers is present.

Any and *some* are singular or plural according to sense:

> There was little coffee to be had, but any *was* welcome.
> There were few signs of spring, but any *were* welcome.

Some of the field *is* already harvested.
Some of the harvesters *are* already in the field.

Shall, Will; Should, Would

The length of the following discussion may suggest that the problem is important. It is not. It is a very minor problem of usage but rather complicated and controversial. If you do not care what the controversy is about, skip to the next section.

Shall and *will* are the helping verbs with which the future tense is formed. There was a time when the following paradigm was rigorously taught:

I shall (go)	We shall (go)
You will	You will
He, she, it will	They will

The forms "I will go" and "We will go" to express simple futurity have been regarded as vulgarisms. The same distinction has been made for the past forms *should* and *would* in clauses depending on a stated or implied *if*-clause:

We should be sorry if you were displeased.
I should like to see you [if I could].

British English maintains these distinctions to some extent (though to judge by the amount of academic grumbling to be heard across the Atlantic, they are breaking down even in England); so do many American writers, especially the more self-consciously "correct." But a great many good writers, and most speakers, of American English do not consistently discriminate among the forms. "I will go" and "I would like to see you" are generally accepted forms in the United States, as even the most perfunctory examination of American prose will demonstrate. In fact, the invariable use of *shall* and *should* in the first person can sound rather prissy to American ears. In very formal writing, they remain the predominant forms. They are rarer in less formal prose, such as good journalism. We would only suggest that if the writer finds himself occasionally using *will* or *would* in the first person, it is nothing to worry about.

With *should*, the trouble is that besides its use in conditional sentences, it also has the regular meaning "ought to." And the sentence "I should go," by itself, can mean only "I ought to go"; it does not imply an *if*-clause ("I should go, if I could"). In some sentences, the difference between the two uses of *should* cannot be seen without an additional clause:

> I should be surprised to learn of his defection [if he did defect].
> I should be surprised to learn of his defection [but I am not].

The meaning of the first sentence would be unambiguous in the form "I *would* be surprised. . . ."

Only *would* is possible in such expressions as the following:

> I would save the Union. [LINCOLN]
> I would be free as air. [MELVILLE]

The use of *should* here would give a radically different meaning to the sentences ("I should save the Union, but I'm not going to"?); no choice, then, is open.

Etymologically, *will/would* connotes desire and resolve; [2] *shall/should* connotes obligation, usually external obligation. But in their use as auxiliary verbs for the future and the conditional, the connotations are seldom discernible. They do not even exist, of course, in the second and third persons: "The sun will rise at 5:30 tomorrow morning" obviously says nothing about the sun's desire or resolve to rise. The same is now generally true for the first person. Theoretically, "I will save the Union" should express desire and resolve, and "I shall save the Union" simple futurity. But few readers would notice any difference between the two. Actually both sentences suggest resolve, but as an implication of the whole sentence and its circumstances, not as a result of the verb forms. Likewise the simple conditional "I should like to know" conveys no sense of obligation; nor does "If this were Monday, it would be time to get up" convey any sense of desire. However, since *should* may, and often does, have the meaning "ought to," preserving the etymological connotation of obligation, the etymological force of *would* has also been preserved to some extent, perhaps as an accident of distinguishing it from the obligatory *should*.

Verbals

The verbals, though formed from verbs, are not verbs proper; they function as some other part of speech. They are the participial forms

---

2 Thus for Fowler, the expression "I would like" (for "I should like") was a low and insufferable redundancy. But it has come into regular use; countless examples could be cited, including some from Sir Winston Churchill and Sir Alec Douglas-Home.

and the infinitive. The present participle is readily recognizable from its *-ing* ending (*running, voting, losing, complaining*). The past participle is the third principal part of the verb (lose, lost, *lost*; sing, sang, *sung*; vote, voted, *voted*). These forms are used as modifiers (*running* water, *voting* machine, *losing* candidate, *lost* cause) as well as parts of compound verbs (he has lost, he is losing, he was voted out). When the present participle is used as a substantive, it is usually called a gerund (*Voting* is the last thing I want to do; Let him try *running* a mile every day; The effect of her *singing* was powerful). The infinitive is the form of the verb that appears with the word *to* in such constructions as "I want *to go*," "*To see* Paris again is all I desire," "You have only one life *to live*." The infinitive is sometimes a modifier, as in the last example, more often a substantive, as in the first two examples.

Although verbals function as substantives or modifiers and are not properly verbs, they nevertheless share with the verbs they are derived from the capacity for having subjects and objects. In participial and infinitive phrases, there is an implied someone or something performing the action represented by the verbal. In the sentence "I want to go," the implied subject of the infinitive "to go" is "I." If it is anyone else it must be stated—"I want *Jones* to go." It is sometimes said that the subject of a gerund is in the possessive case—"*His* (*Smith's*) singing is a joy to hear"; *his* or *Smith's* may also be thought of as merely a modifier of the gerund parallel to "*Good* singing is a joy" or "*Bad* singing is a pain."

Similar looking constructions using respectively the participle and gerund may have distinct emphases:

> I carefully observed him working the abacus.
> I carefully observed his working the abacus.

The object of observation in the first sentence is *him*, in the second *working*; the emphasis in the first sentence is on the man himself, in the second, on what he is doing. (This distinction is not maintained in Great Britain.)

Dangling Modifiers

The problem of the "dangling modifier" arises from the misuse especially of participial phrases and elliptical clauses. Examples:

While eating my dinner, a friend visited me.
Refreshments were served *before taking a nap*.

Having surrounded the fort, the town was soon taken by the invaders.

Sometimes these constructions are obviously silly; sometimes they go unnoticed. Their occasional appearance in the prose of even the most excellent writers should be taken as inadvertent, for there is nothing at all to be said in favor of the dangling modifier; it is pointlessly illogical and can be as grotesque as its name. As mentioned earlier, the participle implies a subject (or "agent"): in the above instances, *someone* eating dinner, taking a nap, surrounding the fort. In normal usage that implied subject is most often the subject of the sentence and appears immediately after the participial phrase. (In other constructions—"I saw *him running* down the street"—there is seldom a problem.) The above sentences sound odd, if not absurd, because another word appears where we expect the subject of the participle. They should be changed accordingly:

While eating dinner, *I* was visited by a friend.
Before taking a nap, *I* was served refreshments.
Having surrounded the fort, *the invaders* soon took the town.

Alternatively, the subjects of the participles may be supplied by changing the phrases to clauses:

While I was eating my dinner, a friend visited me.
Before I took a nap, refreshments were served.
Soon after the invaders had surrounded the fort, they took the town.

A participial phrase before the "anticipatory *it*" (p. 51) is not usually felt to be dangling.

While acknowledging Tubermann's greatness as a scholar, it is still possible to question his morals.

This construction does not jar despite the presence of *it* where we should expect the implied subject of *acknowledging.* Exception must also be made for a few participial phrases of the following type:

Considering her age, she was rather lively.

Judging by appearances, the natives were certainly friendly.

The team did well this season, *always excepting Trumbull.*

Leaving politics aside for the moment, what can be said of the ethical issue?

Allowing for spoilage, forty tons of wheat should be available.

These exceptions have a pattern: they are all adverbial phrases making a conditional qualification of the main assertion; they are equivalent to *if-clauses* ("If we consider her age," "If we judge by appearances," "If we except Trumbull," etc.).

These exceptions do not extend to the construction using "situational *it*" (as in "*It* is snowing," "*It* is very warm today," "I think *it* may rain"), where the dangling modifier may sound strange indeed:

> After sitting there awhile, it began to rain.

The Split Infinitive

An infinitive phrase is "split" by the insertion of a modifier between *to* and the verbal ("to really understand," "to completely be at a loss," "to kindly help"). The old rule "to never split an infinitive," as the waggish have it, has roused extraordinary passion for so trivial a matter. The rule is denounced most hotly by those who have just discovered that language is "living" and changing and perforce not to be cast into arbitrary molds by moss-backed academicians. They point out, quite rightly, that there is no justification for the rule in logic or nature. At the same time, they curiously ignore their own usual shibboleth of usage. The obvious facts of usage are that the split infinitive is commonplace in speech and informal writing, in newspapers and widely read magazines, and that it is rare in formal prose: a split infinitive in the New York *Times* would scarcely be noticed; in a professor's book it would be surprising. The professor, in turn, though seldom surprised to see the split infinitive in a student's essay, is seldom pleased. And he has some reason: to one whose ear for prose has been trained by long acquaintance with good literature and formal writing the split infinitive *sounds* wrong, simply because it is so regularly avoided (logically or not) in the writing he has come to esteem. Would anyone, after all, prefer Hamlet's soliloquy to begin "To be or to not be . . ."? Or consider this example (from a professor's book):

To study them is *to not only master* specific facts but to reap at the same time all the benefits supposed in the past to accompany the study of the classic curriculum.

The split infinitive here, gratuitously disturbing both the formal diction of the sentence and the parallelism of the *not only . . . but* construction, must grate on any ear but a tin one. Conversely, few readers would give a second thought to Lewis Mumford's writing in the *New Yorker* about the Guggenheim Museum's "utility stacks," which house the closets and lavatories on each level, rising against the wall on either side of the elevator *to visually tie* all the floors together.

Adjectives

Any modifier of a substantive is an adjective. A modifier is a word that limits, describes, identifies, or alters in some way the meaning of the word to which it is attached. To say "Women are odious" is obviously very different from saying, "*Garrulous* women are odious." Our conception of the subject *women* (and therefore of the meaning of the sentence) is greatly modified by the limiting word *garrulous*. According to its position in the sentence, an adjective may be classified as an attributive, appositional, or predicate adjective. An attributive adjective precedes the noun it modifies: *garrulous* women; *red* house; *the* man; *an* apple; *tree* house; *back* yard; *the tall, old, dilapidated* mansion. Appositional adjectives, usually in pairs or heading a phrase, follow the word they modify: "The Chief Justice, *keen* and *vigorous* as ever, walked in briskly," "The girl, rather *clever* for a Kallikak, held the book upside down." Predicate adjectives, as the name suggests, follow the verb: "The Chief Justice seemed *keen* and *vigorous*," "The girl was rather *clever* for a Kallikak."

Predicate adjectives are the only type that present any grammatical problem, and even they not often. But sometimes uncertainty arises as to whether a predicate adjective or an adverb should be used in linking-verb constructions (see p. 24). In "He feels badly today," *badly* does not fit the logic of the construction, which requires the adjectival form *bad*, and is not used in good prose. Some verbs may be linking verbs in one sentence and non-linking verbs in another:

> He looked soft in her eyes.
> He looked softly into her eyes.

The meanings are very different, of course. Similarly, "He felt a fool" may have two quite distinct meanings depending on whether *fool* is to be taken as a predicate nominative or as an object. Conversely, some verbs not usually linking verbs may have that function in certain expressions, as "He went blind" (compare "He went blindly down the dark path").

Adverbs

Often ending with the characteristic suffix *-ly*, adverbs modify verbs, verbals, adjectives, and other adverbs. As modifiers of verbs they usually answer the question Where? When? How? or In what circumstances? asked of the verb. Similarly *there, then,* or *thus* can often be substituted for more specific adverbs.

> He went *home quickly yesterday.*

The adverb *home* answers the question Where did he go? The adverb *quickly* answers the question How did he go? The adverb *yesterday* answers the question When did he go?

The adverb modifies verbals.

> They wanted to go *immediately.*

Here the adverb modifies the infinitive, answering the question Go when? (It does not modify the verb, since it says nothing of the time of the wanting—compare "They immediately wanted to go.") Similarly:

> To leave *instantly* is all I desire.
> There was a plot to dispose of Rasputin *quietly.*

Modifiers of participles are adverbs:

> Running *fearfully,* she bolted the door.
> It was a *hopelessly* lost cause.
> Mr. Vasse is renowned for his *masterfully* mixed Martinis.

The modifier of a gerund is an adverb if it follows the gerund within the gerund phrase:

> Planning *badly* will help no one.
> He was charged with driving *carelessly.*

Or if it precedes a transitive gerund:

> He was accused of *badly* planning his strategy.
> He was charged with *carelessly* driving his car into a ditch.

Otherwise, the modifier of a gerund is an adjective:

> *Bad* planning will help no one.
> Their planning was *bad.*
> He was charged with *careless* driving.
> His driving is said to be *careless.*

Modifiers of adjectives are adverbs:

> It was a *wonderfully* fresh performance.
> Adams felt *extraordinarily* happy during those years.
> *Usually* cheery, the President was morose this morning.

In each sentence the italicized adverb modifies—widens or narrows the meaning of—the adjective (*fresh, happy, cheery*) it is attached to.
  Adverbs modify other adverbs:

> It was a *quite* wonderfully fresh performance.
> Adams felt *most* extraordinarily happy.
> The President could be seen *very* clearly.
> He left *just* now.
> *Right* here the city was founded.

Two or more adjacent *-ly* adverbs in sequential modification often have a very jingling sound—

> They are on*ly* apparent*ly* happi*ly* married,
> The executions are usual*ly* private*ly* done—

and are best avoided. A *series* of *-ly* adverbs, however, does not sound awkward:

> Sheridan strode in quickly, purposefully, and authoritatively.

Conjunctions

Conjunctions are treated at some length on pp. 78–79; here we shall sketch briefly their form and function. Conjunctions fall into three major categories: coordinating (and correlative) conjunctions, subordinating conjunctions, and conjunctive adverbs.
  Coordinating conjunctions (*and, but, or, nor, for, so, yet, not*) join only like constructions and must come between the constructions joined.

1. McClellan *and* Beauregard were opposing generals.
2. Let us go across the river *and* into the trees.
3. They often saw Pickett *but* never Lee.
4. They didn't know where they had come from *or* where they were going.
5. There was no answer, *for* no one was at home.

In (1) *and* stands between the parallel subjects *McClellan* and *Beauregard*; in (2) *and* stands between the parallel prepositional phrases *across the river* and *into the trees*; in (3) *but* joins the two verb objects *Pickett* and *Lee;* in (4) *or* joins the two subordinate clauses *where they had come from* and *where they were going;* in (5) *for* joins the two independent clauses.

Correlative conjunctions—*either . . . or, neither . . . nor, both . . . and, not (only) . . . but (also)*—are followed by like constructions.

Both McClellan *and* Beauregard were generals.

They saw *not* only Pickett *but also* Lee.

They knew *neither* where they had come from *nor* where they were going.

Subordinating conjunctions (e.g., *after, although, as, because, before, since, until, when, while*) join adverbial clauses to the main clause. They are always the first word in the adverbial clause, but the position of the clause itself is variable.

> *After* the ball was over, they went home.
> They went home *after* the ball was over.

Relative pronouns and *where, wherever, when,* and *whenever* have a similar function in subordinate adjective and noun clauses, but the position of the clause itself is restricted in normal usage.

> I know *where* I'm going.
> I know *who* is going with me.

Conjunctive adverbs (*however, nevertheless, then, therefore, thus, hence, moreover, consequently,* etc.) join only independent clauses; they differ from coordinating conjunctions joining independent clauses in that their position is variable within the second clause. (They may, in fact, be regarded not as conjunctions at all, but as "transitional adverbs," an accurately descriptive term.)

I know where I'm going; *moreover,* I know who is going with me.
I know where I'm going; I know, *moreover,* who is going with me.
I know where I'm going; I know who is going with me, *moreover.*

Compare the following nearly equivalent constructions:

1. I know him, *but* he doesn't know me.
2. I know him, *although* he doesn't know me.
   Although he doesn't know me, I know him.
3. I know him; *however,* he doesn't know me.
   I know him; he, *however,* doesn't know me.
   I know him; he doesn't know me, *however.*

The paradigm is useful if one is not sure whether *so*, for instance, is to be regarded as a coordinating conjunction or as a conjunctive adverb; since it fits the pattern of (1), not (3), it is a coordinating conjunction.

Prepositions

There are a great many prepositions in English; they connect a substantive object to another word. In the following passage the prepositions are printed in italics, their objects in small capitals.

The sun lay *on* the GRASS and warmed it, and *in* the SHADE *under* the GRASS the insects moved, ants and ant lions to set traps *for* THEM, grasshoppers to jump *into* the AIR and flick their yellow wings *for* a SECOND, sow bugs *like* little ARMADILLOS, plodding restlessly *on* many tender FEET. And *over* the GRASS *at* the ROADSIDE a land turtle crawled, turning aside *for* NOTHING, dragging his high-domed shell *over* the GRASS. [STEINBECK]

Many adverbs have the same form as prepositions, but they do not have objects.

Let us go *on*. (adverb)
Let us go *on* stage. (preposition)
They crossed *over*. (adverb)
They crossed *over* the river. (preposition)
He looked *up* from his book. (adverb)
He looked *up* the chimney. (preposition)

There is still a vagrant superstition that a sentence should not end with a preposition, a rule that hardly anyone pays any attention to. A careless writer may, however, unwittingly duplicate prepositions by combining two constructions, e.g., "a rule *to* which hardly anyone pays any attention *to*."

Subordinate Clauses

We have defined the subordinate (dependent, relative) clause as a grammatically complete group of words containing a subject and predicate and functioning as a part of speech. Only nouns, adjectives, and adverbs have clausal and phrasal equivalents. Thus a subordinate clause acting as a subject, object, appositive, or predicate nominative is a noun clause (often beginning with *that, what, whoever, whatever, whichever*).

That there was a conspiracy is now well known. (subject of the sentence)
Give it to *whoever wants it.* (object of preposition *to*) [3]

> The idea *that chills cause colds* has been recently disproved. (appositive)

> Your life is *what you make of it.* (predicate nominative)

A clause that modifies a substantive is adjectival (usually beginning with a relative pronoun or *where* or *when*).

> The conspiracy, *which was unknown at the time,* has since come to light. (modifying *conspiracy*)

> An old idea *that has been recently disproved* is that chills cause colds. (modifying *idea*—not telling what the idea is, as the noun clause does)

> He *who lives by the sword* will die by the sword. (modifying *He*)

> Zamboanga, *where the monkeys have no tails,* is in the Philippines. (modifying *Zamboanga*)

> Autumn, *when the leaves are turning,* is the best time of year. (modifying *Autumn*)

Adverb clauses usually modify verbs directly.

> He will go *when he is ready.*
> She will go *where he goes.*

Or, more generally, they can be said to designate the time and circumstances of the main clause:

> They couldn't begin the coronation, *because the Queen hadn't arrived.*

> *Although she was late,* she was almost certain to be there.

> There was a further delay *until the crown was located.*

> *After it was all over,* everyone was relieved.

Often within one sentence there are several interdependent subordinate clauses. The subjects and verbs of nine subordinate clauses are italicized in the following (only slightly *outré*) sentence:

---

3 Compare "Give it to *whomever you like*" for another example of how the case of a relative pronoun is determined by its function only in the subordinate clause; in the first instance, it is the subject of *wants* and therefore in the nominative case; in the second instance, it is the object of *like* and therefore in the objective case.

He is the man, *I am told, who was asking* yesterday when the *Senator was* here what *he could do* personally *that might help preserve* those forests which *he had loved* since *he was* a child and *which,* as soon as the new *administration took* office, *would be threatened* with destruction.

Independent Clauses

A clause not used as a part of speech is independent.

I came, I saw, I conquered.

Each clause in the example is independent because it is not syntactically subordinate to any other word or construction. An independent clause and a simple sentence are the same.

Phrases

A phrase is a group of words, not a clause, functioning as a unit and as a part of speech. According to their function, phrases may be classified as noun, adjective, or adverb phrases; according to their form, they may be classified as prepositional, verbal (participle, gerund, infinitive), and absolute.

A prepositional phrase consists of a preposition, its object and any modifiers:

Let us go *into the trees.*
Let us go *into that stand of tall trees.*
Let us go *into those tall trees that are across the river.*

It may be used adverbially, as in the above examples, or adjectivally —"stand *of tall trees,*" "house *by the road,*" "big spender *from the East.*" Rarely is the prepositional phrase used as a noun: "*Across the river* is too far."

A verbal phrase consists of the verbal with its modifiers and complements. The infinitive phrase is used as noun, adjective, and adverb:

To understand Plato thoroughly was his goal. (subject—noun)

To understand Plato thoroughly, he would have to know Greek. (adverb)

He is a philosopher *to respect.* (adjective)

The participial phrase is used as a modifier:

He ran off *tearing his hair.*

It is usually described as adjectival (here modifying *He*), but it obviously has adverbial force in most instances (here denoting *how* he ran off). The gerund phrase is used as a noun:

> *His running off* was a nuisance.

The absolute is like a subordinate clause in that it has a subject, but it does not have a verb. The subject is most often followed by a participle, sometimes by a simple adjective or prepositional phrase:

> *Mrs. DiBona having spoken,* there was no point in further discussion.

> *Drums beating, trombones blaring,* the band came marching down the street.

> *Her eyes red and voice fearful,* she told what had happened.

> He stood there, *his hat tilted on the back of his head, hands in his pockets,* and stared at his son.

The exact syntactical relationship of the absolute to its sentence is not well defined, but it usually has adverbial force. (See further on the absolute, p. 73.)

An appositive phrase is simply an appositive with any modifiers it may have.

Misplaced Modifiers

It is a good principle to keep modifiers, whether words, phrases, or clauses, as close as possible to the words they modify. Prepositional phrases are especially easy to misplace.

> Mr. Harold Wilson, the Leader of the Opposition, is to open an attack on the operation of the Rent Act and on property profiteering in the House of Commons on Monday. [THE *Guardian*]

At first glance, this looks as if the profiteering were going on in the House—awful thought. The phrases "in the House of Commons" and "on Monday" would be less alarmingly disposed at the beginning of the sentence or after "attack." Similarly:

> Yesterday Mr. Thomas gave an account of his recent safari in the McKinley High School auditorium.

> He finally brought in the cow, red with exertion.

Another trap for the unwary is ambiguous parallelism:

> An actor waving a sword and a witch appeared on stage.

A young man vigorously shaking an umbrella and his wife entered the hall.

The modifier *only* should be kept as close as possible to the word it modifies. In speech such a sentence as

General Schmidt only contemplated a quick battle, not a prolonged war

is passable, but careful writers place *only* more accurately:

General Schmidt contemplated only a quick battle, not a prolonged war.

Without the explanatory phrase "not a prolonged war," the first sentence could easily be ambiguous, for it should mean "only contemplated, did not actually start a battle." The proper disposition of *only* is the mark of a careful writer.

Fragments

Expert writers can punctuate almost any word group as if it were a sentence. Because the reader naturally pauses when he comes to a period, the use of fragmentary sentences can provide a certain kind of emphasis, the kind usually associated with a "telegraphic" style. But in most writing, formal and informal, grammatically complete sentences are the rule; and most writers, unless they are quite sure of themselves do well to avoid writing fragmentary sentences. Inexpertly used, they have the appearance of mere ineptness.

The fragmentary sentence is frequent in speech so that in writing meant to suggest the sounds and forms of speech, its use is normal. Exclamatory fragments, particularly, are common: such expressions as "Never!" "Not on your life!" "The idea!" "Anything but that!" and aphorisms such as "Here today, gone tomorrow," "Out of sight, out of mind." The following is an example of an effective variant of the "Anything but that" exclamation:

An almost identical doctrine is to be found in *The Tibetan Book of the Dead,* where the departed soul is described as shrinking in agony from the Clear Light of the Void in order to rush headlong into the comforting darkness of selfhood as a reborn human being, or even as a beast, an unhappy ghost, a denizen of hell. Anything rather than the burning brightness of unmitigated Reality—anything! [ALDOUS HUXLEY]

A not very common form of writing, that meant to suggest impressionistic notes, legitimately employs fragments. In the following example, the first and last sentences are fragments:

An air meet. It took place on the outskirts of Moscow, and we reached it along a road lined with little old mud-brown log houses, which had fancy peaked cornices over the windows and fringes of wood and lace. Some of them seemed to have sunk into the earth till their windows were almost on a level with it.

It was on this field that the crowds were trampled to death at the coronation of Nicholas II. Today there is a loud-speaker and a band playing the *International* through it. Ballet-patterns by gliders, which would sheer off symmetrically from the plane that had trailed them and wheel slowly over on their sides; a regular rocket-burst of parachute-jumpers, some of the women coming down with two parachutes. [EDMUND WILSON]

A third style in which fragments appear frequently is the kind of writing that suggests the hurry and urgency of the telegram. Stylistically, it has important limitations: it should be used only for appropriate subjects, and it should not be prolonged excessively, for it can become oppressive quickly. It is a style with a "punch," as they say, but you don't want to beat your audience senseless. Here is a tolerable example:

With radio on the air continuously during waking hours, the reporters' problems became still more acute. News every hour on the hour, and sometimes on the half hour. Programs interrupted any time for special bulletins. How to avoid deadly repetition, the appearance that nothing was happening, that news gatherers were asleep, or that competitors were more alert? [D. J. BOORSTIN]

The preceding examples illustrate effective, purposive use of the fragment. But what can be said of the following?

Newman did not become converted to Roman Catholicism until middle life. Although he had long tended in that direction. When he took the final step, he was accused of hypocrisy. Which prompted him to write the famous *Apologia*.

The *although* clause and the *which* clause gain nothing whatever from being detached and punctuated as sentences. On the contrary, the passage suggests nothing more remarkable than that the writer doesn't know what a sentence is or how to punctuate it.

Negation

The syntax of simple negative statements is not problematic for native speakers, but double negatives raise questions of economy and precision. It is sometimes said that such expressions as "not unpleasant," "not uninteresting," and "not unhappy" are merely wordy equivalents of "pleasant," "interesting," and "happy" and therefore to be shunned. But they are *not* equivalent to the positive forms. From the statement "Adams was not unhappy," it may not properly be inferred that Adams was happy; the statement implies no more than that Adams was in some middle state between happiness and unhappiness. Sometimes, to be sure, the "double negative" is a form of ironical understatement called litotes (see p. 211): if we say, "Willkie was not unhappy about receiving the nomination," the statement may, in a given context, be an ironical understatement for "Wilkie was wildly joyful." But more often we refer to some middle condition for which there may be no good single word and for which, therefore, the "double negative" is an economical expression. The statement "Coolidge was not unhappy as President" is a reasonably concise way of saying, "Coolidge didn't exactly enjoy being President, but he didn't really hate it either." To say, "This novel is not uninteresting" is about the faintest praise you can give it, but it is still not a condemnation. The construction is frequently used to avoid both outright condemnation and outright praise, as in such assertions as "He is not immoral, but amoral," and "He is not insane, but he is very neurotic." Its use should not, however, be allowed to become a habit of needless hedging.

The "not un-" construction is rarely confusing, but the multiplication of negatives in a sentence can become bewildering:

Yet to say that Augustine was *not* an "intellectualist" is *not* to say that he was *not* acutely conscious of the problem of certitude. [F. COPLESTON]

It is difficult to perceive any advantage in so many *nots*; Father Copleston would have made it easier for us had he written, "Though Augustine was not an 'intellectualist,' he was acutely conscious of the problem of certitude."

PART TWO

RHETORIC OF THE SENTENCE

3

SENTENCE STRUCTURE

ONE tends to think of meaning as the property of words only. The word *dog* "means" a certain animal. But meaning also depends on how individual words are arranged and connected. The words *man*, *dog*, and *bites* do not become news until they are arranged in the order *Man bites dog*. By themselves, words only name things; arranged as sentences, they make assertions. That is what most sentences are for. A sentence may also have the purpose of asking, commanding, or exclaiming; but such sentences, neither frequent nor especially problematic in general writing, need concern us only incidentally. Of much greater importance is the declarative sentence, the purpose of which is to make an assertion.

Structure and Meaning

It is obvious enough that the sentence *Man bites dog* is an assertion; less obvious are two implied assertions, that there is such a thing as *man* and that there is such a thing as *dog*. The sentence *In a fit of pique, the man bit the dog* contains not only the direct assertion of the deed but also the indirect assertion that the man was in a fit of pique. Many sentences convey a multiplicity of assertions, explicit and implicit. Consider this sentence:

Though young and strong, Lester would not engage in any healthful activity such as tennis or swimming.

The principal assertion is that Lester would not engage in any healthful activity, an assertion made in the main clause of the sentence. The sentence also implies that the following statements are all true:

1. There is such a person as Lester and such things as "healthful activity, tennis, and swimming,"
2. Lester is young,
3. Lester is strong,

47

4. Tennis is a healthful activity,
5. Swimming is a healthful activity,
6. There is an anomaly in someone's being young and strong and his not engaging in healthful activities such as tennis and swimming.

None of these statements is directly asserted; their validity is assumed as background for the only direct assertion, that concerning Lester's languor.

Normally, but not invariably, the main point of the sentence is expressed by the main clause; secondary points are expressed in subordinate constructions. The following sentences contain the same information but have different purposes and different effects:

> The house on the hill is to be torn down.
> The house to be torn down is on the hill.

The purpose of the first sentence is to tell the fate of the house; that of the second is to give the location of the house. Exactly the same words and the same word groups are used in both sentences; the difference is in their arrangement. It is the *predicates* of the sentences ("is to be torn down," "is on the hill") that tell us what the sentences are about. Predication is the heart of the sentence, its main focus; other constructions are secondary.

It does not follow that secondary constructions are insignificant; on the contrary, they are often essential. In the proverb "A rolling stone gathers no moss," *rolling* is so essential that the sentence would be meaningless without it. But the *point* of the statement is not that stones roll but that certain stones do not gather moss. It is obviously important for clear communication that the main point of the sentence be expressed in a construction that shows its importance, ordinarily an independent clause.

Predication

We have defined the clause as a group of words that contains a subject and predicate and is grammatically complete (p. 16). What is a "predicate"? Weighty books and learned essays have been written in an attempt to answer that question adequately, but without conspicuous success. In *most* written sentences, the predicate can be defined as the verb plus any modifiers and complements [1] it may

1 A "complement" is any word or words needed to complete the meaning of a verb, as "He is——" does not become meaningful until completed by some such expression as "tall," "a fool," "in trouble," etc.

have. However, since our concern is with the *function* of the predicate, we must resort to the rude expedient of defining the predicate of a sentence as "whatever is said of the subject." A clause, then, has two primary divisions, the subject and the predicate. Something is spoken of (the subject); something is said about it (the predicate).

The grandeur of Thebes/was a vulgar grandeur. [THOREAU]

What is spoken of? The grandeur of Thebes (subject). What is said about it? That it was a vulgar grandeur (predicate).

The very simplicity and nakedness of man's life in the primitive ages/ imply this advantage, at least, that they left him still but a sojourner in nature. [THOREAU]

What is spoken of? The very simplicity and nakedness of man's life in the primitive ages. What does Thoreau say about such simplicity and nakedness? That they imply this advantage, at least, that they left man still but a sojourner in nature. All clauses are divisible in this way, although it is not always possible to draw one line between subject and predicate.

Never in the history of human conflict was so much owed by so many to so few. [CHURCHILL]

What is spoken of? Obviously not "Never in the history of human conflict," but "so much." And what is said about "so much"? That it was never owed by so many to so few.

This way of looking at a sentence clouds up when you are faced with words out of normal word order, as in this sentence:

Bread I at first made of pure Indian meal and salt. [THOREAU]

If you ask what is being spoken of, both *bread* and *I* seem plausible answers, for displaced words (*bread* here) have a center of focus they would not have in normal order (see pp. 61–63). The grammatical subject may, however, be easily found by first locating the verb [2] and asking "who?" or "what?" of the verb.

I saw you on the street.

The verb is *saw*. If you ask, "Who saw you on the street?" the answer will be "I," which is the grammatical subject.

There are four books on the table.

[2] Most readers will know a verb when they see one; in case of doubt, the formal criteria mentioned on p. 23 may be referred to.

The verb is *are*. If you ask, "What are on the table?" the answer, "four books," indicates the grammatical subject.

In most sentences what "is being spoken of" is also the grammatical subject; the subject of discourse is the subject of the sentence. It is a good policy when you are not sure quite how to formulate a sentence to ask yourself exactly what person, thing, or idea you want to say something about and assume that will be the subject of your sentence. (Familiarity with the possibilities of shifting emphasis by manipulating word order will, of course, augment your resources.) As an example, let us consider a general scene we want to say something about: a courtroom scene in which the famous lawyer Clarence Darrow made an impressive defense of his client. Here are three alternatives:

1. *Darrow* impressed the court with his ardent defense.
2. The *court* was impressed with Darrow's ardent defense.
3. Darrow's ardent *defense* impressed the court.

The choice of subjects is determined simply by where you want the focus of the sentence—on Darrow, the court, or the defense. It is often an important choice, which can help avoid logical tangles. There are, in fact, few things more important in writing than attention to basic predication: having a clear idea of what your subject is and what you want to say about it.

Such attention was wanting when a student wrote:

The prehistoric era was a life of many hardships.

If the sentence sounds strange—as it should—it is because *era* and *life* are not ordinarily equatable ideas. Though intelligible, the predication is off-key, and slightly irritating. The writer should have asked himself, "What is my *subject*? The prehistoric era or *life* in the prehistoric era?" Having decided that, he should have gone on to ask, "Exactly what do I want to say about this subject?" Depending on his context, he might then write:

Life in the prehistoric era was full of hardships,

or:

The prehistoric era was a time of many hardships,

or:

In the prehistoric era, life had many hardships.

These do not exhaust the possibilities, but all are better than the original sentence. Another student, writing about political campaign methods, says:

> The use of the "father image" can be carried back to early United States history.

This is not just a little haywire; it is scarcely intelligible. How can you "carry back" such a "use"? The writer was thinking, as it turned out, of such things as the early designation of George Washington as father of his country, and reasoning that the modern exploitation of a candidate's fatherly appearance could not be new in all respects. Yet, as it again turned out, he also did not mean that the Founding Fathers ever consciously used their paternal characteristics for political purposes. What *was* his subject then? What he wanted to talk about was the appeal or effectiveness of the so-called "father image." *That* was not new. Obliged to re-examine the basic predication of his sentence, the student was able to untangle both his syntax and his thought, and write:

The "father image" had as much political appeal in the early days of the Republic as it does now, but only in modern times has that appeal been so systematically exploited in political campaigns.

The result of his close attention to predication was not just an intelligible sentence but the actual discovery and articulation of what he had had "in mind" only vaguely.

A practical guide, then, to meaningful predication is that the "something spoken of" should be clearly formulated and made the grammatical subject of the clause; what is said about it should be exactly stated and should be the predicate of the clause.

The only very important exception to this generalization occurs when the subject takes the form of a clause (or sometimes a phrase). In this case, an "expletive" construction is often used, in the familiar sentence pattern *It* + linking verb + predicate adjective + noun clause or phrase.

> It is possible that this information has been published.

> It is not likely, however, that it has come to the Chief of Staff's attention.

> It is hard to believe that the project is finished.

> It has become increasingly apparent that our present policy toward Monaco is not succeeding.

The *It* of each sentence conveys no meaning by itself. Whether the

It is the grammatical subject is a bit uncertain, for if we ask of the first sentence, "What is possible?" the answer may be either *it* or, just as likely, "that our plans are known." Evidently the *it* refers forward to the clause and is therefore sometimes called the "anticipatory *it*." The reasons for the existence and use of this construction are a matter of the history of the language and need not concern us here. The pertinent question of rhetoric is whether there is any difference between

> It is possible that this information has been published

and the alternative,

> That this information has been published is possible.

In the second sentence the grammatical subject is certainly correct; yet the first construction is so familiar that we hardly notice the "It is"; our attention focuses on the rest of the sentence. Hence no awkwardness or tension results. The choice of alternatives depends, then, on the preferred sequence of ideas, whether the writer wants the predicate ("is possible") or the "semantic" subject to come first. The "It is" form is the more normal one. The second pattern, less common, has some of the effect of the "periodic sentence" (see p. 59): it does not give a sense of completion until the last word is reached; the first sentence gives a sense of completeness with the first three words, since they make up a grammatically complete pattern (subject-verb-complement). There is not much difference of emphasis between the two sentences. The first form is usually to be preferred, simply because it is the more common and therefore less obtrusive (but see p. 55).

A similar construction—*It is* + predicate noun + adjective clause —has a more discernible effect. Compare the following:

> The President must make the appointment; Congress must approve it.

> It is the President who must make the appointment; it is Congress that must approve it.

The second sentence, by subordinating the predicates and thus deemphasizing them, throws greater emphasis to the subjects *President* and *Congress*; the "it is" construction is neutral in effect. In the following passage, using the same construction, it is *woman* that gets the emphasis throughout.

It was woman who wielded the digging stick or hoe: she who tended the garden crops and accomplished those masterpieces of selection and cross fertilization which turned raw wild species into the prolific and richly nutritious domestic varieties: it was woman who made the first containers, weaving baskets and coiling the first clay pots. [LEWIS MUMFORD]

Another exception is a usual form of "indirect discourse," that is, the way of reporting statements. The common alternatives are:

> The President said today that he does not choose to run.
> He does not choose to run, the President said today.

The principal predication of the first sentence is "The President said today," that of the second, "He does not choose to run." But in both sentences the semantic focus is on the President's statement, not on the fact that he made it; the "he said" formula is almost as neutral as the "It is" construction (similarly for most expressions of reporting: "It was announced," "Smith states," "He mentioned," etc.). About the only way to emphasize the predication of "He said" is to add some qualification: "He himself said," "He actually said," etc.

Logical Statement

Evidently what a sentence predicates of its subject should be possible. Failure to see the structure of predication in a sentence can result, especially among inexperienced writers, in illogical and ludicrous statements.

> I, along with other groups, was separated into smaller groups.

Here is inattention indeed, when the writer asserts that he was divided into smaller groups.

> The ever increasing number of super-markets springing up all over gives rise to the fact that ours is an ever-growing population.

Here the writer seems to assert that the increase of super-markets is the cause of population growth. The failure of both sentences could have been prevented had the writers been conscious of subject-predicate structure. If the first writer had asked himself, "What do I want to speak of?" he might have seen that the answer was not "I," but "my group." If the second writer had asked himself, "What do I want to say about super-markets?" he would probably have answered not that they "give rise to" a growing population, but that they "indicate" or "reflect" a growth of population.

Similarly, the failure to keep in mind the principal predication of a sentence often leads to illogical implications in subordinate structures.

> When one walks in these markets, there are many pushcarts.

This suggests that if one did *not* walk in the markets, there would be no pushcarts. The writer fails to see that the principal clause merely asserts the presence of pushcarts, which has nothing to do with one's walking in the store.

> Hawaii is known for her wild orchids and night-blooming flowers because the climate is humid and the temperature high.

The hot, humid climate may account for the *presence* of orchids but hardly for the fact that Hawaii is *known* for its orchids. Again, because the writer has not kept securely in mind his principal predication, the logic of his sentence crumbles.

Full and Empty Statements

Since it is so important in the sentence, the predication should be to the point; it should make a meaningful assertion. One of the most common inadequacies of style is the generalized statement with virtually no content, the kind of statement found particularly as an introduction to a paragraph or essay.

> There are many pros and cons on capital punishment.

The existence of controversy about this subject is too obvious to be announced as if it were news or a judicious opinion. There being so little point in making the statement at all, it is a weak way to introduce a discussion of the subject. Yet it is a favorite device, and a favorite because so easy. The writer dispenses with any thought about meaningful predication.

> Requirements for high-school graduation are becoming stiffer as society places more and more stress on the need for education; these requirements are divided into two categories: grades and units.

The fact of *division* is trivial in the context, yet it is made the principal statement. What *is* the point here? Not, certainly, that the requirements are divided, but rather that the student must achieve better grades and take more units.

Each of the two preceding examples illustrates empty statement. The predication is not illogical; it is just not worth making the primary assertion of the sentence. Another common form of empty predication results from overuse of the "It is" formula described on p. 52.

> It is interesting to note that the king dissolved parliament.
> It may be said that he was within his prerogatives.
> It is no exaggeration to say that the members were outraged.
> It might be argued that they were unjustified.
> It is at this point that legal precedent must be considered.

There is nothing necessarily wrong with such formulations; in fact, they are often indispensable. But if used repeatedly in a passage, they deaden the style, and if used without purpose, they become empty. The first formula—"It is interesting to note that"—is particularly tiresome; if something really is interesting it should be evident without our having to be told so, and if it is merely a note, it is often irrelevant. Usually a transparent excuse for not integrating or indeed even thinking through the material it introduces, the formula could well be dropped from English usage without serious loss. Any tendency to overuse the anticipatory-*it* construction should be checked. This is easily done. Such formulas as "It may be said that" and "It may be argued that" can be reduced to a simple "Perhaps." The kind of circumlocution represented by "It is no exaggeration to say that" can often be simply omitted. "It is at this point that" can be pared to "At this point." These strictures, we repeat, apply only to excessive and purposeless use of the construction.

A number of miscellaneous problems of sentence structure become easier to see and solve when careful attention is given to predication. Consider, for instance, the perennial problem of pronoun reference (see pp. 18–20). Most teachers and editors object to sentences like this one:

> In Hawaii they eat poi.

The pronoun *they* has no antecedent. The lack here may not be a very serious matter since the meaning is clear enough; on the other hand, there is no doubt that the frequent use of imprecise pronouns weakens style and should be avoided. The writer who asks himself what he is speaking of and answers "they," is acquiring the kind of attentiveness that should lead him to ask further who "they" are and to see that the sentence provides no answer. He can then easily write, "Hawaiians eat poi," or, if "poi" seems the better subject, "Poi is a favorite dish in Hawaii," both better sentences.

> Therefore when one says that Dewey is, despite the varieties of experience which he has illuminated, primarily a moralist and a social philosopher, this is a logical consequence of his definition of the philosophical enterprise.

The stilted awkwardness of this sentence stems both from the unclear "this" and from the rather pointless "one says." The consequence of Dewey's definition is more likely to be his actual philosophical role than what "one" may say about it. Surely it is clearer to write:

> That Dewey is, despite the varieties of experience which he has illuminated, primarily a moralist and a social philosopher is a logical consequence of his definition of the philosophical enterprise.

Or:

> As a logical consequence of his definition of the philosophical enterprise, Dewey is primarily a moralist and a social philosopher, despite the varieties of experience which he has illuminated.

Wordiness and emptiness are avoided more readily when attention is given to sentence structure. In what follows—a little case history— a student began an attempted explanation for the defection of an American Negro soldier in the Korean War:

> I feel Red China had two principal ideas to offer him which he might not have been able to attain in the U.S. These two qualities deal with discrimination and education.

The language is both wordy and garbled. The word *ideas* in this context is meaningless; *attain* makes no sense. And how can *ideas* and *qualities* be equated? What does *deal with* mean here? And what, after all, is actually being asserted? Nothing very definite or intelligible, though many words are used. Plainly, the writer had not given much thought to what he was saying. He would have done better to pause before setting pen to paper and ask himself what he wanted to write about. From news accounts, he knew that the ex-soldier had attended a technical school in China and that he had complained of racial discrimination in this country. The problem the writer had set himself was to account for this man's defection. On reflection, he realized that his "subject" was not China but the soldier himself. What did he want to say about him? That he felt attracted to something in Red China. What? "Well, it probably had to do with discrimination and education." "What?" "Well, he may have felt there was less racial discrimination in China and that he might have a better opportunity for an education." At this point the writer dis-covered what he wanted to say. Illumination was nearly visible. The next problem was to put his discovery into a sentence. But the prob-lem had already been solved, for his answers had provided him with the sentence he needed. He proceeded to write, quite intelligibly:

> Unhappy with his life in the United States, this soldier probably felt that in Red China there would be less racial discrimination and that he would have a better opportunity for an education there than in this country.

This was much more satisfactory, but was it quite enough? *Why* should the soldier think this way about China? As a prisoner of war in Korea, what could he know about discrimination and education in China? Obviously, he must have been *told*. This realization led to the unexceptionable sentence:

> Unhappy with his life in the United States, this soldier felt, and was undoubtedly led to believe, that in Red China there would be no racial discrimination and that he would have a better opportunity for an education than in this country.

By giving some thought to what he wanted say in the framework of basic predication, the writer was able to turn a ragout of verbiage into a meaningful statement. Such attentiveness to predication will not solve all writing problems; it is no panacea. But it can help greatly to sharpen one's awareness of sentence content and structure, and it is a helpful guide to constructing clear, meaningful sentences.

4

SENTENCE PATTERNS

THIS chapter is again concerned only with positive statements, since the patterns of negative statements and questions involve no special problems for native speakers of English.

Normal Patterns

In most sentences, the subject and predicate appear in that sequence. Very often the sentence begins with the subject, because we want right away to identify what we are talking about. Probably just as often, however, we begin a sentence with some adverbial modifier in order to provide a preliminary setting for the main statement or to provide transition from previous remarks. The three sentences you have just read are examples; here are some more:

During the winter [time setting] we yearn for summer.

While we were in Washington [time and place], we saw the Smiths.

Though we enjoyed our visit [transition and condition], we were glad to get back home.

Each of these adverbial modifiers could be put at the end of its sentence as well as at the beginning. Does it make any difference where they are put? A transitional structure would seem naturally to go between the statements that it links; it can go elsewhere, but it should not be so far away that the reader misses the transitional effect. For the others there seems little difference. However, when the modifiers are of greater length and the sentence more complex, there are certain rhetorical effects resulting from word order. The controlling element is the principal predication. When the reader comes to the end of that in a sentence, subsequent modifiers may seem comparatively anticlimactic, added on. Conversely, since the reader is, consciously or unconsciously, on the lookout for the principal predication, suspense may be developed by the postponement of the main statement.

The Periodic Sentence

In a periodic sentence, the words are arranged so that the most important part of the sentence—usually all or part of the principal predication—comes at the end; a sense of completion does not develop until the period is reached. When successful, it keeps the qualifications of the main statement in the front of the reader's consciousness as he approaches the conclusion; by developing suspense in the reader's mind, it can dramatize the conclusion. On the other hand, if the suspense is overdeveloped, if the reader has to wait too long for the main statement, he may become confused and have to go back and read the sentence again. There are two principal ways of forming a periodic sentence, postponing the main clause and suspending it.

POSTPONED PREDICATION

A familiar example of postponing the main clause is the beautiful sentence from the New Testament:

And though I have the gift of prophecy, and understand all mysteries, and all knowledge; and though I have all faith, so that I could remove mountains, and have not charity, I am nothing.

A certain tension mounts as we approach the principal assertion "I am nothing," a tension lacking if the word order is turned around. Such a sentence must have a main clause strong enough to bear the weight of expectation placed upon it, as St. Paul's sentence does. A lame conclusion after an extended build-up always sounds ridiculous:

If men cannot restrain their greed, if they must prey on their fellow men, if they must fight wars on that account and spill the blood of countless innocent people, then that seems to me a bad thing.

Though the pattern hints of the oratorical and can degenerate into empty rhetoric, if it is used sparingly and sensibly, it has power. Its strength is in the all-important conclusion, which must justify the tension created. The following illustration, written in a rather leisurely style, contains an extraordinarly long *whereas* clause leading up to the statement "Whitehead's work is perfectly free from all this sort of thing," which, despite its casual wording, rings out forcibly.

His work in philosophy forms part, and a very important part, of the movement of twentieth-century realism; but whereas the other leaders of that movement came to it after a training in late-nineteenth-century idealism, and are consequently realistic with the fanaticism of converts and morbidly terrified of relapsing into the sins of their youth, a fact which gives their work an air of strain, as if they cared less about advancing philosophical knowledge than about proving themselves good enemies of idealism, Whitehead's work is perfectly free from all this sort of thing, and he suffers from no obsessions; obviously he does not care what he says, so long as it is true. [R. G. COLLINGWOOD]

SUSPENDED PREDICATION

This method is quite similar to postponed predication, but is somewhat more literary and artificial. Here the main clause is begun but its completion suspended by interrupting modifiers.

Plato, a man of high authority, indeed, but least of all for his commonwealth, in the book of his Laws, which no city ever yet received, fed his fancy by making many edicts to his airy burgomasters. [MILTON]

The subject "Plato" and the verb "fed" are rather widely separated by modifiers, obliging the reader to keep the subject in mind until the predicate appears.

The person capable of feeling in the given case more than another of what is to be felt for it, and so serving in the highest degree to *record* it dramatically and objectively, is the only sort of person on whom we can count not to betray, to cheapen or, as we say, give away, the value and beauty of the thing. [HENRY JAMES]

Here not only are subject (*person*) and verb (*is*) widely separated, but the following *sort of*, requiring completion, and the transitive infinitives, requiring an object, force us on to the end of the sentence before we can pause. That, of course, is the point of the periodic style—to keep the sentence grammatically suspended up to the period. Carried to such length as the quotations illustrate, the device is rare today and has a contrived air. For most readers, too, it is difficult to follow and has a jerky rhythm. Used in moderation, however, the periodic sentence is effective. It is particularly useful and familiar in constructing a quick vignette, for it allows a good deal of secondary information to be admitted without deflecting the course of the principal predication. The writer may wish, for example, to identify someone in passing:

Roger Morrison, once an active supporter of the Prime Minister, though now old and retired, came out, to the surprise of everyone, in favor of the opposition.

The main point is, of course, that Morrison came out in favor of the opposition, but the additional information is essential to give that statement its force. The facts could have been expressed in different form:

Roger Morrison came out in favor of the opposition. This surprised everyone, since he had once been an active supporter of the Prime Minister, though he was now old and retired.

The first version is more compact and, by reason of the periodic tension, more effective in conveying surprise. Moreover, the second version slightly deflects the reader's attention from the main course of exposition, as the first does not. In the following passage the writer manages to pack a good deal of illustrative material between subject and verb without losing the principal thread of argument:

But modern automatic machines such as the controlled missile, the proximity fuse, the automatic door opener, the control apparatus for a chemical factory, and the rest of the modern armory of automatic machines which perform military or industrial functions, possess sense organs; that is, receptors for messages coming from the outside. [NORBERT WIENER]

Variations of Normal Word Order

In most sentences the subject, verb, and complement appear in that order, and adjectives normally come before the words they modify. Changes in these "regular" patterns stress the constructions displaced. To emphasize the complement, it can be put first in the sentence (thus Thoreau's "Bread I at first made from pure Indian meal and salt"). The usual sequence in the sentence "I call it a crime" may be altered to "A crime I call it." The emphasis may be increased by repetition: "A crime I call it, a crime," or by contrast: "A crime I call it, not a mistake." This kind of inversion can emphasize a comparison or contrast:

Hurricanes the natives had experienced, and monsoons, but never an atomic explosion.

This throws much more weight on the objects of "experienced" than the equivalent normal order:

The natives had experienced hurricanes and monsoons, but never an atomic explosion.

Inversions are often useful for preserving the reader's focus on the subject of discourse. In the following example, the first two sentences follow a normal sequence, but the third, in order to keep the idea of "London" first in the sentence, is completely inverted:

London was, and still is, the political and commercial center of England. It was the seat of the court, of the highest judicial tribunals, the focus of the social and intellectual activities of the country. To it were drawn in a constant stream those whose affairs took them beyond the limits of their provincial homes. [A. C. BAUGH]

The author might well have continued with, say, a sentence beginning "From it," if he had had more to say on the subject. The advantage of such inversion is that it keeps our attention clearly on "London," the subject of the writer's remarks. Another example may be recalled from the familiar pattern of the Sermon on the Mount, where the normal sequence—"The meek are blessed"—is inverted to "Blessed are the meek." The inversion not only emphasizes the complement "Blessed" and contributes to the continuity, but also creates an effective rhythm by the repetition of the formula "Blessed are—."

The same inversion may be used to construct a periodic sentence that emphasizes the complement. For example:

In overwhelming pride, delight in cruelty, neurotic disintegration—in this and not in the Treaty of Versailles or in the incompetence of the German Republic lies the explanation of Fascism. [LEWIS MUMFORD]

Adjectives in pairs or series can be moved about to some extent with varying effects.

1. The haughty and insolent prince soon gained the hatred of the stiff-necked barons.
2. Haughty and insolent, the prince soon gained the hatred . . .
3. The prince, haughty and insolent, soon gained the hatred . . .

The first may be considered the "normal" pattern without special rhetorical effect. In the second pattern, the adjectives are preliminary; we feel them leading up to something, for they more clearly suspend the predication than the same adjectives in the first sentence. The third pattern may have a similar effect, but the adjectives are felt as more parenthetical. The important difference between (1) and the variations (2) and (3) is that in the latter two sentences the adjective phrases suggest predication; indeed they can be readily converted into clauses:

> Because he was haughty and insolent, the prince . . .
> The prince, who was haughty and insolent, . . .

Thus they begin to approach the assertion of an actual clause, which the attributive adjectives of (1) do not do at all.

The position of single adjectives is not so readily shifted. It would sound very odd to say, "Haughty, the prince soon gained the hatred . . . ." However, single past particles follow the pattern easily:

> The enraged king ordered the queen's arrest.
> Enraged, the king ordered the queen's arrest.
> The king, enraged, ordered the queen's arrest.

There Is/There Are

Some rather foolish things have been written and said about this indispensable formula; particularly foolish is the general admonition that it should be avoided. There is nothing wrong with the formula itself—it has a simple, clear meaning; knowing how to use it is what matters, and this again is a matter of paying attention to the predication of a sentence. We have already given an example of an objectionable sentence using this formula: "There are many pros and cons on capital punishment." The trouble here is not the use of "there are" but the triviality of the predication. The formula "there is" simply asserts the existence or presence of something; it does nothing more. To assert the mere existence of differing opinions on the subject of capital punishment is to assert the egregiously obvious. But occasions are numerous when the assertion of existence is precisely the point.

> There are more women than men in New York.
> There is only one way to solve this problem.
> There was enough water on the floor to float a battleship.

When the existence of something is beside the point, the formula is useless:

> There is an old proverb which says that too many cooks spoil the broth.

If the mere existence of the proverb is unimportant, as in most contexts, then it need not be asserted.

> An old proverb says that too many cooks spoil the broth.

Here the existence of the proverb is taken for granted. If greater emphasis is desired on what the proverb says rather than on the fact that an old proverb says it, we may make that statement the main clause and write:

According to an old proverb, too many cooks spoil the broth.

Patterns of Equivalency

The important structures here are (1) subject + linking verb + predicate noun, and (2) the pattern x *as* y, or x *such as* y. They are structures which, by their form, assert one thing to be equivalent to another.

Washington was our first President.

Washington and *first President* are equivalent.

A thing of beauty is a joy forever.

Thing of beauty and *joy* are equivalent.

Augustine defines evil as the absence of good.

Evil and *absence of good* are equivalent.

A great power such as England has great responsibility.

Great power and *England* are equivalent.

The last two examples show *implicit* assertions of identity: that evil *is* the absence of good, that England *is* a great power. The first two are direct assertions.

These structures are often a source of confusion for the beginning writer if he does not pay sufficient attention to the assertions of identity involved. For the sentence of this type to make sense, it must be logically possible for the terms to be equated. We have used one example before: "The prehistoric era was a life of many hardships." The sentence seems garbled because "era" and "life" are not equatable terms.

1. The feeling of helping others is the greatest source of accomplishment that I know.
2. Phoebe is the main way Holden can attain his desire to gain respect or admiration.
3. The third problem to be overcome by the rocket designer is the question of economic feasibility.

Each of these sentences, except perhaps the first, is more or less intelligible, but clumsy. The clumsiness results from the odd equations: *feeling = source of accomplishment, Phoebe = the main way, problem = question of economic feasibility.* The first statement was probably intended to convey the idea that the *fact*, not the feeling, of helping others is the source of the *feeling* of accomplishment. Thus:

Helping others gives the greatest feeling of accomplishment that I know.

In the second sentence, if we wish to retain *Phoebe* as the subject, a more suitable predicate should be found: "Phoebe inspires Holden to attain. . . ." Or if, as is more likely, the appropriate subject is Holden, we might write:

Through his attachment to Phoebe, Holden can attain his desire for respect or admiration.

In the third sentence *that* may be substituted for *the question.*

In each case the principles of the previous chapter can be usefully applied. By asking what he wants to talk about, the writer of the first sentence should be able to see that it is "helping others," not "the feeling of helping others." Similarly the writer of the third sentence, asking, "What *is* the problem?" may see that it is simply "economic feasibility." It is not only beginning writers who have trouble with patterns of equivalency; in a college textbook, we find this strange sentence:

One might fairly say that his position is primarily a motivational psychology.

Assertions of identity must be made continually, particularly in definitions. Frustrating when they are made sloppily, they can have clarity and grace when made precisely—as when Newman says, "Certitude is a mental state; certainty is a quality of propositions."

Most frequently the two things identified have the same grammatical form; that is, they are both nouns (Certitude, state; certainty, quality). But often noun equivalents must be used:

Weaving was Penelope's *salvation.* (gerund, noun)
To drink is *to live.* (infinitives)
Our *plan* is *to leave* instantly. (noun, infinitive)
That men are unhappy is *nothing* new. (clause, noun)
Whatever he said is a *lie.* (clause, noun)

A problem of usage arises with some types of clauses in this construction, particularly clauses that are ordinarily adverbial. Few readers, however grammatically fussy, feel anything wrong with

> *Home is where the heart is,*

or

> *When I am leaving is none* of your business,

though *when* and *where* suggest adverbial clauses rather than noun clauses. Similarly,

> *The Fourth of July is when our family reunion is held.*

But a *definition* in this form is usually frowned on:

> A holiday is when you don't have to work.
> An altercation is when people fight.
> Christmas is when Santa Claus comes.

Whether or not the prevailing prejudice against this form is justified, it does prevail; no writer of acknowledged competence uses the pattern.

Another bête noire is "the-reason-is-because" construction:

> The reason the officer had to resign was because he was involved in a scandal.

Handbooks recommend *that* for *because*, reasoning that this substitution will convert the subordinate clause from an adverbial to a noun clause. There is little basis for the recommendation in either usage or logic. The best writers from Dryden to the present have used the construction freely. The logic is perverse, too, for the identification of a clause as a noun or adverb clause can arise only from the way the clause is *in fact* used. And the fact is that the *because*-clause here is used as a noun. But there are those who, in spite of all, *will* regard the construction as "incorrect"; and a *that* clause in this construction will make no one unhappy.

5

SUBORDINATION

THE ideas in a sentence have varying importance, and their relative importance and relationship to one another are most easily indicated by the grammatical constructions used to express them. Although all constructions are flexible in this respect, there is a general hierarchy of subordination: at the top is the main clause, from which all subordinate constructions depend; next come dependent clauses and verbal and appositive phrases; most subordinate are prepositional phrases and simple modifiers—single adjectives and adverbs. In general, important ideas belong in constructions that make them stand out clearly, secondary ideas in constructions that show their relationship to the main clause. And, of course, "importance" is determined by context and purpose. The statement, "I was buying cigarettes in the drugstore when the radio announced the President's Cuban ultimatum," would be a ludicrous instance of "upside-down" subordination in an objective essay about the Cuban crisis. In an essay about your own experience in those days, it would be entirely apt.

In what follows we treat first adjectival, then adverbial, and finally absolute constructions.

Adjectival Subordination

The function of the adjective is to point to a quality (or property, or attribute) of the substantive it modifies. The adjective in the phrase "a *beautiful* evening" attributes the quality of beauty to *evening*. In the sentence "I am *tired*," tiredness is attributed to the speaker. In "That man I *love* is mean to me," the quality of "being loved by me" is attributed to the *man*. There are several constructions that can function adjectivally; and the type of construction used very often indicates the relative importance of the quality expressed. To illustrate, let us take the simple example of a red house on a hill:

1. The house on the hill *is painted red.*

67

Clearly the most important attribute of the house in this sentence is that it is painted red, for that is the principal predication of the sentence.

2. The house *that is painted red is* on the hill.
3. The house *painted red* is on the hill.

In these sentences the subordinate constructions, an adjectival clause and a participial phrase, show that the redness of the house is of secondary importance. Redness is still important, nevertheless, because it points out which house is referred to. If redness does not identify the house, it will go into even less emphatic constructions:

4. The Throckmorton house, *which is painted red*, is on the hill.
5. The Throckmorton house, *painted red*, is on the hill.

Here the non-restrictive constructions show that the redness of the house is less essential information; the purpose of the sentence—to communicate the locality of the Throckmorton house—is accomplished with or without the modifiers. That purpose could not be accomplished in (2) and (3) without the modifiers (see pp. 283–84). Finally, the idea of redness may be simply taken for granted:

6. The red house is on the hill.

The redness is still important, but not important enough to require assertion. The first five sentences all make an assertion, directly or implicitly, that the house is painted red: the sixth sentence does not assert, but *assumes* the house's redness. The first five sentences imply some necessity for stating, with decreasing emphasis, the color of the house—they make some point of it; the sixth sentence does not. (See also p. 62 for further variations possible with a pair of adjectives.)

The simple adjective modifier can sometimes be put to devious uses. If you say,

Relativity theory is really very simple and explains these phenomena adequately,

or

Relativity theory, which is really very simple, explains . . .

the reader will probably recognize the assertion as one man's opinion and do no more than mutter, "Simple for *you*, maybe," before going on. But if you say,

The simple theory of relativity explains . . .

the reader may quit in despair, for the construction implies that the simplicity of the theory is so universally acknowledged that it may be taken quite for granted. This device is dear to propagandists and other information officers, who believe that if they refer often enough to something as if it were self-evident truth, people will begin to believe that, in fact, it *is* self-evident. Obviously, then, this most subordinate of constructions should be reserved for ideas that are indeed acknowledged facts.

Although we have indicated that the main clause is not subordinate at all, an exception is the independent clause used parenthetically, as indicated in speech by lowered intonation and in writing by the use of dashes or parentheses:

> The Throckmorton house—it is painted red—is on the hill.
> The Throckmorton house (it is painted red) is on the hill.

This construction has about the same force as the nonrestrictive clause in sentence (4), but the implication that the information is additional and nonessential is rather more pronounced.

Adverbial Subordination

Adjectival constructions point out the properties of an object—the redness of a house, for instance—and they can attribute very finely discriminated qualities to the nouns they modify. But adverbial constructions have an additional advantage in that adverbial *clauses*, at least, can express rather precise logical relationships among ideas. This capacity of modern English is extremely advantageous for precision and accuracy. Consider the following sentence with its adjective clause:

> Medea, who sought revenge on her husband, murdered her own children.

The relationship between the ideas of murder and revenge is not expressed and is therefore uncertain. More precise are the alternative interpretations stated in subordinate adverbial clauses:

> *Although* Medea sought revenge on her husband, she murdered her own children.

> *Because* Medea sought revenge on her husband, she murdered her own children.

> *While* Medea sought revenge on her husband, she murdered her own children.

When Medea sought revenge on her husband, she murdered her own children.

Each conjunction expresses quite a different meaning from the others. And it is the subordinating conjunctions themselves that make precision about relationships possible.

Among the principal relations expressed by adverbial clauses are purpose, result, cause, condition, and concession. Often the same relationship can be expressed by several different constructions; the choice among them can be made according to the kind of emphasis wanted, though sometimes there is little discernible difference.

PURPOSE

He grew a mustache so (*or* so that) he would look more dignified.
He grew a mustache to (*or* in order to) look more dignified.

The infinitive phrase to express purpose is normal; it is more economical, a trifle less ponderous than the adverb clause.

He grew a mustache; he wanted to look more dignified.

He grew a mustache, the purpose of which was to make him look more dignified.

Neither of these sentences is felicitous: the first shows no relationship; the second uses a cumbersome adjective clause with a vague relative pronoun. However, a writer might want to give the two ideas equal emphasis and write:

He grew a mustache. His purpose (in doing so) was to look more dignified.

CAUSE AND RESULT

But his wife objected, so he shaved it off.

So or *so that* is the usual way of expressing result.

But his wife objected; therefore he shaved it off.

This is almost equivalent, but the unavoidable emphasis on "therefore" gives more stress to the result relationship and to the equal weight of the two clauses. If the cause seems less important than the result, then one writes:

But because his wife objected, he shaved it off.
But because of his wife's objections, he shaved it off.

A *because*-clause or *because of*-phrase is the normal way to express this relationship. *Since* is usually interchangeable with *because*, but is best avoided whenever its temporal sense might be suggested:

> Her friends avoid her since she insulted the mayor.

There is no way of telling whether the subordinate clause is temporal or causal. The ambiguity might be defensible, but if only one meaning is intended, the sentence should be revised.

> Oedipus blinded himself *inasmuch as* he discovered that he had murdered his father and married his mother.

> Oedipus blinded himself, *being that* he discovered that he had murdered his father and married his mother.

Of these, the first is stuffy, the second not generally regarded as literate. There is nothing wrong, however, with this participial modifier:

> Having discovered that he had murdered his father and married his mother, Oedipus blinded himself.

Though it does not spell out the exact relationship between the two notions, that relationship is almost unmistakable.

> Oedipus blinded himself, for he discovered . . .

There is a rhetorical difference between *for* and *because*, but it is subtle and probably of no great importance. The coordinating conjunction *for*, indicating that an independent clause is to follow, leads to a distinct pause before it and suggests (very slightly) a somewhat weightier statement to follow than the subordinating conjunction *because* suggests. *For* looks forward to an explanation for the preceding statement; *because* points only to the cause for the preceding predicate.

> Oedipus blinded himself. The reason for his doing so was that he discovered . . .

This uneconomical expression of the causal relationship is rarely used, but conceivably could be if unusually heavy emphasis on the reason were desired.

The use of *whereas* to introduce causal clauses is best restricted to legal writing.

CONDITION
Equivalent constructions are these:

If the weather permits, we will go sailing. (adverbial clause—perhaps a trifle old-fashioned now is the subjunctive here: If the weather *permit* . . .)

With good weather, we will go sailing. (prepositional phrase)

Weather permitting, we will go sailing. (absolute)

As would be expected, the first clausal form is somewhat slower and more formal than the phrasal equivalents. In the past tenses there is an alternative clausal form still quite common in formal prose, though not heard so often in speech:

Had he arrived a day earlier, he would not have been defeated,

equivalent to

If he had arrived a day earlier, he would not have been defeated.

CONCESSION

He was a remarkably intelligent man, but he had no grasp of practical affairs.

He was a remarkably intelligent man; nevertheless (however, yet) he had no grasp of practical affairs.

Although (though) he was a remarkably intelligent man, he had . . .

Although (though) a remarkably intelligent man, he had . . .

Semantically these are more-or-less equivalent, with decreasing emphasis given to the idea of intelligence. In the first two sentences, a good deal of importance is obviously attached to the idea, where it is expressed in independent clauses. Put into subordinate and elliptical clauses, the idea seems of much less importance than the idea that the man had no grasp of practical affairs.

In spite of the fact that he was a remarkably intelligent man, . . . etc.

This is an uneconomical and rather graceless construction, but is used occasionally when the *fact* of the matter is to be underlined but still subordinated. Often then the word *fact* will be qualified: "In spite of the indubitable fact that . . ."

Prepositional phrases are also used to express concession without strong emphasis:

Despite (Regardless of) his remarkable intelligence, he had no grasp . . .

The qualifier *no doubt,* as in

No doubt he was a remarkably intelligent man, but he had no grasp . . .,

carries the suggestion that what follows, though true, is also trivial, perhaps barely worth mentioning.

The Absolute

The absolute (p. 40) nearly always has adverbial force, but its *exact* relationship to the main clause is unexpressed. Though the absolute usually has only one sense in context, its occasional ambiguity can be a virtue, for it can express more than one relationship simultaneously and compendiously. For example:

The wind rising, we took in sail.

Was sail taken in *because* the wind was rising or *while* it was rising? Surely both. Similarly:

Our train having already gone, we had to spend the night in a hotel.

We spent the night in a hotel *because* the train had gone and *when* it had gone.

The absolute is also invaluable for descriptive purposes:

As he stood there, mouth twitching, sweat pouring from his forehead, the police continued to question him.

There is no other way to state this as economically and expressively.

Special Uses of Subordination

DESCRIPTION

Besides the usefulness of subordinate constructions for accurately expressing relationships among ideas, they are also indispensable for packing a lot of information into a brief compass. Descriptive material particularly, though it may be necessary to the meaning and interesting in itself, is often best handled in secondary constructions. By so doing and at the same time making the more essential statements in comparatively lean main clauses, the writer can clarify the structure and direction of his discourse:

Here we landed, and leaving our equipment in charge of Colonel Chick, whose log-house was the substitute for a tavern, we set out in a wagon for Westport, where we hoped to procure mules and horses for the journey. . . . At length we ascended a high hill, our horses treading upon pebbles of flint, agate, and rough jasper, until, gaining the top, we looked down on the wild bottoms of Laramie Creek, which far below us wound like a writhing snake from side to side of the narrow interval, amid a growth of shattered cottonwood and ash trees. [FRANCIS PARKMAN]

The main predications ("we landed," "we set out," "we ascended") provide a clear narrative sequence; they are simple and unencumbered by descriptive detail, which is kept in subordinate constructions. Parkman draws freely on the wealth of subordinate constructions available to the writer who is aware of the syntactical resources of his language. In the second sentence, besides numerous prepositional phrases and vivid adjectives (*rough, wild, writhing, shattered*), Parkman uses an adverbial clause ("until we looked . . ."), an adjective clause ("which wound . . ."), a participial phrase ("gaining the top"), and an absolute phrase ("our horses treading . . ."). And for all its complexity, the sentence reads smoothly.

The Musketaquid, or Grass-ground River, though probably as old as the Nile or Euphrates, did not begin to have a place in civilized history until the fame of its grassy meadows and its fish attracted settlers out of England in 1635, when it received the other but kindred name of Concord from the first plantation on its banks, which appears to have been commenced in a spirit of peace and harmony. It will be Grass-ground River as long as grass grows and water runs there; it will be Concord River only while men lead peaceable lives on its banks. [THOREAU]

Turn only the subordinate clauses in Thoreau's first sentence into independent clauses, and see how much is lost:

The Musketaquid, or Grass-ground River, did not begin to have a place in civilized history until 1635. It is probably as old as the Nile or Euphrates. The fame of its grassy meadows and its fish attracted settlers out of England in 1635. Then it received the other but kindred name of Concord from the first plantation on its banks. This plantation appears to have been commenced in a spirit of peace and harmony. The river will be. . . .

Such writing approaches what is sometimes called "primer style." More important, the second version loses the focus and organization of the original, where there is a clear central predication (about when the river began to have a place in civilized history) and where the proper relationship of the other matters of information is indicated by sentence structure. Probably the greatest loss is the concessive relationship of the original *though*-clause. The revision also forces the otherwise pointless repetition of *plantation* and *river*, since *it* can not be substituted in either place without confusion. Finally, the revision does nothing to prepare for the idea that follows in the second sentence of Thoreau's text; if anything, in fact, it leads us in the wrong direction. This subtly ironic reflection of Thoreau's on the "civilized history" of his first sentence follows smoothly from what he has already written, in great part because he can so easily pick up the subject of the first sentence and give it a new turn— which can be done only very clumsily in our version. Furthermore, Thoreau undoubtedly wanted the philosophical observation of his second sentence to stand out prominently over the descriptive first sentence: he achieves this effect by sharply contrasting the terseness, simplicity, and careful balance of the second sentence to the length and multiple subordination of the first.

TRANSITION

Another valuable use of subordination is for purposes of transition. It is often desirable to sum up very briefly in the same sentence one portion of an argument or description while announcing a new topic; this can often be done economically by summarizing in a subordinate clause and turning to the next subject in a principal clause. This method reminds the reader of what has just been said and at the same time shows him the direction next to be taken. The method is probably most familiar in chronological description:

In the meantime, while the Democrats at the national capital were wrestling with the dislocations in economy and trying to get it into a higher speed of production, politics was gaining power over economics. [C. A. BEARD]

The preceding exposition is summarized in the *while* clause, and the next matter to be described is announced, in general terms, in the main clause. If the language of this kind of transitional statement is too general and vague ("While all this was going on, a new factor was entering the picture"), you might as well forget about summarizing and introducing and simply say, "Next."

The following transitional sentences refer succinctly to rather long passages preceding and following them. In the first, the writer moves, with the help of a short absolute phrase, from an explanation for the long period of infancy in the human species to a discussion of the family:

Helpless infancy being prolonged by these interrelated causes, if the species is to survive, at least one social group must keep together for several years until the infants are reared. [V. GORDON CHILDE]

The following, even out of context, is plainly a turning point in the argument:

It is clear that if the geneses of civilization are not the result of biological factors or of geographical environment acting separately, they must be the result of some kind of interaction between them. [TOYNBEE]

Such transitional sentences are useful "signposts." They tell the reader where he has been and where he is going, but they do so without clubbing him, as do these graceless but familiar announcements: "In the preceding paragraphs, I have tried to show . . ." "Now let us turn to my second point. . . ."

6

COORDINATION

THE principle of coordination is so fundamental a part of English that it would be almost impossible to write a paragraph of normal prose that did not rely again and again on coordinate structures. The various forms of coordination, or parallelism (balance, comparison, series, and repetition), are probably the most powerful rhetorical tools at the writer's disposal, and therefore repay close study. The fundamental fact about coordination is the joining in some way of identical or recognizably similar constructions. The fundamental principle of its use is that constructions so linked should express coordinate ideas. Coordination is essential not only for clarity but also for emphasis and rhythm; it is the heart of the ceremonial style and the rhetoric of emotional persuasion. Coordination is particularly useful as a means of organization, of holding together sentences and groups of sentences.

At times in the history of English literary style, an extravagant use of the devices of coordination has been thought elegant. One of our first great stylists, John Lyly, was writing in the sixteenth century like this:

Young gentleman, although my acquaintance be small to entreat you, and my authority less to command you, yet my good will in giving you good counsel should induce you to believe me, and my hoary hairs (ambassadors of experience) enforce you to follow me, for by how much the more I am a stranger to you, by so much the more are you beholding to me. . . .

This is, of course, a highly artificial style; the elaborate balancing is mostly ornament only. In more restrained form, the style dominated formal prose of the eighteenth century:

It is the fate of those who toil at the lower employments of life to be rather driven by the fear of evil, than attracted by the prospect of good; to be exposed to censure, without hope of praise; to be disgraced by miscarriage, or punished for neglect, where success would have been without applause, and diligence without reward. [DR. JOHNSON]

77

Similar passages are to be found throughout the writings and speeches of our own Founding Fathers (thus the judicious use of this style in contemporary political discussion may happily evoke a sense of the American tradition).

In this century, a plainer style generally prevails, a style closer to conversation, so that excessive use of coordination may have the effect of artificiality. Parallel structures lend themselves to pomposity and to what we think of as "empty rhetoric," and their steady rhythms can induce sleep. Thus their effective use requires some caution and common sense. In modern prose, readers expect coordination to arise naturally from the substance of the statements. When used for decoration or when forced on material for which it is unsuitable, it distracts the reader's attention from content to manner and thus undermines the communicative function of language. History is full of renowned orators much admired for their eloquence who nevertheless were ineffective speakers simply because their audiences, lost in admiration of the eloquence, hardly knew what the orators were saying. There are, to be sure, a very few occasions when content is of secondary importance, particularly ceremonial events (funeral eulogies, commemorative celebrations, ribbon-cutting, etc.), from which we do not expect more than general praise, promise, or vague exhortation. But the more common function of language to explain or persuade requires something to be communicated; and the function of rhetoric is to enhance communication, not get in its way.

"Natural" coordination simply expresses equivalent ideas by equivalent constructions. This is very obvious in simple cases. No one is tempted to say, "Having an apple, I have a pear." One says naturally, "I have an apple and a pear" because of the normal equivalence of attitude towards the two objects. Conversely, "I walked to school this morning and found a fifty-dollar bill" would ordinarily sound odd because one does not usually attach equivalent importance to walking to school and finding fifty dollars. We should rather expect the first idea to be subordinated: "On my way to school this morning, I found a fifty-dollar bill."

The Conjunctions

Like constructions are usually joined by conjunctions. These are as follows (see also pp. 35–37):

Coordinating Conjunctions		Correlative Conjunctions
and	for	both . . . and
or	nor	either . . . or
not	so	neither . . . nor
but	yet	not only . . . but (also)
		not . . . but

Of these, *for, nor, so,* and *yet,* like the conjunctive adverbs (p. 36), normally join independent clauses only. A few other words are occasionally used as coordinating conjunctions, but these are the most common. The coordinating conjunctions stand between the constructions joined. They join only like constructions, i.e., two subjects, two prepositional phrases, two objects of a verb, etc. This rule has occasional exceptions, but they are infrequent, and you will never be wrong following the rule whenever possible. Sometimes it is not possible: "My case was handled efficiently and in a friendly way"—you cannot very well say, "and friendlily." "I am going home or to the movies." "You can go with Mary or Jane or whomever you please." Note, however, that though the constructions may sometimes differ in *form,* they always *function* alike in the sentence: *in a friendly way* is a prepositional phrase used adverbially and joined to an adverb, both modifying the verb; similarly, *home* and *to the movies* are both adverbial constructions modifying the verb; *whomever you please* is a noun clause, object, along with *Mary* and *Jane,* of *with.*

Parellelism is not affected by the presence of modifying and parenthetical constructions.

Dreams, which would seem to be completely private experiences (though Jung has suggested a collective, or racial, as well as personal unconscious), *and* primitive *rituals,* whose very essence, surely, is that they are public, *and art,* even in its very self-conscious manifestations, are all thought to be phenomena closely related to the unconscious mind.

In this sentence, despite their wide separation, the three subjects of the sentence—*Dreams, rituals,* and *art*—are properly parallel.

Balance

Jack and Jill went up the hill [*and* joins two subjects] . . .

Jack fell down and broke his crown [*and* joins the two predicates *fell down* and *broke his crown*],

And Jill came tumbling after [*And* joins two independent clauses].

The coordination in the old nursery rime is proper: from the standpoint of formal syntax, the conjunctions correctly join equivalent constructions; from the standpoint of rhetoric, the constructions so joined express ideas of equivalent importance. Other examples:

> Did you drop the eggs in the kitchen or in the hall? [*or* joins prepositional phrases]

> It is a simple but attractive dress. [*but* joins two adjectives modifying *dress*]

> She is pretty, not beautiful. [*not* joins predicate adjectives]

Again, the constructions joined do not have to be immediately adjacent to the conjunction:

> It is a simple but in some indefinable way an attractive dress.

But it must be clear to the reader which constructions are joined. (See pp. 40–41 for examples of ambiguous parallelism.)

The syntactical rule for the use of *correlative* conjunctions is that each element should be followed by the same construction. If, for example, *either* in a sentence is followed by a prepositional phrase, we must subsequently have *or* and another prepositional phrase.

> I am going *either* to church *or* to bed.

This rule is also ignored occasionally, but again you will never go wrong to follow it strictly. You may see or hear, "I am either going to church or to bed," where the correlatives are followed by different constructions, but the first statement is generally to be preferred because of its sharper and more logical form. It lets the reader see exactly the coordination wanted by the writer. The more complicated a sentence is, the more desirable it becomes to follow the rule. Other examples:

> This policy is followed *both* in this country *and* in England. (correlatives followed by prepositional phrases modifying the verb)

> In *neither* this country *nor* England has it been successful. (correlatives followed by objects of the preposition *in*)

> *Neither* in this country *nor* in England has it been successful.

> This policy is followed *not only* in this country *but also* in England.

> I *neither* went to the meeting *nor* intended to go. (correlatives followed by predicates)

Not only did I go to the meeting, *but* I enjoyed it. (correlatives followed by independent clauses. Note that a clause following the negative correlatives, *not only, neither,* and *nor,* inverts subject and verb order.)

He found *not* a house *but* a crater. (correlatives followed by objects of the verb *found*)

Coordination in pairs, then, is a simple matter, requiring only a knowledge of the coordinating conjunctions and an awareness of structure in the sentence. The writer should be alert for the presence of these conjunctions in his writing and ask himself, first, whether they are in fact joining like constructions, and second, whether these constructions contain ideas in some way equivalent. Much syntactical looseness, and even confusion, can be cleared up by such attention. One brief example:

If consumers could learn to recognize the value of a product and not its appearance, they would be better off.

Here the writer, inattentive to structure, makes "value" and "appearance" both objects of "recognize." The result is the meaningless notion that customers should learn not to recognize a product's appearance. What the writer intended can be properly put in coordinate form: consumers should learn (1) to recognize the value of a product and (2) to disregard its appearance. Elementary awareness of structure would show that there are two things to be *learned*, not two things to be *recognized*; or, alternatively, that the two things to be recognized are not value and appearance, but value and the irrelevance of appearance.

A note on the joining of verbs. Some teachers and traditional handbooks insist that if two tenses of the same verb are joined by a coordinating conjunction, the complete form of both must be given. According to this view, the following sentence is "incorrect":

But the world has never succeeded, nor ever will, in making itself delight in black clouds more than blue sky, or love the earth better than the rose that grows from it. [RUSKIN]

For it should read, "But the world has never succeeded, nor ever will succeed. . . ." As usually stated, the traditional rule is unjustified, for English has many such elliptical constructions which are logical and unambiguous. Ruskin's usage is idiomatic and can be paralleled in other writers of his stature. Nevertheless, the ear rebels at hearing two incompatible verb forms *together*. A contemporary political

writer, who may remain anonymous, has perpetrated in print this
ear-rattling sentence:

> I have not—because truthfully I cannot—treated contemporary Liber-
> alism except as a contemporary phenomenon.

But so clumsy a construction is rare simply because it is so unidio-
matic.

Another note on joining prepositional phrases. When two prepositional phrases have the same object, the two common constructions
are these:

> He is proud of, and kindly to, his children.
> He is proud of his children and kindly to them.

Both are logical and correct, but to many the first pattern sounds
jerky and suggests pedantry; consequently the second pattern is often
preferred.

Ironic Parallelism

The fact that coordinate constructions ordinarily convey ideas of
equivalent significance lends itself to manipulation for special effects.
Consider, for example, the famous statement "We have met the
enemy, and he is ours." Here *and* joins two independent clauses. Are
they of equivalent significance? No, ordinarily we should expect the
fact of victory to carry more weight than the fact of military engagement, a difference we should expect to see reflected in the structure.
The laconic force of the statement derives from the deliberate coordination of ideas which are not inherently equivalent; the victory is
treated as a matter of course, almost to be taken for granted.

Ironic parallelism is the basis for a kind of wit immortalized by
Alexander Pope, who liked to write such couplets as this:

> Not louder shrieks to pitying heav'n are cast,
> When husbands, or when lap-dogs breathe their last.

The humor derives, of course, from making "husbands" and "lap-
dogs" of equal significance; it also derives from the element of surprise: the coordinate construction leads us to expect something very
different from "lap-dogs." Not to labor the point unduly, here are
some more examples of ironic parallelism:

He was a fairly humane man towards slaves and other animals. [TWAIN]

Californian fruits and heiresses appeared seasonably in New York and were absorbed. [THOMAS BEER]

There was a time, during the prime of the late Senator Joseph McCarthy, when a large section of the press held that to say a man had a right to a fair hearing was equivalent to approving of whatever he was accused of —Communism or subversion or consorting with Harvard professors. [A. J. LEIBLING]

Another variation uses parallel constructions dependent on one word with more than one sense:

In the end she throws caution to the winds and herself at him. [PETER GOOLDEN]

Similarly:

Dr. Brinley turned even more confidentially towards the bishop, breathing at him a blast of whiskey and old age. [RICHARD HUGHES]

Epigrammatic Balance

The epigram derives its value from being striking to the eye and ear and from being easily remembered. It is the sort of thing people underline in their reading and remember from a speech. The epigram must be concise and express a kind of unity in itself. This unity is usually accomplished by certain balancings of constructions and words. The precise analysis of the various kinds of balance (antithesis, chiasmus, etc.) need not concern us here; a few illustrations will speak for themselves.

Prisons are built with stones of Law, Brothels with bricks of Religion. [BLAKE]

The cistern contains: the fountain overflows. [BLAKE]

Books are the best of things, well used; abused, among the worst. [EMERSON]

Having wonderful dreams, telling wonderful lies, was a temptation Whitman could never resist; but telling the truth was a temptation he could never resist either. [RANDALL JARRELL]

President Kennedy's Inaugural Address showed a liking for epigrams:

Ask not what your country can do for you—ask what you can do for your country.

If a free society cannot help the many who are poor, it cannot save the few who are rich.

Let us never negotiate out of fear. But let us never fear to negotiate.

As a rather artificial mode of expression, it should be used sparingly, for excessive use of the epigram can easily produce an effect of ornamental triviality. Judiciously used, it will be memorable—like a slogan. But unlike most slogans, it is also a meaningful statement. Don't use the epigram unless you want its message to be comprehended and remembered.[1]

Comparison

Grammatical comparison may be considered an aspect of coordination, since similar constructions and principles of usage are involved. The formal (grammatical) signs of comparison are as follows:

POSITIVE: *as . . . as*

John is as old as George. (Negatively often: John is not *so* talented *as* George.)

COMPARATIVE: *-er than, more (less) . . . than*

John is older than Mary.
John has more money than George.
John has less talent than George.

SUPERLATIVE: *-est (of, in), most (least) . . . (of, in)*

He is the richest of all.
He is the tallest man in his class.
He is the least talented of the group.

All forms of comparison require two things: the thing to be compared (*John, He*) and the thing it is compared with (*George, Mary, all, class, group*). Comparison will not make sense unless the things we compare on paper *can* really be compared and unless the terms of the comparison are known. Of the first stricture, little need be said; illogical or meaningless comparison is usually the result of semantic confusion, that is, simply faulty vocabulary. The second condition is more to the point here.

There is a familiar—and notorious—advertising slogan that a certain

1 The first quotation of Mr. Kennedy's above was very well remembered; people *did* start asking what they could do for their country. And for a while the President was twitted in the press for not having a ready answer.

beer "is *more* refreshing!" Without a context the statement is meaningless. More refreshing than what? Gin? Sorghum? Incomplete comparisons are more often than not inherently absurd. However, the second term of the comparison does not have to be stated in the same sentence; it is sufficient that it be clear in context. The sentence "Smith has better sense and greater initiative" conveys little meaning by itself, but if it is preceded by "Smith should have this job rather than Jones," it is perfectly clear and correct since we know the two terms of the comparison, "Smith" and "Jones." But both terms must be expressed somewhere. Similarly, the superlative degree of comparison requires identification of the category in which the subject is outstanding.

> Henry is the tallest man —on the team.
> —in the world.
> —I have ever seen.

Incomplete exclamatory superlatives—"Oh, that's the sweetest kitten!"—are generally considered unsuitable for even remotely formal writing and speech.

There are two traditional problems associated with comparison which we may consider briefly: first, the form of comparing one thing with every other thing in the same category (equivalent to a superlative). The best form includes an *else* or *other*:

> Mr. Warbucks has more money than anyone *else* in the world.
> There are more skyscrapers in New York than anywhere *else*.
> There are more skyscrapers in New York than in any *other* place.

Sometimes you will hear (less often see) this pattern:

> Mr. Warbucks has more money than anyone in the world,

where the *else* is omitted. Logically, "anyone in the world" includes Mr. Warbucks himself, so the sentence says that Mr. Warbucks has more money than he himself has—which is indeed beyond the dreams of avarice. The intended meaning is evident, of course, and the omission of the *else* or *other* is common in conversation; it is, nevertheless, an illogical form avoided by most good writers.

Secondly, the problem of pronoun case arises (see pp. 20–21). In popular speech *than* is sometimes treated as a preposition taking a pronoun object in the objective case: "Herman is bigger than *me*." In relatively formal writing and speaking *than* is treated as a conjunction and the following pronoun regarded as part of an elliptical clause, in this case the subject: "Herman is bigger than *I* [am big]."

True, no one in his right mind would actually say, "Herman is bigger than I am big," and there is some justification for the colloquial usage. Nevertheless, the form "Herman is bigger than I am" is idiomatic at any level of usage, *am* certainly demanding the subjective case *I* (not even the illiterate would say, "Herman is bigger than me am"). In writing, it is logical, traditionally correct, and normal to regard *than* as a conjunction. The case of the pronoun, then, should be determined by the terms of the comparison, not by the word *than*.

> Herman is taller than I. (comparison of subjects)
> Herman's arms are longer than mine. (comparison of possessives)
> He likes her better than me. (comparison of objects)

Colloquial usage has given a slight sense of uncertainty to the form "He likes her better than I," so we usually see and hear, "He likes her better than I *do*."

Series

The same principles of coordination apply to series as to pairs. Three or more coordinate elements constitute a series; the important rule for forming a correct series is simply that the elements should be like constructions and that they should express notions in some way equivalent. Most people are familiar with intelligence tests that require one to find the element in a series "that shouldn't be there."

> Apples, pears, bulldogs, bananas.

It is just a way of testing the ability to categorize; our language conventionally requires that a series contain only things in the same category. Sometimes the category may be relatively subtle:

> In the state mental hospital I saw alcoholics, drug addicts, juveniles, and insane patients.

No doubt the writer was telling the truth, but to include "juveniles" without qualification, as if all juveniles were somehow in the same category as the others, seems excessively invidious.

Furthermore, the elements in a series have equal rhetorical weight. To say,

> We want life, liberty, and happiness

is quite different from saying,

> We want liberty and happiness as well as life.

The first sentence presupposes some lack of all three, the second of only two; in the first sentence the words have equal weight, in the second they do not.

Almost all grammatical constructions can be put into series, but they should (ordinarily) be the same kind of constructions (always) used in the same way.

> John, Mary, and I are going to the beach. (subjects in series)

> We met Tom, Dick, Harry, and Mike. (objects of *met* in series)

> He rode across the meadow, over the brook, and into the cabbage patch. (series of prepositional phrases modifying *rode*)

> Your mother has told you, your father has told you, and I have told you to stay out of that cabbage patch. (series of clauses)

It is not difficult to make mistakes in series if you let your awareness of sentence structure lapse:

> One is able to go swimming in the ocean, hiking in the mountains, or whatever his sport may be.

Here we have three objects of the infinitive *to go*. To go swimming, to go hiking—yes. But "to go whatever his sport may be"? The three elements look all right in isolation (they are not the same constructions, but they are all noun equivalents functioning as objects), but they do not all look so well with the word they depend on.

Conjunctions in a Series

All the examples given so far use only one conjunction, before the last element of the series: a, b, *and* c. This is the commonest form, but a series may also have the form a *and* b *and* c, or a, b, c. These, being comparatively uncommon, have different rhetorical effects. The repetition of the conjunction, because it is ordinarily unstressed, may give a more rhythmic and fluid effect to the series, emphasizing the joining of the elements. The absence of any conjunctions, on the other hand, encourages a somewhat more staccato, more forceful reading of the series. It is probably easier to illustrate than explain the differences involved. Compare the different effects of series in these very simple sentences:

> There I saw a bird, a frog, and a snake.
> There I saw a bird and a frog and a snake.
> There I saw a bird, a frog, a snake.

The structure of the first sentence is the ordinary one; it does not call attention to itself in any way. The other two sentences are different. Read them aloud, and you will hear a distinct difference of tone: a rather matter-of-fact tone in the first, a suggestion of tranquillity in the second, a note of harshness in the third. The second and third patterns should be used only for special effect and only where justified by the context. Observe the fitness of the following:

> Science is again, as in the days of the alchemists and the necromancers, awesome, threatening, uncanny, sinister. [ROBERT PLANK]

Extended Series

Another case where structure enhances style is the extended series. One way to produce the effect of a multitude, a crowd, a great variety, is to expand a series to abnormal length. Compare the following descriptions:

> The city was very colorful. On the river there were many boats of all shapes and sizes; in the stalls along the banks were flowers of many different colors; and people were coming and going.

> The city was colorful. The river was filled with boats—big boats, small boats, row boats, sail boats, red, blue, green, orange, yellow boats; the flower stalls along the bank exploded with daffodils, tulips, roses, forget-me-nots, violets, hyacinths. . . .

One could go on, but hopefully this will suffice to make the point. Part of the greater vividness of the second paragraph is due to the concrete imagery (see pp. 179ff.), but the structure too contributes to the effect of variety and multiplicity. Here is another example:

> How much more genuine an education is that of the poor boy who contrived from the beach, and the quay, and the fisher's boat, and the inn's fireside, and the tradesman's shop, and the shepherd's walk, and the smuggler's hut, and the mossy moor, and the screaming gulls, and the restless waves, to fashion for himself a philosophy and a poetry of his own! [NEWMAN]

Effective humorous exploitation of series structure can be seen in the following passage by Sir Arthur Quiller-Couch, arguing against certain Teutonic critics who would have it that the witches in *Macbeth* are not really witches at all, but goddesses, Norns, Fates, or what-have-you (notice, too, how postponed predication contributes to the wit of the passage):

But if the reader insist on my being definite, when a lady wears a beard on her chin and sails to Aleppo in a sieve, and sits at midnight boiling a *ragoût* of poisoned entrails, newt's eyes, frog's toes, liver of blaspheming Jew, nose of Turk and Tartar's lips, finger of birth-strangled babe, to make a gruel thick and slab for a charm of powerful trouble—I say, if he insist on my giving that lady a name, I for one am content with that given in the stage-direction, and to call her "witch."

Mark Twain, in the following passage of invective, achieves a grandly tumultuous effect by piling up invidious adjectives. He describes a famous American woman as

grasping, sordid, penurious, famishing for everything she sees—money, power, glory—vain, untruthful, jealous, despotic, arrogant, insolent, illiterate, shallow, immeasurably selfish. . . .

A final example is a justly famous passage in which Henry James reflects on the absence of the amenities of (English) civilization in mid-nineteenth-century America:

One might enumerate the items of high civilization, as it exists in other countries, which are absent from the texture of American life, until it should become a wonder to know what was left. No State, in the European sense of the word, and indeed barely a specific national name. No sovereign, no court, no personal loyalty, no aristocracy, no church, no clergy, no army, no diplomatic service, no country gentlemen, no palaces, no castles, nor manors, or old country-houses, or parsonages, or thatched cottages, or ivied ruins; no cathedrals, nor abbeys, nor little Norman churches; no great Universities nor public schools—no Oxford, nor Eton, nor Harrow; no literature, no novels, no museums, no pictures, no political society, no sporting class—no Epsom nor Ascot! [2]

It will be evident from these examples that any very great expansion of the series readily takes on a humorous tone. All three passages, though essentially very critical, indicate, simply by excess, that they are not to be taken with total seriousness.

Repetition

All coordination is, of course, a kind of repetition, a repetition of constructions. We turn now to the repetition of words as well as constructions. This is the very essence of oratory and the grand style. But it is also essential to plain communication. The reason is simple. Few readers, and fewer auditors, really grasp a point unless it is re-

[2] Famous race tracks in England.

peated and thus emphasized—made to stick in one's mind. (The opposite danger is obvious: excessive repetition is boring and offensive; thus discreet variation often becomes necessary.) Once more, the important principle to be observed is that the use of repetition should always be purposeful; the writer should know exactly why he repeats himself. The device should never be gratuitous.

A frequent occasion for effective repetition is in argumentation. When an essay is devoted to the establishment of one principal point by a series of arguments or by accumulation of evidence, it may be very effective to repeat exactly the statement to be proved at the end or at the beginning of each argument or bundle of evidence. It provides emphasis on the conclusion to be drawn, defines the organization of the argument, and strongly enhances the effect of piling up evidence. Similarly, an essay attempting to prove a group of closely related statements may conclude, or introduce, all the arguments with sentences which *begin* the same way. The Sermon on the Mount,, repeating the formula "Blessed are," uses such a principle. This device requires too much space to illustrate at length, but take as a hypothetical example an argument for the independence of some group, which we shall call "we." We wish to promote self-government on the grounds of sufficient education of the group, ability to manage our own affairs, inherent moral right, and strong desire for independence. Each argument should be developed and exemplified; the overall argument may be punctuated by structural and verbal repetition.

> We have sufficient education for self-government.
> (argument)
>
> We have sufficient training and ability for self-government.
> (argument)
>
> We have the moral right to self-government.
> (argument)
>
> We have a passionate desire and need for self-government.
> (argument)

Such repetition organizes the specific arguments clearly, and strongly emphasizes the overall argument.

Repetition is particularly useful in a summary conclusion to an essay or speech. Even if your reader has been wool-gathering during the course of your arguments, you may, in your conclusion, arouse his attention to your principal points by the device of repetition. Here, for a simple but potent example, is Emerson summarizing his argument for the independence of American culture from that of Europe:

We will walk on our own feet; we will work with our own hands; we will speak our own minds.

Franklin Roosevelt had considerable facility in this respect. A speech in which he has argued for certain reforms in American institutions concludes:

We cannot go back to the old system of asylums. We cannot go back to the old lack of hospitals, the lack of public health. We cannot go back to the sweatshops of America. We cannot go back to children working in factories. Those days are gone.

Observe, too, the force of the short concluding sentence, often to be found at the end of a summary repetition of this sort.

Repetition may also be effective in the kind of conclusion which does not summarize but rather announces the result or advocates a certain action as a result of the preceding argument. Thus William Jennings Bryan, concluding his arguments for "bi-metalism" in his famous Cross of Gold speech, defines his (and presumably his party's) position on the issue:

We have petitioned and our petitions have been scorned. We have entreated and our entreaties have been disregarded. We have begged and they have mocked when our calamity came. We beg no longer; we entreat no more; we petition no more. We defy them.

At any point within an essay, repetition may be useful for underlining the similarity of ideas and for emphasizing addition or contrast.

Certainly there is no freedom where there is self-complacency about the truth of one's own beliefs. There is no freedom but demonic bondage where one's own truth is called the ultimate truth. [PAUL TILLICH]

7

VOICE

O NLY transitive verbs (that is, verbs that take objects) have an
active and a passive voice; intransitive verbs do not have voice.
The traditional way of stating the difference between active and
passive is to say that in the active voice the object "receives the action
denoted by the verb"; in the passive voice, the subject receives the
action. This terminology is not very attractive, but it will do for
practical purposes. (On the form of the passive, see p. 24.) To illustrate:

1. ACTIVE: Congress defeated the President's bill.
   PASSIVE: The President's bill was defeated (by Congress).

2. ACTIVE: Engineers are sending a satellite into orbit today.
   PASSIVE: A satellite is being sent into orbit today (by engineers).

3. ACTIVE: People throughout the nation mourned Miss Adams's
             death.
   PASSIVE: Miss Adams's death was mourned (by people) through-
             out the nation.

In the active voice, the bill which was defeated in (1) is the object of
the verb; in the passive voice, it is the subject; similarly for the satellite sent in (2) and the death mourned in (3).

The words in parentheses indicate the chief advantage of the passive voice, namely that the agent of the verb (whoever is doing the
defeating, sending, and mourning) need not be expressed. And there
are countless situations in which the agent is unknown, unimportant,
vague, or general, and therefore need not and should not be expressed. For instance:

Shakespeare was buried in Stratford on Avon.

We do not know and ordinarily would not care who actually did the
burying. Similarly:

In the year 1054 a new star was suddenly seen in the constellation of
Taurus.

92

Who saw it? Well, presumably everyone who looked. That is, the agent is general and indefinite. Again:

> If sulfuric acid is added to nitric acid, a chemical reaction is obtained.

The implicit agent here is "anyone." But what possible advantage can come of writing: "If anyone adds sulfuric acid to nitric acid, he will obtain . . ."?

Active or Passive

The agent of an action, then, is frequently irrelevant, especially in scientific writing and in exposition that aspires to the objective, factual atmosphere of science. There is a prevailing superstition that the active voice is somehow superior to the passive; and the wholesale admonition to "avoid the passive" is regularly sounded in rhetorical handbooks. To put it bluntly, this is plain nonsense. Each voice has its own value and should be used where it is appropriate. The common-sense criterion of propriety is, above all, the importance of the agent: if the agent of the action is important, it should be made the subject of the active verb; if the receiver of the action is more important, then it should be the subject of the passive verb. The active voice focuses attention on the doer *and* the doing; the passive voice focuses attention on what is done. Compare the following:

> Babe Ruth set a home-run record in 1927.
> A home-run record was set in 1927 by Babe Ruth.

The focus of the first sentence is on Babe Ruth and what he did; that of the second sentence is on the setting of the home-run record. The first sentence would be most appropriate in a context devoted to Ruth; the second would be most appropriate in a context devoted to baseball records. In any context, to be sure, the need for some variety of structure should prohibit exclusive use of one voice or the other; but, in general, the choice of voice should be determined by context and purpose.

The following passage, written by an award-winning expositor of science, illustrates the ease and propriety of the passive voice:

> In 1941, experiments *were conducted* with uranium-graphite mixtures, and enough information *was gathered* to lead physicists to decide that even without enriched uranium, a chain reaction *might be set up* if only the lump of uranium *were made* large enough. . . .

The Manhattan Project in 1942 set out to build a uranium chain-reactor of critical size at the University of Chicago. By that time some six tons of pure uranium were available; this *was eked out* with uranium oxide. Alternate layers of uranium and graphite *were laid down* one on the other, with holes through them for insertion of the cadmium control rods. The structure *was called* a "pile"—a non-committal code name which did not give away its function. [ISAAC ASIMOV]

Of the ten verbs here, one is a linking verb, two are in the active voice, and seven in the passive. Dr. Asimov did not *have* to use the passive so extensively, but by doing so he avoided much possible cumbrousness, which could easily have become absurd. He might have written, for example:

In 1941, Professor Urey and his associates at Columbia University and other physicists elsewhere conducted experiments with uranium-graphite mixtures, and they gathered enough information to lead them to decide that even without enriched uranium, someone might set up a chain-reaction if only someone else made the lump of uranium large enough.

Specifying the agents in this context would be clumsy, to say the least, and unfortunately the clumsiness would be nearly unavoidable, for the three different activities referred to were being undertaken by three different groups.

The propensity of scientific writing for the passive voice is observable in the following parallel passage by an equally renowned scientific writer, who is also a well-known scientist:

A large "pile" of graphite bricks with small pieces of natural uranium included in the structure *was constructed* in great secrecy under the grandstand of the University of Chicago Stadium, and on December 2, 1941, Professor A. Compton phoned to his colleague, Professor Conant of Harvard, the guarded message: "The Italian navigator has landed. The natives are friendly." This *was* quite correctly *interpreted* to mean: Fermi's pile works successfully. The first successful nuclear chain reaction *has been achieved.*
In the pile, the fission chain reaction *could be maintained* in natural uranium, but the natural uranium *was* so highly *diluted* by carbon that high efficiency in energy production *could* not *be achieved.* . . . [The ten lines omitted here contain four intransitive verbs, two passive verbs, only one active verb.]
Although the energy released in the fission of U^{235} nuclei *could* not *be utilized* and *was* literally *sent* down the drain by means of the water-cooling system, a new fissionable element *was produced* inside the pile during its operation. The neutrons that *were* not *used* in the maintenance

of the chain reaction in U^{235} nuclei *were captured* by U^{238} nuclei, producing the heavier isotope. [GEORGE GAMOW]

Both writers have used a very similar style; its excellence attests to the perfect suitability of the passive voice in the right context.

Conversely, there are situations where the active voice naturally predominates. The following brief passage, for example, about General Sheridan and what he was doing, contains not one passive construction; even the participles are transitive, varying the same active structure (and notice, too, how in the last clause the author avoids the more usual passive construction "when the advance *was* sounded"):

Sheridan was the man for it. As Warren's brigades struggled into position Sheridan was everywhere, needling the laggards, pricking the general officers on, sending his staff galloping from end to end of the line. He rounded up the cavalry bands, which had made music on the firing line the evening before, and he put them on horseback with orders to go into action along with the fighting men when the advance sounded. [BRUCE CATTON]

It is also sometimes said that the passive is "weaker" than the active; this is also a highly dubious generalization. Consider:

Yet Sheridan still was not satisfied. The enemy must be annihilated, all escape must be cut off, that railroad line must be broken, no one must relax or pause for breath as long as there was anything still to be accomplished. [CATTON]

Surely there is nothing "weak" about this; in fact, it is obviously comparable to the intense rhetoric of a Bergson or Lewis (see pp. 125–26). To turn the verbs into their active forms would be destructive, if indeed it is even possible to do so. For what can you supply as agents? "The Union army must annihilate the enemy?" "Sheridan must annihilate the enemy?" Not only are these less forceful than the original, they are erroneous. For the idea attributed to Sheridan here is that it doesn't matter *who* does it or *how*, it must be *done*; the focus is all on what is to be done, not at all on the doer.

Continuity

Especially in writing where the interest is continuously focused on one person or object, voice may vary from active to passive as the central figure acts or is acted upon. In the following excerpt from a case-history, observe how "Johnny" or "he" is the subject of every clause, keeping our attention fixed on the boy being written about, while the voice of the verbs alternates:

A few days after Johnny's arrival at the home he ran away after becoming involved in a series of thefts from parked cars, along with two older boys from the home. In court, at Baldwin, Johnny cried continuously for three quarters of an hour. He had been treated roughly, he said, had been glared-at at the table and whipped for picking grapes from the vines in the yard. He had not wanted to stay in this place, so he had committed the thefts in the hope that he would be transferred immediately. Then he had become frightened and ran away. [JEAN EVANS]

Passive as Imperative

The passive voice is often used as the approximate equivalent of an imperative, but has a different force, which can be exploited advantageously.

> Never dilute good scotch.
> Good scotch should never be diluted.

These sentences convey a very similar message, but the first, because it is in the imperative mood, speaks directly to the reader, commands him personally, while the second, in the indicative mood (the mood of general truth), sets up a supposed fact, merely implying the command; it is more impersonal, less direct. The force of the passive here is very familiar in the form "That just isn't done in polite company." In *fact*, of course, you have probably just committed the very outrage that "isn't done" and hence elicited the remark. The passive here is, then, a kind of indirect imperative passing itself off as an impersonal statement of fact. The usefulness of the construction is self-evident. It is, however, no substitute for the imperative where the situation calls for direct command or admonition. "That car should be looked out for" will hardly do for "Look out for that car." Nor does "He should be shot" mean at all the same thing as "Shoot him!"

8

POINT OF VIEW

B Y point of view we mean the way a writer presents himself in his writing and the kind of relationship he establishes with the reader. The broadest distinction is between a personal and impersonal point of view, a matter of distance between the writer and reader. If a writer uses the personal pronouns *I* and *you* regularly, if he addresses himself directly to the reader, he establishes a personal, perhaps even intimate, tone. Similarly the somewhat vague *we* (meaning "you and I and others," not the "editorial we") helps establish a certain amount of rapport. The extended use of *I* without reference to the reader may give the impression that one is overhearing a monologue rather than sharing a conversation. A very impersonal style avoids the personal pronouns, using when necessary the indefinite pronouns (*one, someone, anyone,* etc.) and, of course, the passive voice. The usual problem with point of view is in trying to maintain a reasonable balance, a tone that is neither too intimate nor too aloof.

Personal

The grammatical person (first, second, or third) which is to predominate in a passage or a whole essay should be determined by subject matter and intention. If you are writing of personal experience, then the natural point of view is from the first person singular: "*I* was there," "*I* did thus-and-so." The circumlocutions sometimes used in this situation are often clumsy and unnatural. The "editorial we" for a single person is at best seldom felicitous; at worst it can be absurd.

> The other day we went to the barber-shop to get our hair cut.

As light humor, this might be tolerable; in a serious context it would be grotesque. This same "we" can also seem devious, as if the writer were evading personal responsibility for his words.

> We do not like murder mysteries; we regard them as a waste of time.

This may give the impression of widespread agreement; it is more likely to give the impression that the writer is too pusillanimous to say "I."

The "editorial we" is appropriate in editorials and wherever the writer is speaking for a group. But as a substitute for the natural "I" in ordinary exposition, it is inept. The same is true for such substitutes as "the present writer," "the author," "the undersigned," etc. There is nothing inherently egotistical about the pronoun "I." And, in fact, if you *are* singing your own praises, it will be all the more obvious from coy references to yourself as "the author" or "this writer."

The use of "you" and the imperative mood is right for any context that directly addresses the reader, particularly hortatory and directive contexts. If, for instance, you are telling the reader how to do something, the imperative mood is natural, as in any recipe. Discretion is important, for few people much like the idea of taking orders; the unnecessary or unwarranted use of the imperative can easily alienate the reader.

An occasional problem arises with the use of "you" when it means not so much "you the reader," but "anyone," as in "To get to Woodlake, you have to ride on the morning milk-truck." This usage frequently appears in contexts where there is no suggestion that the *reader* might be doing anything of the sort; it is simply equivalent to saying, "*Anyone* who goes to Woodlake must ride on the morning milk-truck." The usage is quite acceptable, appearing in the best authors. The unwary writer, however, may unconsciously blend this indefinite "you" with the pronoun of direct address, slip into the imperative, and thus muddle his point of view. The result can be ludicrous. We know of an essay, for example, describing the concoction of an elaborate dish, which proceeds easily, using the indefinite "you" ("You must be sure the oven is preheated to exactly 350 degrees . . ." etc.), only to end with the dismayingly aggressive command, "Now eat it!" Here are two more examples of inept shifting of point of view:

> Compare this world of French society with America and one will find a sordid world giving way to a better world.

> There lies within man a desire to cast off from the lee shore and to take your chances in an unknown nature.

In contexts which do *not* give directions or make appeals, the true second-person point of view can be helpful in bringing the reader into the experience a writer is attempting to communicate. The following passages, for example, have substantially the same content:

> The pond is no longer the same. Where Thoreau once hoed his beans there is now a gas-station; there are hot-dog stands and summer cabins now where there had been only the quiet woods.

> Go now to the pond, and you will see a gas-station where Thoreau once hoed his beans. You will see hot-dog stands and summer cabins where there had been only quiet woods.

The first version is impersonal; the second attempts to draw the reader into the scene. When this device works, the reader may feel a closer involvement, feel himself in some way present at the scene. He may also get the feeling of being spoken to personally, as if the author really cared about his seeing what the author has seen. On the other hand, the exclusive use of the *imperative* widens rather than narrows reader distance:

> Look at the pond now. See the gas-station where Thoreau once hoed his beans. See the hot-dog stands . . .

This does not encourage imaginative participation in the subject. Hearing commands, we think of the commander; and where the writer's presence is scarcely felt in the first two examples, here we are much aware of it and to that extent distracted from the scene.

Besides drawing the reader into an experience, a writer may wish to establish some rapport between the reader and himself. Then the use of "I" and "you" and the "we" that means "you and I" is natural. Effectively used, this point of view encourages the reader to identify himself with the author's point of view and thus follow sympathetically the author's train of thought. It can also create a sense of ease and informality. Here, for example, is Sir Arthur Eddington speaking conversationally to the reader—speaking about himself, the reader, and both together:

> At the moment I am not insisting on the shadowy and symbolic character of the world of physics because of its bearing on philosophy, but because the aloofness from familiar conceptions will be apparent in the scientific theories I have to describe. If you are not prepared for this aloofness you are likely to be out of sympathy with modern scientific theories, and may even think them ridiculous—as, I daresay, many people do.

> It is difficult to school ourselves to treat the physical world as purely symbolic. We are always relapsing and mixing with the symbols incongruous conceptions taken from the world of consciousness. Untaught by

long experience, we stretch a hand to grasp the shadow, instead of accepting its shadowy nature. Indeed, unless we confine ourselves altogether to mathematical symbolism it is hard to avoid dressing our symbols in deceitful clothing. When I think of an electron there rises to my mind a hard, red, tiny ball; the proton similarly is neutral gray. Of course the colour is absurd—perhaps not more absurd than the rest of the conception—but I am incorrigible.

This passage has a graceful ease of manner (a quality, by the way, which many Englishmen have in their writing) that makes the reader feel that he is sharing in an intellectual enterprise. Eddington manages this with simplicity and honesty; he has avoided condescension, and, most importantly, he has avoided that wearisome and offensive "I'm-just-folks-too" approach which is a danger of an intimate conversational tone.

How far to go in this direction is a delicate problem. It is frequently good to establish a close relationship with the reader; it is also quite possible to go too far, become too intimate, too friendly, too confidential, causing the reader to draw back in discomfort and distaste. In the following excerpt, Eddington is probably approaching the limit:

Infinite space cannot be conceived by anybody; finite but unbounded space is difficult to conceive but not impossible. I shall not expect you to conceive it; but you can try. Think first of a circle; or, rather, not the circle, but the line forming its circumference. This is a finite but endless line. Next think of a sphere—the surface of a sphere—that also is a region which is finite but unbounded. The surface of this earth never comes to a boundary; there is always some country beyond the point you have reached; all the same there is not an infinite amount of room on the earth. Now go one dimension more; circle, sphere—the next thing. Got that? Now for the real difficulty. Keep a tight hold of the skin of this hypersphere and imagine that the inside is not there at all—that the skin exists without the inside. That is finite but unbounded space.

No; I don't think you have quite kept hold of the conception. You overbalanced just at the end. It was not the adding of one more dimension that was the real difficulty; it was the final taking away of a dimension that did it. I will tell you what is stopping you.

Is this perhaps excessive? Do we feel that Sir Arthur is about to sit in our laps? [1] Well, reactions will vary from one reader to another, of

<hr/>

[1] For purposes of comparison, the following piece of fatuous familiarity may be instructive:

Of course, emptying the mind is not enough. When the mind is emptied, something is bound to enter. The mind cannot long remain a vacuum. You can-

course, but it may at least be said that a writer will do well to keep before him a picture of his potential audience and judge his limits accordingly.

Impersonal

An impersonal point of view means primarily that the reader is not referred to or directly addressed in any way. Hence the pronouns "you" and "we" (meaning "you and I") are avoided. Secondarily, the impersonal point of view usually avoids the pronoun "I," though a writer can refer to himself quite often and still sound impersonal if he does not address his reader. Much of T. S. Eliot's prose (see p. 121) is of this kind; then the reader may feel that he is overhearing the writer rather than being spoken to. The impersonal point of view naturally predominates when the subject matter is impersonal—in history, for instance, and scientific writing. However, there is certainly no rule about the propriety of point of view to subject matter; it all depends on what kind of tone the writer wants to maintain and what kind of relationship he wants to establish with the reader. As it happens, most scientists and historians prefer an objective, impersonal tone; but there are plenty of exceptions. Several examples of the impersonal point of view have been given or will be (see the passages from Asimov, p. 93, Gamow, p. 94, Trevelyan, p. 128, and Schlesinger, p. 129). A danger of this point of view is that the writing can become so objective that it seems cold and inhuman, repelling the reader by its frigidity; but the impersonal style can be humanized by the use of effective imagery, metaphor, concreteness, lightness of style, and occasional humor. Most good writers, furthermore, naturally vary their implicit distance from the reader as their subject changes and develops.

Of the impersonal and indefinite pronouns, only *one* is trouble-

---

not go around permanently with an empty mind. I admit that some people seem to accomplish that feat, but by and large it is necessary to refill the emptied mind or the old, unhappy thoughts which you have cast out will come sneaking in again.

To prevent that happening, immediately start filling your mind with creative and healthy thoughts. Then when the old fears, hates, and worries that have haunted you for so long try to edge back in, they will in effect find a sign on the door of your mind reading 'occupied.' They may struggle for admission, for having lived in your mind for a long time, they feel at home there. But the new and healthy thoughts which you have taken in will now be stronger and better fortified, and therefore able to repulse them. Presently the old thoughts will give up altogether and leave you alone. You will permanently enjoy a mind full of peace.

some. It is a meaningful and useful word for the appropriate occasion. If used extensively or even more than occasionally, however, it quickly begins to sound stuffy. More often than not, the misuse of this pronoun is due not to any inherent inadequacy in the word but to the writer's using it where it is not appropriate. For example:

When one speaks of Dewey's metaphysics, one refers neither to a construction of pure reason nor to a cosmology organizing the conclusions of the special sciences.

If this seems wooden, it is probably because the writer has not made the best choice for the principal predication; "one refers" certainly doesn't sound very essential. Both *ones* seem to be cluttering up the sentence, which might as well be written:

What is called Dewey's metaphysics is neither a construction of pure reason nor a cosmology organizing the conclusions of the special sciences.

Commitment

Point of view also indicates the relationship between the writer and what he is saying. If the writer believes something to be a fact, if he has no doubts of the matter, then he should simply state it as a fact. If he is confident of his zoology, he will say, "Pigs do not have wings," not "It is my belief that pigs do not have wings." But there are many occasions when the writer, quite properly, does not wish to commit himself so unequivocally, and employs some means to weaken his own expressed relationship to the statement. Among such means, the verb *seem* instead of *be*, the subjunctive, and qualifying words and phrases are the most common.

> They do not seem hostile.
> They would not seem to be hostile.
> I do not think they are hostile.
> As far as one can judge, they do not appear to be hostile.

Too often such qualifications are merely an evasion of moral or intellectual commitment, but they may express as well a proper tentativeness of judgment. Even so gingerly an approach as "It would seem then that we are justified in holding that they are not hostile," if not elegant, might be defended as accurately implying tentative conviction on the basis of available evidence. The following is a good illustration of an eminent writer's cautious approach to a statement:

But, granting the complexity of the subject, I would yet venture to deal with it to the extent of proposing the idea that . . . [LIONEL TRILLING]

Too much of this sort of thing weakens one's style, for it leaves the impression that the writer lacks conviction.

A report of general opinion must often be stated vaguely:

> It is often said that . . .
> They say that . . .
> One often hears . . .
> The opinion is current . . .

Or, as Emerson nicely varied the expression:

> There goes in the world a notion that the scholar should be a recluse.

In reporting general opinion, precise attribution is unnecessary. If the opinion is in fact general, the statement will be accepted without a catalogue of sources. Examples are often useful, of course, but a long list beginning with the *Times* and ending with your barber is likely to be superfluous.

If the opinion is not general, or if it is not known to be authoritatively held, then the citation of sources is necessary. What authorities to cite and how many must be determined by the needs of the context and the nature of the audience. The only guide we can suggest is common sense, which tells us, above all things, that authorities must indeed be authoritative. The only common rhetorical problem is how to cite authorities briefly without losing continuity; the most convenient solution is to put the identifications in subordinate structures.

That capital punishment is not a deterrent to crime—a view held by many law enforcement officers, sociologists, and psychologists—can be shown by statistics.

The citation of names can be handled in the same way:

The relationship between pornography and sexual crime, attested to by J. Edgar Hoover among others, has been a major concern in this community.

Consistency

It is reasonable to expect a fairly consistent point of view in an essay —violent or unmotivated shifts are certainly distracting. Most good writers maintain a predominant point of view which answers to their intentions and often to their personalities. But while one point of view may predominate, it will rarely be exclusive, and the point of view will naturally change in the course of exposition as propriety dictates. In the following selection, the point of view, though predominantly impersonal, easily modulates to *we* to *one* to *you* and back to the impersonal. The changes of point of view are smooth and right because they exactly suit their context.

Thus measurements of space and time are "relative" to some arbitrarily chosen frame of reference—and that is the reason for naming Einstein's idea the "theory of relativity."

To illustrate. Suppose we on earth were to observe a strange planet ("Planet X"), exactly like our own in size and mass, go whizzing past us at 163,000 miles per second relative to ourselves. If we could measure its dimensions as it shot past, we would find that it was foreshortened by 50 per cent in the direction of its motion. It would be an ellipsoid rather than a sphere and would, upon further measurement, seem to have twice the mass of the earth. Yet to an inhabitant of Planet X, it would seem that he himself and his own planet were motionless. The earth would seem to be moving past *him* at 163,000 miles per second, and it would appear to have an ellipsoidal shape and twice the mass of *his* planet.

One is tempted to ask which planet would *really* be foreshortened and doubled in mass, but the only possible answer is: that depends on the frame of reference. If you find that frustrating, consider that a man is small compared to a whale and large compared to a beetle. Is there any point in asking which a man is *really*, large or small?

For all its unusual consequences, relativity explains all the known phenomena of the universe at least as well as pre-relativity theories do. But it goes further: it explains easily some phenomena which the Newtonian outlook explained poorly or not at all. Consequently Einstein has been accepted over Newton, not as a replacement so much as a refinement. The Newtonian view of the universe can still be used as a simplified approximation which works well enough in ordinary life and even in ordinary astronomy, as in placing satellites in orbit. [ISAAC ASIMOV]

In some special forms of writing, particularly formal reports of experiments, surveys, and the like, it is often necessary to maintain a fairly rigid distinction of point of view because of the necessity of sharply distinguishing observed facts from the writer's interpretation of them. Thus factual evidence (data) is properly presented in an impersonal mode; the conclusions drawn from the data in a personal mode. On the one hand, for example:

Forty subjects answered the question affirmatively.

The tobacco mosaic virus was identified under the electronmicroscope.

On the other hand:

> We conclude from this sampling . . .
> I believe other viruses can be isolated by similar methods.

These examples are obvious enough. Less obvious are such statements as "All forty subjects were nervous and apprehensive," where the more accurate statement would probably be "All forty subjects *appeared to be* nervous and apprehensive." That is, the predicate is an interpretation of appearances. Similarly, "This conformation is the result of volcanic pressure," if not an indisputable fact, may need to be prefaced by the phrase "In our judgment. . . ."

This is partly a matter of normal caution about generalizations; more importantly, it is a matter of not misleading the unwary reader into regarding your own interpretation of evidence as unquestioned fact or generally received opinion.

9

AURAL EFFECTS

Most readers, though they do not read aloud, hear in their minds the sounds of the words before them (as witnessed by the way most of us, even in silent reading, pause over words that we do not know how to pronounce); and good writers may take advantage of the fact to create atmosphere and enforce emphasis and contrast by their manipulation of rhythm. By rhythm we mean the repetition of the same or recognizably similar stress patterns.

Syllabic Rhythm

The regular metrical patterns of verse are seldom found in prose, except sometimes in brief passages; they seem too contrived, normal stress in prose and speech being irregular. Sometimes a writer will accidentally compose a line or two with the metrical pattern of blank verse, but if he does so often enough to call attention to the fact, he is likely to dissipate the attention of his reader, who in this context neither expects nor wants metrical prose.

However, because English has so many polysyllabic words and so many unstressed function words—particularly the articles, prepositions, and conjunctions—and because accented words are heavily stressed (much more so than in French, for instance), the predominant pattern of English prose is an alternation of stressed and unstressed syllables. For this reason the juxtaposition of two or more stressed syllables tends to attract the reader's attention:

> He took the final step in *cóld blóod*.
> It is *hére, nów* that we must act.

But the sounds of prose are subtle, and such juxtapositions are rhetorically forceful only as they are supported by meaning and sentence structure. For example, the contrast of a short summarizing, central statement to longer, more complex secondary statements in a paragraph (see pp. 75, 91) may be enhanced by the contrast of rhythm. To illustrate:

One can understand the fearlessness of the skunk. Nearly every creature but the farm dog yields to him the right of way. *All dread his terrible weapon.* If you meet one in your walk in the twilight fields, the chances are that you will turn out for him, not he for you. He may even pursue you, just for the fun of seeing you run. He comes waltzing toward you, apparently in the most hilarious spirits.

The coon is probably the most courageous creature among our familiar wild animals. Who ever saw a coon show the white feather? He will face any odds with perfect composure. I have seen a coon upon the ground, beset by four men and two dogs, and never for a moment losing his presence of mind, or showing a sign of fear. *The racoon is clear grit.* [JOHN BURROUGHS—italics added]

Each italicized sentence is the most important in its paragraph, an importance emphasized by the brevity and simplicity of the two sentences in contrast to the others. But notice also the rhythmical contrasts. "Áll dréad" and "cléar grít" have equal stress on adjoined syllables, adding to the emphasis of these sentences. In the rest of the passage, the same stress pattern in "fóur mén" and "twó dógs" gives desirable emphasis to the odds against the racoon. And the second most important sentence in the second paragraph has, similarly, "cóon shów" and "white féather." Otherwise the predominant stress pattern in the passage is an alternation of stressed syllables with one or more unstressed syllables.

The two kinds of rhythm have a quite discernible difference of effect, readily apparent if we take the famous line of Tom Paine's—

These are the times that try men's souls—

and change it to

These times try men's souls.

The first, with its regular alternation of stresses is dignified, sonorous, almost incantatory. The second, with its unrelieved heavy stresses, has a greater effect of urgency and anger—it may even sound querulous. The first stress pattern can be effectively used to suggest quietude. For example:

When the sun withdraws the sand ceases to flow, but in the morning the streams will start once more and branch and branch again into a myriad of others. [THOREAU]

Here the regular rhythm creates a lulling effect suitable to the content. To be sure, very much of this at a time may lull the reader to sleep. Some writers and speakers, probably attracted by the sonority of a regular rhythm, tend to overuse it, forgetting how soporific it can be—as anyone who has heard many sermons can testify. The second stress pattern is useful for breaking up rhythmic monotony; more importantly, it can sharpen emphasis at critical moments. This pattern, though virtually impossible to sustain for long, if used often enough, creates a kind of nervous rhythm:

There they were, walking forward in battle lines that were a míle wíde and many ránks déep, sunlight glinting on thousands of bríght múskets, flágs snápping in the breeze, brigáde frónts táut with paráde-gróund Régular Army precision. [BRUCE CATTON]

Another familiar, brief quotation (from Patrick Henry) will illustrate the meaningful variation of stress patterns:

The gentlemen may cry Péace, Péace! but there ís no peace.

The juxtaposed stresses of the first sentence contribute strongly to its exclamatory force. In contrast, the rising to "is" and falling away from it in the second sentence contribute to the gravity of that statement.

Phrasal Rhythm

A second type of rhythm grows out of the repetition of structural patterns. The same structure or the same words repeated create a larger, more general rhythmic pattern, which is simply an adjunct of parallelism. Although some writers consciously manipulate structures to produce certain rhythms, more often phrasal rhythm is an accident, as it were, a by-product of structure.

He may still be in the bondage of dogmatic self-assurance but he has begun to be free of it. He may still be in the bondage of cynical despair, but he has already started to emerge from it. He may still be in the bondage of unconcern about the truth that matters, but his unconcern is already shaken. [PAUL TILLICH]

Each sentence has the same balanced structure and repeats the same words "He may still be in . . . but . . ."; each sentence has the same rhythm. The result is a strengthening of the semantic parallelism. The passage is dignified, solemn, sermonlike (as a matter of fact, it is taken from a sermon), a quality enhanced by the regular syllabic rhythm, which is rhetorically effective but could not go on too much longer without becoming boring or irritating.

The effect of phrasal rhythm depends not on repetition in itself, but on *what* is repeated. The repetition of fairly long balanced structures, as in the above example, has an effect different from that resulting from the repetition of, say, short, simple clauses, for example:

> He was born a fool, he grew up a fool, he died a fool.

Basic to the use of rhythm in prose is the fact that one reads in units: words, phrases, clauses. Shorter, simpler units one usually feels to be somehow more forceful than longer equivalents. Thus monosyllabic words may seem more virile than their polysyllabic synonyms (compare: *hope* and *optimism, house* and *domicile, tough* and *resilient, big* and *capacious,* etc.), and short simple sentences more telling than long complex ones (compare: "Down with Jones!" and "It is my unshakable conviction that Jones should be removed from office forthwith."). The reason for this commonly felt difference lies, possibly, in the difference between an uninterrupted flow of syllables and semantic units on the one hand, and on the other, a frequent starting and stopping of such units. We have a sense, largely unconscious, of stopping at the end of a word, phrase, or clause; hence the more often we stop and start again, the faster the rhythm and the greater the feeling of quickness, activity, even nervousness.

The following passage illustrates the effective use of contrasting rhythms to underline contrasting situations:

After all these years I can picture that old time to myself now, just as it was then: the white town drowsing in the sunshine of a summer's morning; the streets empty, or pretty nearly so; one or two clerks sitting in front of the Water Street stores, with their splint-bottomed chairs tilted back against the walls, chins on breasts, hats slouched over their faces, asleep—with shingle-shavings enough around to show what broke them down; a sow and a litter of pigs loafing along the sidewalk, doing a good business in watermelon rinds and seeds; two or three lonely little freight piles scattered about the "levee"; a pile of "skids" on the slope of the stone-paved wharf, and the fragrant town drunkard asleep in the shadow of them. . . .

Then the steamboat arrives:

The town drunkard stirs, the clerks wake up, a furious clatter of drays follows, every house and store pours out a human contribution, and all in a twinkling the dead town is alive and moving. Drays, carts, men, boys, all go hurrying from many quarters to a common center, the wharf. [MARK TWAIN]

The first part, mostly a string of long absolute constructions, has a slow, leisurely rhythm, which seems to be the result of the comparatively few stopping places at the end of the absolutes. The second part has a quicker rhythm because of the stops at the end of each short clause and, similarly, because of the string of stressed monosyllables in "Dráys, cárts, mén, bóys, áll." The feeling of torpor in the first part and the feeling of bustle in the second are due above all to the words used—to the meaning of the passage; but the contrasting rhythms undoubtedly contribute to the final effect.

Alliteration, Assonance, Rime

All three terms refer to the proximate repetition of sounds: alliteration to the repetition of initial sounds of words ("spic and span"), assonance to internal sounds ("reaping wheat in the field"), rime to syllables ("gruesome twosome") or part of syllables ("true blue"). All have a limited use in prose, chiefly for epigrammatic purposes. Since they are great aids to memory they are used prodigiously in slogans: "Peace, Progress, and Prosperity," "Win With Willkie," "Fifty-four Forty or Fight," "Tippecanoe and Tyler Too," etc., etc., etc. Thus they can be useful, if not too laboriously contrived, to sharpen an epigrammatic remark.

> [In the movies] the salable blending of the pious and the prurient has long been a fine art. [HENRY POPKIN]

> . . . the kind of entertainment that used to be furnished by Errol Flynn, a blade and a babe. [POPKIN]

> He was carnivorous, bibulous, querulous, cantankerous and poisonous as a snake. [HENRY MILLER]

To be effective, such devices should be used very sparingly and only where the meaning and purpose of the expression justify their use. Overused, they are merely cute.

Another danger is the accidental sound cluster which grates on the ear, but which the eye may not behold. Accidental alliteration, particularly, can produce some hair-raising sounds. For example, while writing this book, we discovered that we had at one point advised the reader to "notice the succinctness of the sixth sentence." To avoid such cacaphony, it is well to read one's work aloud before committing it to its final form.

10
LENGTH
AND COMPLEXITY

THE question how long a sentence should be is very like the old query about how long a man's legs should be. A sentence should be long and complex enough to accomplish its purpose effectively —anywhere from one word to half a page or more. The most effective sentence structure, as we have said before, corresponds to the thought it conveys. There is no inherent virtue in either brevity or length for its own sake. Moreover, short, simple sentences are not necessarily easier to read than long, complex ones. On the contrary, a long string of simple sentences can actually be harder to understand than relatively complex statements if it fails to show the comparative importance of assertions and the logical relationships among ideas. If simple sentences are generally more forceful, it is only when they are used in contrast to more complex structures. Brevity and simplicity are not to be confused with economy. Economy *is* a virtue in writing, for unfunctioning, purposeless language impedes communication. Unnecessary complexity, redundancy, empty verbiage may bore and exasperate the reader to the point where he ceases to be open to the content of the writing; and if communication fails, any hope of persuasion disappears. On the other hand, a false economy of oversimplification may just as easily confuse and alienate the reader. The economical structure, then, is the one that conveys the writer's intention in the minimum number of words *necessary to that intention.*

Simplicity or Complexity

Complexity is often desirable, most importantly when predication needs qualification.

Patterns of meaning are arbitrary if they do violence to the facts, or single out correlations or sequences of events which are so fortuitous

111

that only some special interest or passion could persuade the observer of the significance of the correlations. [REINHOLD NIEBUHR]

It would not do to simplify this structure, for the proper understanding of the central predication requires the close dependence of the qualifications. Two more sentences of Niebuhr's will illustrate the situation where the subject of discourse must be carefully identified, in the first case what kind of an observer can apprehend irony, in the second what kind of a nation is involved in incongruities.

The knowledge of irony depends upon an observer who is not so hostile to the victim of irony as to deny the element of virtue which must constitute a part of the ironic situation; nor yet so sympathetic as to discount the weakness, the vanity and pretension which constitute another element.

There are so many obviously ironic elements in current history, particularly in our own national history, because a nation which has risen so quickly from weakness to power and from innocency to responsibility and which meets a foe who has transmuted our harmless illusions into noxious ones is bound to be involved in rather ironic incongruities.

There is also the matter of tone, which depends usually on the kind of audience the writer has in mind. If he is writing to a limited audience of fellow professionals, for example, he may strive for a terse, precise, rigidly formal tone; but if he contemplates a wider audience, he may well desire a more easy-going, conversational tone, which, perhaps paradoxically, usually involves a more complex sentence structure. The difference may be illustrated by two passages of philosophical exposition.

An occasion of experience is an activity, analysable into modes of functioning which jointly constitute its process of becoming. Each mode is analysable into the total experience as active subject, and into the thing or object with which the special activity is concerned. This thing is a datum, that is to say, is describable without reference to its entertainment in that occasion. An object is anything performing this function of a datum provoking some special activity of the occasion in question. Thus subject and object are relative terms. An occasion is a subject in respect to its special activity concerning an object; and anything is an object in respect to its provocation of some special activity within a subject. Such a mode of activity is termed a "prehension." [ALFRED NORTH WHITEHEAD]

Throughout the long tradition of European thought it has been said, not by everyone but by most people, or at any rate by most of those who have proved that they have a right to be heard, that nature, though it is a thing that really exists, is not a thing that exists in itself or in its own right, but a thing which depends for its existence upon something else. I take this to imply that natural science, considered as a department or form of human thought, is a going concern, able to raise its own problems and so solve them by its own methods, and to criticize the solutions it has offered by applying its own criteria: in other words, that natural science is not a tissue of fancies or fabrications, mythology or tautology, but is a search for truth, and a search that does not go unrewarded: but that natural science is not, as the positivists imagined, the only department or form of human thought about which this can be said, and is not even a self-contained and self-sufficient form of thought, but depends for its very existence upon some other form of thought which is different from it and cannot be reduced to it. [R. G. COLLINGWOOD]

The two passages have in common a very abstract language, but the first employs a rather simple sentence structure, the second a very complex one; yet the second is plainly easier to read. We seem to be listening to Collingwood thinking out loud, so that we can follow his thought processes to their conclusions; Whitehead, on the other hand, gives us only the results of his thinking in a precise, almost mathematical way. A writer desiring bare accuracy would strike out Collingwood's "not by everyone but by most people, or at any rate . . ." and try to define right off exactly who is meant without, as it were, publicly making up his mind. Similarly he would be suspicious of saying something "in other words," thinking he should get it said in exactly the right words in the first place. But, though Collingwood is copious, he is not uneconomical. All the words count, either for explanation or for establishing an easy tone; the result is an attractive handling of a forbidding subject.

Structural simplicity is most useful for emphatically communicating essential points, ideas the writer particularly wants his readers to remember. The mere statements themselves will not, of course, be persuasive if they are not supported by convincing argument; hence they are most effective as a means of forcefully summarizing an argument or stating the conclusion to be drawn from presented evidence. We have already given many examples of this rhetorical device (recall, for example, "Those days are gone," p. 91, "The racoon is clear grit," p. 107). Here is another illustration:

Language is more than a vehicle of tradition. It affects what is transmited. The socially accepted meaning of a word (or other symbol) is almost necessarily somewhat *abstract*. The word "banana" stands for a *class* of objects having in common certain visible, tangible, odorous and above all edible qualities. In using it we make abstraction of, that is, we ignore as irrelevant, details—the number of spots on its skin, its position on a tree or in a trap, and so on—that are qualities of any real individual banana. Every word, however gross and material its meaning, possesses something of this abstract character. By its very nature language involves classification. On the practical side, by example you learn to imitate accurately and in detail a particular set of manipulative movements. By precept you can be taught the sort of movements to perform, but you are still left a little room for variation. In engineering the contrast between apprenticeship and a university education really goes back to this. Language makes tradition rational. [v. GORDON CHILDE]

The last brief sentence, epitomizing the whole paragraph, gives a sense of point and conclusion to the paragraph. This device, to refer to another realm of discourse, is exactly comparable to the punchline of a joke.

Similarly, a brief, compact sentence may open a paragraph or essay with good effect (as in the above quotation). The summarizing sentence is probably most effective at the end of a section; at the beginning, a concrete, exemplary statement often serves to catch the reader's attention, particularly if it has a dramatic quality. Bacon, for example, began his famous essay on truth thus: "*What is truth?* said jesting Pilate; and would not stay for an answer." In recent years, a journalistic exposé of the "shame" of New York City began something like this: "There are seven million people in New York City; there are ten million rats"—an arresting introduction.

Simple, terse statements, if well handled, often have an epigrammatic flavor and therefore stick in the memory. Everyone remembers "War is hell," though few of us remember any arguments Sherman may have adduced to support the statement. One remembers "Life is nasty, brutish and short," but not what considerations led Hobbes to his conclusion. How are such statements "well handled?" Besides the application of strictly rhetorical devices—such as the aural effects discussed in Chapter 9, for example—there is one principle of far greater importance than any other: the *meaning* conveyed by such means must be worthy of emphatic treatment. Succinct conclusions and summaries must indeed conclude and summarize. Since these simple, forceful statements are mnemonic, they must embody ideas that are indeed worth remembering. The quasi-dramatic introductory statement must indeed introduce: it must be strictly relevant to what follows. Otherwise, the device is worse than wasted; it is confusing, for it prepares the reader for a sequence of ideas that is not forthcoming. Impressive techniques are worthwhile only so far as content justifies them.

Conciseness

Whether or not a given piece of writing should be terse or leisurely in style depends on the writer's intentions. In general, however, conciseness is the more frequently sought after goal; it is particularly in demand in all kinds of technical exposition. In any writing wastefulness is a self-evident vice.

Conciseness and structural simplicity are not the same things at all. Consider the following:

> Cedar Rapids is known as the 'Garden City of Iowa.' It is situated on the Cedar River. It has a population of about 90,000. It is the second largest city in the state.

> The 'Garden City of Iowa,' Cedar Rapids, situated on the Cedar River, is, with a population of about 90,000, the state's second largest city.

The first version, than which nothing could be more painfully simple, is yet nine words longer than the second. Simplifying the syntax will not automatically lead to conciseness, though it sometimes may.

From a structural standpoint, the way to achieve conciseness is by substituting shorter constructions for equivalent longer ones, a phrase for a clause, a word for a phrase. (In addition to the following illustrations, see pp. 67–73 for other equivalent constructions.)

> 1. McPartland, who was still vigorous at the age of eighty, was presiding over the Senate.

This can easily be reduced to:

> McPartland, still vigorous at eighty, was presiding over the Senate.

Similarly:

> 2. The *Queen Mary*, which was at that time the largest ship in the world, keeled over in the harbor.

This can be reduced to:

> The *Queen Mary*, then the world's largest ship, keeled over in the harbor.

Almost all adjective clauses whose subject and verb are the relative pronoun and the verb *be* can be reduced by eliminating the subject and verb. Further examples:

3. Elizabeth, *who is* generally thought to be England's greatest queen, reigned forty-five years.

   Elizabeth, generally thought to be . . .

4. The wine, *which had been* in the cellar for twenty years, was brought out for the wedding.

   The wine, in the cellar twenty years, . . .

This generalization is limited by possible confusion and by idiom. You would probably not say, for instance, "We opened the wine, in the cellar for twenty years," because "in the cellar" here might at first be taken for an adverbial phrase describing where the wine was opened. The writer's ear should be a sufficient guide in such cases.

Other clauses can also be reduced to phrases:

5. When all the measurements of the specimen had been taken, it was disposed of.

   All its measurements taken, the specimen was disposed of.

   Measured completely, the specimen was disposed of.

6. When the convict's sentence had been completed, he was released.

   His sentence completed, the convict was released.

7. We did the best we could, although the equipment was not adequate.

   We did the best we could with inadequate equipment.

8. In order that an answer might be obtained quickly, they called Washington.

   To get a quick answer, they called Washington.

9. He postponed the meeting so that he could gain time to prepare his argument.

   He postponed the meeting to gain time for preparing his argument.

Sentences (8) and (9) illustrate the equivalence, as already noted on p. 70, of purpose clause and infinitive phrase.

Several reductions can be observed in the following pair of sentences. An author in a leisurely style might have written:

10. In 1831 he was fifty-four years old and was practicing law in the state of Maryland; he had at one time been a Federalist, just as McLane had been.

A. M. Schlesinger, Jr., a concise writer, actually wrote:

A Maryland lawyer, fifty-four years old in 1831, he had once, like McLane, been a Federalist.

With a little practice and a little ingenuity, anyone alert for equivalent constructions can apply the principles sketched here and can achieve structural conciseness.

There are other aspects of the problem, which involve vocabulary and often basic predication. In the search for conciseness one should be on the watch for redundancy and unnecessary periphrasis. For example:

11. It was found necessary to dilute the mixture further with an additional amount of water.

Surely anyone writing this would suspect there might be a more concise way to put it. But how to find the way? First of all, the writer should, as always, consider the basic predication. Does "It was found" really get at what he wants to say? He might ask himself whether there is some *thing* here that might be an appropriate subject. If he comes up with "water" he has won half the battle. Now he may also speculate about the equivalent constructions. Is there a shorter equivalent for "it is necessary to"? Well, the idiom "to have to" also expresses obligation and necessity. What about redundancy? Are "further" and "additional" both necessary? What about unnecessary words? The word "amount" is too vague to mean much; and "the mixture," which has obviously been referred to already in the context, could probably be omitted. All things considered, then, he might say simply:

More water had to be added.

This is a problem, primarily, of eliminating useless verbiage; fundamental to its solution is a firm grasp on essential predication. If you are quite sure what basically you want to talk about, conciseness comes much more easily than if you are not sure. As a final illustration we shall venture, with due apologies, to tamper with the prose of a very eminent and brilliant and not very concise linguist. This is how he begins an argument that psychologists need to know something of linguistic science before they embark on psychological studies of language:

The above remarks will serve to emphasize that one of the most important methodological considerations is a scientific conception of the nature of language in general and of the characteristics of the particular language or languages involved in any investigation.

Now what does it mean to say that a consideration is a conception? Surely the predication here is not as lucid as it might be. Secondly, is anything to be gained from the principal, but not very meaty, clause "The above remarks will serve to emphasize"? Transition, perhaps, but a simpler transitional device ("Evidently, then," for example) would be more effective and help put more weight on the important predication, now in a subordinate construction. The idea conveyed in the phrase "involved in any investigation" is already implied in "methodological" and therefore unnecessary. Finally, nothing seems to be gained from distinguishing between "language in general" and "particular language or languages," especially since the distinction is not taken up in the following context, and since the general term "language" logically implies particular languages. We would venture, assuming we understand the writer's meaning, to rewrite the sentence thus:

A sound methodology requires a scientific conception of language.

A later paragraph begins with these sentences:

One of the basic drawbacks in the available research literature is that it is based mainly on observations in naturalistic settings. Theories of language learning cannot ultimately be tested unless an experimental approach is adopted.

Again we would inquire about the basic predication. We could be wrong, but it looks as if the focus ought to be less on the research literature than on the research itself. Furthermore, the relationship of the second sentence to the first seems so inexplicit as to be obscure. "To adopt an experimental approach" seems, in context, to mean no more than "to experiment." The passage can probably be reduced to this:

A basic drawback of present research, because it is conducted mainly in natural settings, is that its results are not tested by experiment.

Subsequently we read:

Despite the fact that the phonetic diversity noted during the period of babbling increases considerably, these phenomena have little specific relevance for the development of true language.

Something is not altogether satisfying about "these phenomena." Besides the inherent semantic thinness of the words (meaning no more than "these things" here), what do they refer to? Why not preserve the more meaningful subject and perhaps abandon the wordy "Despite the fact that" concessive clause as well? Then we can write:

The increase of phonetic diversity noted during the period of babbling has little specific relevance to the development of true language.

Only the writer himself can know exactly what he means, and we may have distorted the sense in these suggested revisions. Be that as it may, the lesson to be learned here is that the original passages are difficult to follow, and the difficultly arises from a lack of conciseness. Whether or not we have done it properly, the original sentences *need* considerable paring to communicate effectively. A salubrious by-product of the attempt to be concise is often a sharpening or redefinition of the thought itself.

11
STRUCTURE IN STYLE

A WRITER's style arises in great part from the structure of his sentences. What we call metaphorically a "crisp" or "weighty" or "flowing" or "crabbed" style is as much a matter of syntax as of vocabulary. A prose with many subordinate clauses, parenthetic qualifications, and suspended predications makes a very different impression from a prose of simpler structure. There is a wide range in which stylistic excellence can be, and has been, attained. There are also dangerous extremes, which require considerable virtuosity to bring off successfully: at one pole, the kind of long and involuted structures that flirt with unintelligibility; at the other, the "news-flash" manner, which often seems merely simple-minded. Brilliant stylistic victories have been won at both extremes, but they are tours de force.

The first bull was Belmonte's. Belmonte was very good. But because he got thirty thousand pesetas and people had stayed in line all night to buy tickets to see him, the crowd demanded that he should be more than very good. Belmonte's great attraction is working close to the bull. In bull fighting they speak of the terrain of the bull and the terrain of the bull-fighter. As long as a bull-fighter stays in his own terrain he is comparatively safe. Each time he enters into the terrain of the bull he is in great danger. Belmonte, in his best days, worked always in the terrain of the bull. This way he gave the sensation of coming tragedy. People went to the corrida to see Belmonte, to be given tragic sensations, and perhaps to see the death of Belmonte. [HEMINGWAY]

In this passage the norm is short sentences without elaborate subordination, heavy adjectival modification, or parenthetical qualification. They suggest a clear-eyed, unemotional, rather laconic observer setting down matters just as they stood. Only in the infinitive series of the last sentence do feeling and complexity of tone enter when Hemingway evokes the image of a crowd gathered to experience tragic sensations and perhaps witness a death. Even then, the evocation is very restrained, controlled by the stylized simplicity of the writing.

Here, in contrast, is Henry James:

It is very true that Fielding's hero in *Tom Jones* is but as "finely," that is but as intimately, bewildered as a young man of great health and spirits may be when he hasn't a grain of imagination: the point to be made is, at all events, that his sense of bewilderment obtains altogether on the comic, never on the tragic plane. He has so much "life" that it amounts, for the effect of comedy and application of satire, almost to his having a mind, that is to his having reactions and a full consciousness; besides which his author—*he* handsomely possessed of a mind—has such an amplitude of reflection for him and round him that we see him through the mellow air of Fielding's fine old moralism, fine old humor, and fine old style, which somehow enlarge, make every one and every thing important.

These two Jamesian sentences, weighted with subordination and qualification, make a subtle critical point about *Tom Jones;* they also express the richness and subtle modifications of James's sensibility. Both the Hemingway and the James passages are good, indeed eloquent, English prose, delicately controlled instruments of their authors' purposes. But both stand at, or beyond, the extreme limits of "normal" English prose. In weaker hands the stylized simplicity of Hemingway might well suggest empty-headedness or affected toughness; without James's richness of mind, the elaborations of his prose would seem only pompous spluttering. Any inexperienced writer who ventures into James's or Hemingway's stylistic territory is on dangerous ground. But in the territory between these two extremes there is room for great variation of effective style.

The use of heavily subordinated, complex sentences leads to a slow-moving, comparatively "heavy" style that is a suitable vehicle for a thoughtful, reflective attitude. It is a style suitable to complex ideas which the writer feels must be stated with qualifications if they are to be stated accurately. In the following passage the writer is discussing the function of literary criticism.

When I say criticism, I mean of course in this place the commentation and exposition of works of art by means of written words; for of the general use of the word "criticism" to mean such writings, as Matthew Arnold uses it in his essay, I shall presently make several qualifications. No exponent of criticism (in this limited sense) has, I presume, ever made the preposterous assumption that criticism is an autotelic activity. I do not deny that art may be affirmed to serve ends beyond itself; but art is not required to be aware of these ends, and indeed performs its function, whatever that may be, according to various theories of value, much better by indifference to them. Criticism, on the other hand, must always profess an end in view, which, roughly speaking, appears to be the elucidation of works of art and the correction of taste. The critic's task, therefore, appears to be quite clearly cut out for him; and it ought to be comparatively easy to decide whether he performs it satisfactorily, and in general, what kinds of criticism are useful and what are otiose. [T. S. ELIOT]

The syntax is dominated by devices of qualification, much of it in parenthetical constructions: "of course," "in this place," "(in this limited sense)," "I presume," "whatever that may be," "according to various theories of value," "in general." There are many subordinate clauses: "When I say . . .," "as Matthew Arnold uses . . .," "that criticism is . . .," "that art may be affirmed . . .," "whatever that may be," "which appears to be . . .," "whether he performs . . .," "What kinds of criticism are . . .," "what are. . . ." In fact there are no simple sentences in the passage. Contributing to the heavy atmosphere of qualification are also such noncommittal verb forms as "appears to be" (twice) and such circumlocutions as "I do not deny that art may be affirmed to" (equivalent to "Art may"). There is almost no structural repetition; and almost no sentence proceeds to its period without some kind of interruption.

Certainly this prose does not race or drive to a conclusion; it is a series of careful, gingerly steps. Its complexity and its twitchy rhythms prohibit hasty reading, thus forcing the reader to proceed as cautiously as the writer. The style, then, suits the context, where great (perhaps excessive) care is being given to the statement of a position, for it solicits the reader's careful attention. However, it is not a style to everyone's taste; for some it will suggest more pedantry than thoughtfulness and more complexity than the material warrants. The rather fancy vocabulary ("commentation," "autotelic," "otiose") does nothing to discourage such a reaction. It is a style with potential pitfalls, certainly. Yet it is Eliot's *own* style; it is to a considerable extent determined by his personality, which Eliot himself has, in a pleasant mood, written of thus:

How unpleasant to meet Mr. Eliot!
With his features of clerical cut,
And his brow so grim
And his mouth so prim
And his conversation, so nicely

> Restricted to What Precisely
> And If and Perhaps and But.
> How unpleasant to meet Mr. Eliot!

Needless to say, many readers, including the Nobel Prize Committee, have found it pleasant enough to meet Mr. Eliot in both his poetry and his prose.

Here is another example, from an earlier generation, of the same general kind of style:

> One has often wondered whether upon the whole earth there is anything so unintelligent, so unapt to perceive how the world is really going, as an ordinary young Englishman of our upper class. Ideas he has not, and neither has he that seriousness of our middle class which is, as I have often said, the great strength of this class, and may become its salvation. Why, a man may hear a young Dives of the aristocratic class, when the whim takes him to sing the praises of wealth and material comfort, sing them with a cynicism from which the conscience of the veriest Philistine of our industrial middle class would recoil in affright. And when, with the natural sympathy of aristocracies for firm dealing with the multitude, and his uneasiness at our feeble dealing with it at home, an unvarnished young Englishman of our aristocratic class applauds the absolute rulers on the Continent, he in general manages completely to miss the grounds of reason and intelligence which alone give any colour of justification, any possibility of existence, to those rulers, and applauds them on grounds which it would make their own hair stand on end to listen to.
> [MATTHEW ARNOLD]

Even more than the passage by Eliot, this quotation exemplifies what is sometimes called the Mandarin style. It assumes that both writer and reader are highly cultivated persons with enough leisure and free play of mind to explore all the (frequently ironic) ramifications of the topic at hand. The choice of words—particulary such ironic expressions as "young Dives," "whim," "sing the praises," and "firm dealing" and the colloquial flavor of "Why," and "make their own hair stand on end"—gives the passage a somewhat lighter tone than the Eliot quotation, but the general effect is still distinctly heavy. There are many subordinate clauses: "whether there is . . .," "how the world is really going," "which is . . .," "as I have often said," "when the whim . . .," "from which . . .," "and when . . .," "which alone . . .," "which it would make. . . ." The sentences are long and complex and use suspended predication (especially the last sentence). The frequent modifying clauses interrupt the rhythm and slow down the pace. They are not used, however, as in Eliot, to subtract anything from the principal idea, but rather to amplify the circumstances. The style suggests a rich and reflective mind. For example, in the last sentence there is no absolute necessity for the long phrase "with the natural sympathy . . . at home" that interrupts the course of the *when*-clause it appears in. But we should not want to do without it; it is a side observation that palpably enriches the statement.

Again, this style has the vices of its virtues. Its complexity smacks somewhat of the schoolmaster. Its richness detracts from its strength. Though essentially Arnold is making a very strong statement indeed about young Englishmen of the upper class, it doesn't *sound* very strong; the force of the condemnation is somewhat dissipated by structural complexity.

The principal rhetorical danger of the style represented here by Eliot and Arnold is that of being too demanding on the reader. It is a style that requires more than a minimum effort on the reader's part. Now the writer has every right to expect such an effort, and any intelligent reader is willing to make it. But self-evidently, there should also be a reward for his effort. If the ideas are not in themselves complex, it is a great mistake to couch them in very complicated language. For if the reader makes the effort to grasp your pearl of wisdom and finds only a clod, he will, quite justly, dismiss your writing as bloated.

Another problem is the use of humor in this style. Arnold's relatively quiet ironies sit well on his style, but a more obvious wit combined with this heavy style may produce a curious result. For example, in speaking of Nathaniel Hawthorne's early career, Henry James says:

Certain of his tales found their way into one of the annuals of the time, a publication endowed with the brilliant title of *The Boston Token and Atlantic Souvenir*. The editor of this graceful repository was S. G. Goodrich, a gentleman who, I suppose, may be called one of the pioneers of American periodical literature.

The phrases "endowed with the brilliant title" and "graceful repository" have a nice ironic wit (at least *we* think so), but the final effect is a unique combination of the airy and elephantine. There is nothing wrong with this at all, but it is very special. If the wit is not genuine, the effect can be heavy-handed or grotesque.

A quite different style is achieved by shunning heavy subordination, suspended predication, and parenthetic phrases and depending instead on relatively simple sentences and the repetition of structures. Here is C. S. Lewis saying how, as we read English literature of the sixteenth century,

[1]we come to dread a certain ruthless emphasis; bludgeon-work. [2]Nothing is light, or tender, or fresh. [3]All the authors write like elderly men. [4]The mid-century is an earnest, heavy-handed, commonplace age: a drab age. [5]Then, in the last quarter of the century, the unpredictable happens. [6]With startling suddenness we ascend. [7]Fantasy, conceit, paradox, colour, incantation, return. [8]Youth returns. [9]The fine frenzies of ideal love and ideal war are readmitted.

This prose is terse and crisp; it reads quickly; it strikes directly at its subject. The effect is gained from the kind of syntax Lewis uses. Only simple sentences appear. There are no subordinate clauses in the passage, no interruptors to slow it down. The importance of the syntax can be seen if we consider how another writer might have written the fifth and sixth sentences:

Then in the last quarter of the century, the unpredictable happens, when, with startling suddenness, we ascend.

This is good English, but how much better the original syntax reflects "startling suddenness." We feel as well as read what Lewis is talking about. The effect is enhanced by the series constructions, particularly those without connectives. Finally, the constructions echo one another to produce a lightly hammering rhythm. Consider the fifth and sixth sentences again, where the same sentence pattern is repeated: an adverbial prepositional phrase followed by a simple subject-verb clause. Observe, too, how the structure of the seventh and eighth sentences echoes that of the fourth:

[4]The mid-century is an earnest, heavy-handed, commonplace age: a drab age.

[7]Fantasy, conceit, paradox, colour, incantation, return. [8]Youth returns.

The emphasis of reiteration heightens the contrast and the lyrical quality of "Youth returns." Lewis's style here corresponds to the content, just as Eliot's and Arnold's do in their very different way.

The dangers of this style are almost the reverse of those attaching to the heavy style. As the sentences move forward with such briskness and sparkle, such directness and lack of qualification, the reader may be led to ask himself whether something, possibly the inherent complexity of the subject, has been sacrificed to a rather tinselly effect. Lewis's syntax gratifies the dramatic instinct, but it can also arouse the suspicion that one is being offered an arbitrarily simplified map of a complicated intellectual terrain.

The following quotation from Henri Bergson catches in its syntax some of the compulsive quality of passionate love.

Analyse the passion of love, particularly in its early stages; is pleasure its aim? Could we not as well say it is pain? Perhaps a tragedy lies ahead, a whole life wrecked, wasted, ruined, we know it, we feel it, no matter, we must because we must. [Tr. by R. A. AUDRA and C. BRERETON]

Again the constructions are simple and serial; conjunctions are avoided: "wrecked, wasted, ruined," "we know . . . we feel . . . we must . . . we must." The jabbing intensity of the style, achieved mainly by the manipulation of syntax, again helps us *feel* the content and the writer's attitude.

A similar style can be attained with much more complex sentence structure, as this galloping prose attests:

How easy it is now to understand the prodigious success of *The Innocents Abroad*, appearing as it did at the psychological moment, at the close of the Civil War, at the opening of the epoch of industrial pioneering, at the hour when the life of business had become obligatory upon almost every American! How easy it is to understand why it was so generally used as a guidebook by Americans travelling in Europe! Setting out only to ridicule the sentimental pretensions of the author's pseudo-cultivated fellow-countrymen, it ridiculed in fact everything of which the author's totally uncultivated fellow-countrymen were ignorant, everything for which they wished just such an excuse to be ignorant where knowledge would have involved an expenditure in thought and feeling altogether too costly for the mind that was fixed upon the main chance. It attacked not only the illegitimate pretensions of the human spirit but the legitimate pretensions also. It expressly made the American business man as good as Titian and a little better: it made him feel that art and history and all the great, elevated, admirable, painful discoveries of human kind were not worth wasting one's emotions over. [VAN WYCK BROOKS]

Here there are many subordinate clauses, but they do not slow the pace very much, if at all, because they never suspend the predication; they never interrupt the invariable sequence of subject-verb-complement. This repeated sentence pattern carries the reader's attention forward in a straight line, without pause or backtracking, to a concluding statement that seems inevitable because of the energetic syntactical thrust that leads up to it. There is an abundance of structural repetition and a minimal use of conjunctions: "How easy it is now to understand . . . How easy it is to understand . . ."; "at the psychological moment . . . at the close . . . at the opening . . . at the hour . . ."; "pseudo-cultivated fellow-country-men . . . totally uncultivated fellow-countrymen . . ."; "everything of which . . . everything for which . . ."; "not only the illegitimate pretensions . . . but the legitimate pretensions . . ."; "It attacked . . . It expressly made . . . it made . . ."; etc. It is particularly these structural and verbal repetitions that produce the hammering rhythm of the passage, a rhythm that sweeps the reader along with it.

All three of these illustrations exhibit the velocity and intensity and exclamatory quality characteristic of this style. The words rush along. It is the antithesis of the slow and meditative style of Eliot and Arnold. Its dangers are also the opposite of those inherent in the heavier manner. While Arnold's style may tend to be stuffy, Brooks's may become glib and even a trifle hysterical. And while the one style may expect too much effort from the reader, the other may not ask enough. The two styles seem to be, by nature, primarily suitable for different modes of thought and feeling; one lends itself to reflection and amplification, the other to a more emotional and dramatic approach. It is, for example, very hard (though not impossible) to infuse Eliot's prose style with lyricism; it is a style that cannot easily be taught to sing. Conversely, it is hard to seem dispassionate or aloof in the style of Brooks. Injudiciously used, both styles can easily be unconvincing. (In philosophy John Dewey and Bertrand Russell are fairly representative of the two styles, and one student of philosophy has observed that he can hardly help thinking that the writing of Dewey is too dull to be credible, that of Russell too clever.) Judiciously used, however, both styles can provide the strongest support for effective communication because they can add a dimension of feeling to the communication.

Not many accomplished writers employ one style or the other exclusively. When they do, it is probably because of very strong and relatively inflexible personalities or because they have evolved such a characteristic manner that they cannot convey their thought apart from it. D. H. Lawrence, for example, was a man of great personal passion, and especially his non-fictional writing is generally in a passionate style, sometimes almost apocalyptic. Some political writers, too, normally write in a passionate, sometimes almost apoplectic manner. Conversely, T. S. Eliot, who praises objectivity and has deplored emotionalism, rarely departs from the prose style that suits his temper and beliefs. But probably the bulk of good writers find a middle way, usually a combination or alternation of the styles just discussed. When they are themselves reflective or wish the reader to reflect, they will use the syntax that is most conducive to the desired effect. When they are themselves excited or wish to excite the reader, they use the kind of syntax most suitable to that end. Most of their sentences are neither stuffed nor starved and follow normal sentence patterns. Here is an illustration from an eminent historian and accomplished writer:

> In the Middle Ages men thought and acted corporately. The status of every man was fixed by his place in some community—manor, borough, guild, learned University or convent. The villein and the monk scarcely existed in the eye of the law except through the lord of the manor and the Abbot of the monastery. As a human being, or as an English subject, no man had "rights" either to employment or to the vote, or indeed to anything very much beyond a little Christian charity. The unit of mediæval society was neither the nation nor the individual but something between the two,—the corporation.
>
> By thus strictly formulating on the group principle the relation of every man to his fellows, civilization emerged out of the Dark Ages into the mediæval twilight. Only in the later age of the Renaissance and Reformation, after the emancipation of the villeins had shattered the economic system on which the feudal world rested, was it possible to take another step forward towards personal freedom. Then indeed many of the mediæval corporations went down before the omnipotent State on the one hand and the self-assertive individual on the other. [G. M. TREVELYAN]

The style is lucid, easy to read, lively, and authoritative. The thesis is stated briefly and economically in a simple sentence. The rest of the sentences being longer and more complicated, the first statement gains force from its succinctness. Normal word order prevails throughout. The first paragraph has no interrupters, no suspensions. The second paragraph begins with a rather long participial phrase, preparing the way for the more lengthily postponed predication of the next sentence, which has a long prepositional phrase and a long qualifying complex subordinate clause ("after the emancipation . . . had shattered the . . . system on which . . .") before the principal predication ("was it possible"), which itself leads on the rest of the complement ("to take . . ."). This rather complicated sentence is followed by another forcefully simple sentence. Like Brooks and Lewis, Trevelyan depends much more on coordination than on subordination; unlike them he also uses the normal series construction (a, b, *and* c) and the coordinating conjunctions.

The middleness of the middle way can be illustrated from the fourth sentence. Trevelyan writes:

As a human being, or as an English subject, no man had "rights" either to employment or to the vote, or indeed to anything very much beyond a little Christian charity.

To play at reconstruction, we might, from a writer in another style, expect something like this:

No man, even though he were an English citizen and a human being, had "rights" either to employment or to the vote or indeed, besides a little Christian charity, to anything very much,

And from a stylist of another school, we might read:

As a human being, as an Englishman, no man had "rights"—to employment, to the vote, to anything beyond a little Christian charity.

Between the two possibilities of expression—the one leisurely and parenthetical in its syntax, the other terse and abrupt—Trevelyan has found a very readable middle way.

Here is another example from a contemporary prize-winning historian, writing of economic and moral changes in the age of Jackson:

[1]But industrialism brought the growing depersonalization of economic life. [2]With the increase in size of the labor force, the master was further and further removed from his workmen, till the head of a factory could have only the most tenuous community of feeling with his men. [3]With the development of manufacturing and improved means of distribution, the seller lost all contact with the buyer and feelings of responsibility to the consumer inevitably diminished. [4]The expansion of investment tended to bring on absentee ownership, with the divorce of ownership and management; and the rise of cities enfeebled the paternal sentiments with which many capitalists had regarded their workers in towns and villages. [5]Slowly the vital economic relationships were becoming impersonal, passing out of the control of a personal moral code. [6]Slowly private morality and business morality grew apart. [7]Slowly the commercial community developed a collection of devices and ceremonials which enabled businessmen to set aside the ethic which ruled their private life and personal relations.

[8]Of these devices the most dramatic and generally intelligible was the corporation. [9]For a people still yearning for an economy dominated by individual responsibility, still under the spell of the Jeffersonian dream, the corporation had one outstanding characteristic: its moral irresponsi-

bility. [10]"Corporations have neither bodies to be kicked, nor souls to be damned," went a favorite aphorism. [11]Beyond good and evil, insensible to argument or appeal, they symbolized the mounting independence of the new economy from the restraints and scruples of personal life. [A. M. SCHLESINGER, JR.]

Again, the topic sentence is stated briefly and precisely in a simple sentence, of which every principal word will be developed in what follows. Complex sentences there are, but predication is never interrupted by extended modifiers. Several sentences postpone the predication, though not very elaborately; they alternate with sentences beginning with the subject (or single adverb followed by the subject). Thus sentences 2, 3, 9, and 11 postpone predication by phrases of varying length; of these only the ninth has an unusually long postponement. One sentence is moderately inverted, the eighth, where the phrase "Of these devices," appearing at the beginning instead of in its more usual position after "intelligible," is used as a transition from the first to the second paragraph. Regular word order of subject-verb-complement is invariable; most often the subject and verb are contiguous and are never separated by parentheses.

Though there is no series, there is abundant coordination, usually with the conjunction *and*. There is also a good deal of structural and verbal repetition: "With the increase . . . With the development . . ." (2 and 3), "Slowly . . . Slowly . . . Slowly . . ." (5, 6, 7), "still yearning . . . still under the spell . . ." (9), and the parallel adjectival phrases "Beyond good and evil, insensible to argument and appeal" (11). There are relatively few subordinate clauses, and these are all in the first paragraph. Observe here the difference between the sixth and seventh sentences: the one compact, the other, with its two adjective clauses ("which enabled . . . which ruled . . .," *not* parallel), long and stringy.

The general effect of the coordination and repetition is that of balance and cohesion; the whole passage is carefully knit together. Everything follows from the opening sentence. The transition between paragraphs is neatly accomplished by picking up the word "devices" of sentence 7 and giving it a prominent place in sentence 8; similarly the words "economy" and "personal" of the last sentence echo "economic" and "depersonalization" in the first. By such means an impression of unity emerges from the passage. From the extensive use of coordination, a sense of balance arises. Together they suggest rationality and objectivity, precisely the qualities most historians strive for.

Yet the writing is not cold and completely dispassionate; there is some sense of the writer's involvement. The passage increases in intensity as it goes along; there is a quiet but discernible movement, a growth to a climax. This development is, in the first place, lexical; that is, the vocabulary gradually changes from the mildness of such expressions as "depersonalization," "tenuous community of feeling," and "diminished" to such strong expressions as "moral irresponsibility," "kicked," "damned," and "Beyond good and evil." In the second place, the structure and rhythm of the sentences contribute to the same development. The first paragraph ends almost languidly. Not only has the repetition of "slowly" had its effect, but the complex seventh sentence is leisurely. But this is followed by attention-getting variations of syntax: the inversion of sentence 8 and the lengthily postponed predication of sentence 9. The suspense of this sentence is enhanced by the further semantic postponement of the critical phrase "moral irresponsibility," which gains much emphasis from the structure of the sentence. The subtle intensity of the second paragraph is enhanced further by the elimination of the coordinating conjunction twice ("still yearning . . ., still under . . ."; "Beyond good and evil, insensible . . .") and the avoidance of subordinate clauses. Notice how the force of sentence 9 is vitiated if we write:

For a people who were still yearning for an economy which was dominated by individual responsibility and who were still under the spell of the Jeffersonian dream, the corporation had one outstanding characteristic, which was its moral irresponsibility.

This would not have the incisiveness demanded by the content. Conversely, consider the effect of eliminating the last *and* from the closing sentence and writing, ". . . . from the restraints, the scruples of personal life." This would be more forceful than the present syntax. But would it be more desirable? From Schlesinger's viewpoint, probably not. He has so modulated the passage that it rises to a climax in the ninth sentence and returns to a comparatively restrained tone at the end, in keeping with the general style. He has made his point and yet avoided any hint of being carried away with it.

PART THREE

THE CHOICE
OF WORDS

12

WORD MASTERY

. . . as a boy of fourteen I stood motionless on the street wondering if it were possible to ask my way in what would be recognized at once as fine prose. It was so hard to believe, after I had heard somebody read out let us say Pater's description of the Mona Lisa, that "Can you direct me to St. Peter's Square Hammersmith" was under the circumstances the best possible prose. [WILLIAM BUTLER YEATS]

YEATS's question is indeed the best prose possible under the circumstances. Its meaning is unmistakable; it suits the purpose of the speaker; it is decently attentive to English idiom and to the requirement of politeness toward an auditor. It is neither longwinded ("I am very sorry to bother you, but could you possibly direct me . . .") nor curt ("Direct me to . . .). It is neither pompous ("Could you inform me of the whereabouts of . . .") nor vulgarly familiar ("Say, bud, where is . . .). It is also good prose because it should get the right response: directions to St. Peter's Square Hammersmith. The language of the question is concise, correct in form, and clear; it is as eloquent and expressive as the occasion permits; it is appropriate to the circumstance, the speaker, and the audience.

The writer setting out to discover the words that will meet all these requirements is confronted by the often bewildering richness of the English vocabulary—particularly its wealth of synonyms. He must discriminate among words closely related to one another; for, with their subtle variations in tone, emphasis, and reference, they are seldom completely interchangeable. He must search out from a multitude of words the ones that correspond most closely to the ideas in his mind.

How words "correspond" to "ideas" and how "ideas" in turn "correspond" to phenomena are complex problems still being diligently investigated by philosophers, logicians, semanticists, psychologists, and literary critics. Fortunately, the thorny difficulties that confront theories of meaning, symbolism, and communication are not of a kind to prevent us from applying helpful rules of thumb to problems of vocabulary. The theory of language is, to say the least, still incomplete, but there is nevertheless a fund of practical wisdom to guide us through the maze of alternatives presented by our immensely large English vocabulary.[1]

Size of Vocabulary

No one uses or recognizes all the words in English, or needs to. Widely read people might *recognize* a quarter of all English words on coming across them in conversation or in print. But their own speaking and writing vocabulary would certainly be much smaller. The words one actually uses—his active vocabulary—are far fewer than the words he knows on sight or hearing—his recognition vocabulary. Active vocabulary grows through annexations from the recognition vocabulary, and the strategy of such annexations is a practical concern for the writer.

Many beginning writers complain about "lack of vocabulary." Sometimes this feeling of wordlessness drives them to memorize word lists, to search a thesaurus repeatedly as they compose, to buy books that purport to "build vocabulary." But words are vehicles for meanings; they have contexts, overtones of feeling, and associations that cannot be recorded in even the most elaborate definition in a dictionary or word list. For these reasons, memorizing new words as a means of increasing one's *active* vocabulary has at best a severely limited usefulness. Imagine yourself learning the meaning of the word *introjection* from a dictionary:

in *psychiatry*, the incorporating of external events into the psyche and reacting to them as though they were internal, as when a person suffers the same pains as another, without physical cause: opposed to *projection*. [*Webster's New Collegiate Dictionary*]

In the restricted space at his disposal, the lexicographer has managed

---

1 It is hard to say how many words there are in English. The *Oxford English Dictionary* has some 250,000 *main* words; *Webster's Third New International* has over 450,000 *entries*, many of which are derivative forms of the same word—e.g., *integrate, integration, disintegrate, reintegrate.* Many localisms, slang words, trade terms, scientific names, and nonce words never get into dictionaries at all. If one counts all derivative words and compound words (*gin palace, marketplace*) as separate words, and then estimates the number of unrecorded words, a total of a million or more words seems likely.

to say much about this word. If you memorized the definition, you would have a reasonably clear notion of the core meaning of *introjection* the next time you came across it—especially if you had gone on to look up its opposite, *projection*. Thus your bit of memory work would help fix the word as a stable part of your recognition vocabulary. But a sensible person would hesitate to use the word in his own writing until he knew more about this obviously complicated psychic mechanism and the system of ideas of which it is part. He would want to meet the word repeatedly in a variety of contexts so that he could come to understand the area of its use and the range of its meanings. Enlargement of one's speaking and writing vocabulary, then, follows from enlarging one's circle of ideas. Wide reading, attentive listening, and careful observation are the ways to increase vocabulary. So-called "vocabulary-building" devices, like most hopeful short-cuts in intellectual matters, usually turn out to be dead ends.

Most people are reasonably prudent about adding concrete words to their active vocabulary. Few are tempted to talk about *magenta* before they have some acquaintance with that particular shade of purplish red, or to discuss a *jack-hammer*, a *pediment*, or a *sonnet* before knowing what they are. This prudence, unhappily, is less in evidence when it is a matter of adding more general and abstract words to the active vocabulary. Such abstractions as *projection* (or *baroque, charismatic,* or *transcendental*) are all too often used by people for whom their meaning is a misunderstanding based on rumor. Among the supposedly educated, indiscriminate additions to the active vocabulary of speaking and writing cause more confusion, failure of communication, and addled thought than mere poverty of vocabulary. Such additions unleash into a writer's or speaker's discourse notions that he is not really master of, and he is lucky if they do not turn on him at some point and take their revenge. A secure mastery of the meaning of words is more important in writing than their number and variety.

Denotation

What constitutes a minimum mastery over a new word? First, obviously, is a knowledge of the *denotation* of a word, that is, its dictionary meaning: the essential and distinguishing characteristics of the phenomenon to which the word refers. That phenomenon may be called the word's *referent*. A formal definition is usually a successive narrowing of the classes to which the referent belongs.

Thus the definition "A harp is a musical instrument of strings generally set in an open frame and plucked with the fingers" moves from the large class of musical instruments to the narrower classes of stringed instruments, open-framed stringed instruments, and open-framed stringed instruments plucked by hand. To know, then, what a word denotes—or what it "means"—you should know what class its referent belongs to and what characteristics distinguish it from other members of the same class.

This kind of minimal definition is not always easy to pick up in reading: one could see again and again such concrete words as *ibex*, *gnu*, *blini*, and *basilica*, or such abstract ones as *pointillism*, *sensibility*, and *picaresque* without ever discovering their denotation. Hence the wisdom of consulting dictionaries after a first encounter with a word; otherwise its meaning is likely to remain a vague cloud of suggestions. This warning may seem too obvious to deserve attention, but overconfidence about the meanings of words can beget blunders even in the writing of the highly taught. Here are two examples from the work of a respectable scholar: ". . . the context of even the most *obtuse* statements almost always provides the materials needed to make them clear." A dictionary would have informed the writer that *obtuse* does not mean "hard to understand" but rather "dull of apprehension, thick-witted." He means *abstruse*. The confusion is impressively elementary. A less obvious slip: ". . . if the purpose of this edition *mitigated* the profound argument of *Walden* . . ." Again, a look into a dictionary might have led the writer to ask himself if he wanted to speak of making the argument of *Walden* "less harsh, severe, unpleasant." He perhaps means "vitiated."

In conversation, the somewhat off-center use of these two words would probably go unnoticed. We may talk of such things as *neuroses* or *atoms* or *vitamins* or *parity* or *historical necessity* or *evolution*, yet few of us could give a respectable account of what we mean by such words. In talk among friends, we seldom feel a need for rigorous definition. Indeed, the man who always interrupts with the command "Define your terms" is rightly regarded as a boor.

But writing makes stricter demands. A reader who discovers that an author has unwittingly confused vitamins with enzymes, or caste with class, may reasonably doubt that he has much to learn from that source, and go elsewhere. Without a mastery of the basic denotations of words, the writer loses his authority as soon as his failure is discovered.

Since most words have a reasonably limited denotation, care and common sense will protect the writer from error. Even most words that have a multitude of potential referents present no difficulties. Unabridged dictionaries list several hundred meanings each for common verbs like *run, make,* and *do,* yet they are seldom misused even by the most inept writer or misunderstood by the most befuddled reader. Consider the astonishing ease with which we grasp the relevant sense of *run* in the following series of statements:

Joe *runs* to the station every morning.
The fence *runs* around the field.
The engine *runs* best just after it has been cleaned.
The freeway *runs* from Los Angeles to San Francisco.
My brother *runs* a filling station.
The Mississippi *runs* into the Gulf of Mexico at New Orleans.
This stocking *runs* every time I look at it.
His tax *runs* to five figures.
Cretinism *runs* in the family.
His rhetoric *runs* away with him.
Time *runs* out too soon.

In each instance, the context automatically guides the reader to the meaning. Despite their wide range of potential referents, common words like "run" are used easily and clearly because there is universal agreement among speakers of English about what they mean in different contexts. Anyone who is suspicious of every word having more than one sense should consider the efficient flexibility of our most common verbs.

Divided Usage

Difficulties do arise, however, when there is no common agreement about the signification of a word. A *babe* is one thing in a sermon on the Nativity and another on the streets of Brooklyn. A *projection* is one thing to a psychiatrist and another to an economist. A *plausible fiction* means one thing to a lawyer and another to a literary critic. A statistician means something more precise by *probability* than the rest of us do. Usually such words belong to what is rather loftily called a "universe of discourse" that makes clear which signification is intended. For instance, the language of the law and the language of literary criticism are sufficiently remote from one another to prevent either the lawyer or the literary critic from mixing up the two senses of *plausible fiction.*

But sometimes universes of discourse meet, and definitions are needed. Clergymen talk to cab drivers, economists consult psychiatrists, lawyers and literary critics converse, and statisticians address the general public. When they do, they need to be alert to words that may mean one thing to them and another to part of their audience. A literary critic speaking to a biologist does well to remember that he does not mean by *genetic* quite what his biologist friend does. A few words of explanation can prevent a serious muddle.

Another difficulty arises from changes in usage: words take on new meanings and drop old ones; they widen or narrow their range of reference, lose or gain dignity, pick up or drop associated ideas. To Chaucer, *silly* usually meant *innocent, blissful,* to Milton it meant *helpless, defenseless,* to Coleridge it meant *empty,* and to us it means *foolish, feeble-minded. To counterfeit* once meant merely *to copy, to reproduce;* now it always indicates falsification. No living person is likely to call a woman *silly* when he means that she is helpless, or to call an accurate portrait a *counterfeit,* as Shakespeare does. But what of words that are undergoing changes of meaning now?

The divided usage of *disinterested* has aroused lively debate.[2] It is used both as a duplicate for *uninterested* or *bored* and as a synonym for *detached.* Thus a *disinterested* judge may be either asleep on the bench or impartial in hearing the case before him. *Awful* is another word in which older and newer meanings are contending; in the most formal English and in poetry it may still mean *awe-inspiring— the awful Pacific,* but in speech and familiar writing it means *bad, undesirable, unpleasant.* "I had an awful time getting a taxi this morning." *Nice* once had the narrow and precise meaning of *fastidious, discriminating,* but in ordinary speech has widened its meaning to become a vague epithet of general approval. Only in prose addressed to a highly educated audience could one feel sure that the stricter meaning would get through in such a phrase as "a nice distinction."

Here are more common words in which the newer use is at odds with the older, more formal usage:

Aggravate. The colloquial meaning is *to annoy.* "Baby Leroy greatly aggravated W. C. Fields by dropping his gold watch into a bowl of oatmeal." The formal meaning is *to make worse or intensify.* "The government crisis was only aggravated by foreign intervention."

2 See Donald J. Lloyd, "Snobs, Slobs, and the English Language," and Jacques Barzun, "The Retort Circumstantial," both in the *American Scholar* (Summer 1951). The two articles provide an entertaining picture of the all-out verbal battles that take place over changes in language.

Criticism. Often the colloquial meaning is restricted to *find fault with.* "Mary's husband criticized her new hat." The formal meaning is wider: *to analyze and judge.* "Coleridge criticized Shakespeare's plays with a nicer discrimination than any other Romantic critic."

Majority. In speech it is sometimes treated as a synonym for *most.* "The majority of the flies disappeared at the end of the summer." In formal writing the word refers to more than half of a group that can be counted for the purpose of registering a decision or preference. "Pearson won a bare majority in the 1963 election."

Peculiar. In general use it often means *odd, strange,* as when Iris Murdoch writes "This peculiar book lives on many levels." But in the most formal prose, it means *unique* or *distinctive,* as when Coppleston writes "St. Thomas Aquinas, who has in recent times been accorded a peculiar status among Catholic philosophers. . . ."

Unique. The word is very widely used in the sense of *unusual, outstanding.* Thus a billboard advertisement: "The Most Unique Musical Comedy on Broadway Today!" Among the cultivated, it still means *the only one of its kind* and cannot be used with the comparative or superlative: a thing is either unique or it is not. "Dickens' gallery of misers is unique in literature."

In choosing between the two senses of such words, the best course is to prefer the older and more conservative meaning. If you call something *rather unique* you may inflame the heart of the purist against you, but if you use the word in its formal sense, you offend no one.

Elusive Abstractions

Words that change their meanings in different contexts and at different levels of usage can be handled by any writer who is attentive to his craft and to the needs of his audience. But some highly abstract words mean so many different things to so many different people that they are notoriously difficult to use. Words such as *democracy, freedom, beauty, law, morality, happiness,* and *tradition* stand for clusters of ideas complicated in themselves and often inconsistent with one another. Strong feelings and value judgments are attached to them. Some imply metaphysical assumptions that are fiercely debated; some have been misused and debased by irresponsible writers. A few students of language have concluded in despair that all such equivocal abstractions are meaningless and should be banished from the language. Certainly these words are the most difficult of all to use without vagueness or evasion, and present the strongest temptation to the rattle-brained, the impassioned, or the intellectually dishonest. But it is hard to see how we can get along without them: they stand for important ideas that must be dealt with, whatever the terms which represent them.

There is no fully satisfactory solution to the problems presented by abstract words that seem to defy adequate definition, but two procedures can help the writer to reduce the amount of possible confusion. First, if he finds it necessary to use such a word incidentally, he should stipulate the sense in which it is to be taken. This can often be done by adding a simple qualification to the word when it first appears: "direct democracy," "representative democracy," or "parliamentary democracy as it is practiced in Great Britain," and so on.

Second, if a difficult abstraction is one of a writer's key terms, he can often benefit from writing a full definition for himself, even if it never appears in his final paper. If he sets before himself an explicit statement of what he means by a term (and, almost as important, what he does not mean), he can check what he writes against his definition to ensure consistency. This is by no means to say that a word must retain a single, unequivocal meaning throughout a piece of writing. Indeed, most serious writing seeks to complicate and widen our understanding of what, say, *patriotism*, *comedy*, or *scientific method* mean. The point is that each addition of meaning should be controlled and explicit rather than haphazard.

When to Define

Every writer must time and again decide when his audience needs to have a term explicitly defined. Obviously, no writer wants to clog his prose by stopping to define every word that might be unfamiliar to a few of his readers. Nor does he want to confine himself to the vocabulary of a school primer in order to avoid possible misunderstanding. But whenever a good number of readers are likely to be ignorant of a word's meaning, he has an obligation to provide a definition. If a writer is presenting a scientific paper to an audience of specialists, he can assume a shared technical vocabulary for which he need not supply definitions. But if a general audience is addressed, even the most common technical terms should be defined. Before a non-scientific audience, the physicist does well to indicate what he means by even such elementary terms as *work* or *mass*, the engineer to explain even *fulcrum* or *stress*. Laboring the obvious is a lesser evil than leaving out information essential to a large part of an audience. The same is true of all but the most commonly used foreign words. If a writer or a speaker for a general audience quotes from even such relatively familiar languages as French or German and does not supply translations, he is guilty of bad manners and bad rhetoric. The assumption that any educated audience will know these languages is no longer justified.

How Much to Define

How much definition any particular word needs is determined by the author's purpose, subject matter, and audience, and by the inherent complexity of a word's meaning. Sometimes a single word may be enough (*tripterous*—three-winged); sometimes a whole volume may be too little for a writer to set down all he means by *freedom*, *beauty*, or *tradition*. It is the author's purpose, above all, that determines how extensive a definition should be. If a word stands for an idea tangential to his main line of thought, he will be brief. Rachel Carson, writing about the sea around us, gives a definition of *chlorophyll* in a dependent clause: "It is doubtful that this first plant life possessed the substance chlorophyll, with which living plants in sunlight transform lifeless chemicals into the living stuff of their tissues." A textbook might have a whole chapter on chlorophyll; a biologist might write a monograph about it. Here we will confine ourselves to definitions that can be put into a few words or sentences. (For more extended forms of definition, see p. 245–46.)

Relatively brief definitions can be expressed in a variety of syntactical patterns, according to the degree of emphasis the writer wants. When a writer wants to emphasize the importance of a definition, he will make it the main predication of a sentence or two:

> The gnu is an African antelope. One of its most striking characteristics is its head, which is like that of an ox.

When he wants less emphasis, the definition should go into a subordinate structure. Often a definition is given in a dependent clause or an appositive:

> The gnu, which is an African antelope with an ox-like head, . . .
> The gnu, an African antelope with an ox-like head, . . .

Sometimes a single synonym used as an appositive is sufficient:

A hexagonal, or six-sided, building has always been a rarity.
Venitone, a marbelized wallpaper, has of late become very popular.

The main requirement here is that the synonym be a familiar word that will identify the word it is substituting for. To explain *bellicose* as *pugnacious* may not be helpful. Sometimes a definition is given parenthetically, between dashes or parentheses:

The romance (by which I mean any work that flouts probability) nowadays tries to hide itself in the trappings of realism.

Usury—the practice of lending money for interest—was regarded as a deadly sin in the Middle Ages.

Types of Definition

The most familiar type of definition uses the pattern of narrowing classes discussed on p. 137. The definition "A hookah is a pipe with a long flexible stem so arranged that the smoke is cooled by passing through water" states what more inclusive class a hookah belongs to and then states how it differs from other members of the pipe class. Outside a dictionary, this type of definition is no more common than others, appearing usually when a writer wants to give a precise account of something that he assumes is unknown to his readers. But almost all definitions use some part of the material that appears in an inclusive formal definition: they say what large class something belongs to, or they name one or several of its distinguishing characteristics. The choice of which characteristics to name is determined by the context and the author's purpose:

A hookah cools the smoke by passing it through water.

A proper hookah is a pipe, not a complicated cigarette holder.

Those Dutch pipes you see in paintings do not have stems as long as a hookah's.

Most definitions are implicit or explicit assertions of equivalency. "Hookah" *equals* a pipe with certain characteristics; "gnu" *equals* an African antelope with an oxlike head; "hexagonal" *equals* six-sided. Many useful definitions, however, do not use this neatly balanced pattern of $A = B$.

Stipulative definitions—definitions indicating that a word is being used in a special sense—in effect say to the reader: "For the time being, take A to be the equivalent of B." By this means a writer may make the reference of a word narrower and more precise than general usage does:

I here use the word *mystery* in its theological sense of an article of faith beyond intellectual comprehension.

Decisions about atomic weapons are vital in the strictest sense of that word; they affect our ability to go on living on this planet.

Many common words are converted into scientific terms by stipulative definitions which narrow and sharpen their meaning:

A machine is any apparatus by means of which, when a force is exerted at a given point and in a given direction, a force available for doing external work is exerted at some point or in some other direction.

Stipulative definition may also make the reference of a word wider than usual:

In *metaphysics* I include all the more abstruse philosophical disciplines, not merely cosmology and ontology.

Language includes gesture and facial expression as well as speech.

A gentleman is anyone who shows a delicate regard for the feelings of others.

It may explain what a term means to a special group: what *wit* meant to eighteenth-century poets and critics, or what *witness* means to modern Quakers. Or it may indicate that the older sense of a word is the relevant one:

In this passage, *uncouth* means *strange* or unknown rather than our modern *boorish*.

Sometimes a single adjective is sufficient to do the work of stipulation: *Marxist* economic theory, *capitalist* economic theory; *professional* ethics, *Aristotelian* ethics; *raw* sugar, *refined* sugar.

Stipulative definitions require discretion on the author's part. If he tries to wrench words too far off their normal paths, he will lose his audience. If he likes, he *may* stipulate that "The brown cow is in the field" means that "Banana cream pie is messy to eat," but he need not expect anyone to read beyond that point.

Functional definitions use the pattern *A performs the function B* rather than *A = B*. They stress what a thing does rather than what it is:

A butttress supports a wall or building.
The stethometer measures the expansion of the chest during breathing.
Tragedy arouses fear and pity and effects a catharsis of these emotions.

Closely related to these functional definitions are definitions that stress purpose: A is *for* B.

Barbiturates are good for insomnia.
Milton's *Areopagitica* advocates freedom of opinion.
Soft words are used to turn away wrath.

Negative definitions explain a term by what it is *not*. *Eternity, infinity, vacuum, point*, and the like are usually best defined by negatives (e.g., *eternity*: that which is timeless, of boundless duration). Words with several potential meanings can be clarified if a writer specifies which senses are *not* part of his use of the term:

Health is not the absence of disease. It is the positive state of well-being.

To the Greeks, democracy was not a way of life nor an ideal of justice and equality. It was a particular kind of political structure in which all adult male citizens participated directly in the making of political decisions.

Analytic definitions enumerate the parts of which something is composed:

This cake is made with flour, eggs, milk, butter, vanilla, almond extract, and slivered almonds.

The North Germanic languages are Old Norse, Icelandic, Swedish, Danish, and Norwegian.

Grammar is the study of classes of words, their inflections, and their syntactical relations and functions.

Analytic definitions such as these may make good introductory statements about a cake, North Germanic languages, or grammar, but they almost always need the support of further explanation about the parts themselves and their relationship to one another. A list of ingredients is only the first part of a recipe, which goes on to say how they are combined and how the mixture becomes a cake. The statement that certain languages are grouped together as North Germanic is merely a preliminary to telling us something further about the structure and substance of these languages.

Closely related to analytic definitions are definitions by example:

Revenge tragedies—plays like *Hamlet* and Kyd's *The Spanish Tragedy* —have very ancient roots.

American advertising ignores the existence of the American poor: the unemployed, the tenant farmers, the migratory workers, and the casual laborers.

It will doubtless occur to some that I may have overlooked the "Old South,"—the South of the Cotton Kingdom and plantation slavery. [c. vann woodward]

He was a product of the old West, a "provincial" in the best sense of the term, in whose character there was reflected something of the "show-boat" Mississippi: the vigor, the earthiness, the slightly flamboyant elegance, and the uninhibited enjoyment of the good things of life. [G. F. kennan]

Such definitions do not tell a reader what revenge tragedy or poverty *is*, but they show what kind of thing the writer has in mind. By converting the abstract into the concrete, they give the reader something tangible to grasp.

Definition can be given by analogy, a form of extended comparison that often helps a writer to translate a complicated idea into simpler terms more easily grasped. It is particularly useful in explaining technical matters to a layman:

The human brain operates something like an electronic computing machine. It contains millions of short nerve-lengths comparable to wires, and millions of nerve-connections comparable to switches. [L. M. myers]

Until quite recently, atoms were regarded as the permanent bricks of which the whole universe was built. All the changes of the universe were supposed to amount to nothing more drastic than a rearrangement of permanent indestructible atoms; like a child's box of bricks, these built many buildings in turn. [sir james jeans]

Analogies between one art and another often help a writer to make his point succinctly and concretely:

Faberg's paintings are rather like epigrams: compact, neatly balanced, and witty.

In the foreground of Jane Austen's group portraits are three or four families living in a country village; in the background are their servants, friends, and relatives.

A writer should always test his definitions to see whether they include what he wants to include and leave out what he wants to leave out. Many definitions are too wide:

> Democracy is a form of government in which there is universal suffrage. (Does the writer really want to include the Soviet Union and Communist China in his definition, and exclude Switzerland, which denies votes to women?)

> Works of art are characterized by form, order, and inner vitality. (So are many other things.)

Some definitions are too narrow:

> Democracy is a republican form of government. (Does the writer think that Great Britain, Sweden, Norway, Belgium, and the Netherlands are not democracies?)

> A work of art is a representation of human action. (What about music, abstract painting and sculpture, and architecture?)

A writer should also guard against circular definition, which is really a kind of non-definition, since it uses some form of the term to be defined as part of the definition.

> A beast of burden is an animal that is used to carry burdens.

> A sophism is a particular kind of argument frequently used by the Greek Sophist philosophers.

> Freedom always implies choice; it involves being free to choose one course of action rather than another.

Connotation

Assuming that one masters the denotations of words and learns to supply appropriate definitions when they are needed, there is still the problem of the connotations of words: their implications, emotional overtones, and levels of formality and informality—in short, whatever a reader associates with a word beyond its simple referent. For the word *meadow*, the dictionary definition is "Grassland, especially a field on which grass is grown for hay; often, a tract of low or level grassland." Very good. But when you see or hear the word *meadow*, what comes to mind? Grassland, certainly, but if you are like most people, you will probably also think vaguely of rusticity, very likely of sunshine and perhaps of cows or a Constable painting, and almost certainly you will have some sense of tranquility, of a quiet peacefulness. Such things come to mind despite the fact that rain and snow fall on meadows as much as anywhere else, despite the fact that up to the present century meadows have been favorite sites for the bloodiest battles. In fact, meadows have no more claim to serenity than Death Valley. The connotations are nevertheless there; they are quite as important a part of the word's meaning as the definition *grassland*, and as necessary to master. Does a word suggest approval or disapproval? Is it intimate or impersonal, formal or colloquial? Does it suggest a particular region or country, or a particular period in history? Does it belong to common speech, to sport, to science, to juvenile slang, to the jargon of a particular profession or social group? If you can answer questions like these about a word, you almost certainly have a "feel" for the connotations that cluster around it.

Consider the following group of related words:

plump	fat
hefty	overblown
beefy	overweight
fleshy	heavy-set
heavy	stout
corpulent	porcine
obese	

All these words refer to some form of overweight, and, in a loose way, are synonymous with one another. But as any English speaker will recognize, they refer to different degrees and kinds of fatness, they suggest masculinity or femininity, they imply different attitudes toward overweight. *Overweight* itself is the least specific and most neutral of the group. *Corpulent* and *obese* suggest extreme forms of overweight that verge on illness. *Heavy-set* and *stout* are euphemisms that may or may not console fat, middle-aged men and women. *Porcine* is straightforward invective. *Overblown* suggests voluptuous femininity run to seed. A fullback might be called *beefy* or *hefty* but scarcely *plump*.

Or consider this less corporeal group of related words:

spirit	spook
ghost	revenant
apparition	ectoplasmic manifestation
specter	banshee
phantom	poltergeist
shade	vampire
haunt	

All these words refer to the dead who have returned. In more careful usage, some of these words have denotative differences: banshees must wail to be proper banshees, vampires must suck blood, and poltergeists must go bump in the night. But the important differences in ordinary usage are connotative. *Spook* and *haunt* suggest folk superstition, *revenants* belong to anthropology, *ectoplasmic manifestations* appear at seances. *Banshees* are Irish; *vampires* are mostly Central European. *Shades* are classical and poetic; *ghosts* are English and American. Behind the image presented by each of these words is a cluster of associations, a milieu, that is part of its total meaning.

Closely related words can convey a wide variety of attitudes toward what they describe:

foolhardy	brave
rash	courageous
daring	heroic
bold	

All these words could be used to describe, say, the rescue of a valuable painting from a burning building. But *foolhardy* and *rash* condemn the imprudence of the deed, while *brave* and *courageous* indicate unqualified admiration. *Daring* and *bold* stress the risk involved.

The connotations of words can be much modified by the context in which they appear. Some words take on favorable connotations in one context and unfavorable ones in another:

Isabel Archer's *girlish* trust in the good will of others is one of her greatest charms.

Late in life, Mrs. Wishfort sprouted *girlish* ringlets of blonde hair, so that she looked like an elderly beagle peering out from under a Shirley Temple wig.

Boyish enthusiasm and good will can sometimes sweep away difficulties that baffle older, more cautious heads.

With *boyish* directness, the lecturer set out to demolish Schopenhauer, floundering ahead cheerfully in his ignorance.

The task of mastering connotations is complicated by the need to separate private associations from those generally accepted. You may find the very mention of "plum pudding" sickening if you were once made ill by it, but few people share the feeling, and mentioning "plum pudding" is no way to evoke feelings of revulsion. For you, "the Fourth of July" may be associated with the delicious coolness of swimming in a remote mountain lake on a soft grey day, but for most people it means crowds and hot weather. Private paths of association have to be explained before they can have any meaning for a reader.

Another complication arises with words that arouse divergent feelings in different groups of people. The word *socialism* inspires quite different feelings at a meeting of the National Association of Manufacturers and at a convention of the British Labour Party. When a word elicits opposing reactions, the writer must amplify, illustrate, and define if he is to make *his* connotations dominant in the reader's mind.

Even though words often evoke private associations or opposing reactions, most words have a fairly stable range of connotations that is recognized by everyone. Even a man who hates his mother knows what the generally accepted connotations of *mother* are. The many people who believe that government officials are usually competent and fair-minded are aware that *bureaucrat* carries unfavorable suggestions.

The more expert the writer, the more aware he is of the connotative possibilities of words. In reading and listening, he will be alert to the shades of feeling and tone that accompany words. In writing, he will choose words for the associations they will bring to the reader's mind as well as for their denotative meaning. He will search out words that are both accurate and rich in suggestion.

On occasion, the writer may also want to exploit the kind of suggestiveness afforded by allusion, and by archaic, euphemistic, and foreign words. These devices are often mere verbal ornaments, but even mere ornament is not to be despised if it really *is* decorative and sparingly used. Occasional gratuitous allusion or word-play can be enlivening, but a constant stream, like a steady diet of bon-bons, soon cloys.

The more important use of these devices is functional. They can create evocations of particular persons, places, and eras very concretely and economically. They can enrich a statement without lengthening it. As an illustration, consider this allusion by the editor of the English magazine *Encounter:*

Mr. Fairlie is angry with *The Times*, the mores, and Mr. Muggeridge.

As a denotative statement, this merely sums up the three objects of Mr. Fairlie's anger: the London newspaper, certain modes of behavior, and the writer Malcolm Muggeridge. But those who hear the punning allusion to Cicero's famous cry "O *tempora! O mores!*" (Oh, the times! Oh! the customs!) are rewarded not only with the simple delight of recognition but also with rich historical associations. Mr. Fairlie is immediately linked with the great but rather pompous and self-important Roman orator and with the immemorial tradition of pious despair over the wickedness of the current generation, a tradition for which Cicero's words have become a motto. These connotations invest the statement with a tone of amiable mockery, heightening its meaning and effect.

Allusion

An allusion is a brief, indirect reference, a passing mention or a bit of quotation; its purpose is to call to mind a whole complex of facts or attitudes by means of a few words or a proper name. Allusions can evoke associations in the reader's mind and present briefly something that might require several sentences or even pages if explained in full.

In the past English prose has been highly allusive. If you turn over the pages of any anthology of prose of the eighteenth or nineteenth century, you find its pages filled with echoes from other literature—especially the Bible, Shakespeare, Milton, and the Latin poets Vergil and Horace. Earlier writers could feel sure that they and their readers shared a common fund of literary knowledge. In our own time, prose addressed to a general audience is far less allusive; writers can no longer be certain that their readers know even Shakespeare and the Bible well, much less Vergil and Horace.

If, in the last fifty years, the quantity of allusion in general prose has dwindled, in specialized prose it has probably increased. Essays in literary criticism, history, psychology, sociology, and economics are often filled with allusions to materials within their own province. The same is true of sports reporting, theatrical reviewing, the financial news, and gossip columns. Here are two highly allusive quotations which assume a community of interest and knowledge in the writer and his audience. The first is from a magazine article on football:

A onetime single-wing tailback at Louisiana State, Tittle started his pro career in 1948 when many of his teammates were still in grammar school. He spent two years with Baltimore in the old All-America Conference (1949 record: 1 win, 11 losses), put in ten years with the San Francisco 49ers. Everyone agreed that he could pass, but he was no twinkle toes as a runner, and when the 49ers shifted to a ground game last year, he was traded to the Giants. . . . Against the Pittsburgh Steelers in the season's second game, Tittle got the kind of protection a passer needs, completed ten of twelve passes for a 17–14 victory that started the Giants on the road to the Eastern Conference championship.

A sidearm passer in the mold of Slingin' Sammy Baugh, Tittle throws one of the longest (up to 60 yards) passes in football. [*Time* Magazine]

The second quotation is from the historian G. M. Young:

> Of Tennyson, Jowett once observed, mysteriously, that he was a good scholar in the Oxford sense of the word. Of Mr. Gladstone's scholarship, and his philosophy it would be equally true to say that he remained to the end a Christ Church man of the 1830's.
>
> But ah! what days were those Parmenides!
>
> when, if we had entered the room next to the great staircase, that last glory of the Gothic world, we should have found Gladstone, Sidney Herbert, Robert Lowe, Dalhousie, Elgin, and the Younger Canning, translating the *Rhetoric* by turn at the feet of Mr. Briscoe.

The anonymous writer in *Time* assumes that his readers know about the Giants, the 49ers, Slingin' Sammy Baugh, a ground game, and the Eastern Conference. G. M. Young assumes that his readers will recognize the *Rhetoric* as Aristotle's, Sidney Herbert as the leader of medical reform in the British Army, Dalhousie as the governor-general of India, and so on. Through allusion, both bring a great deal of background to bear on the immediate topic. In skilled hands, an allusive style can pack a remarkable amount of material into a narrow compass and give an effect of concentrated richness. But it is not possible to a writer addressing a general audience with no specialized fund of information.

Allusions in general prose must be used with discrimination. If they are stock phrases already used countless times, they have become clichés with no powers of evocation. Probably most of the people who speak of "Achilles' heel" or "crossing the Rubicon" have forgotten what was wrong with Achilles' heel, and who crossed the Rubicon. Certainly, almost everyone who says "The die is cast" has forgotten that the die was one of a pair of dice, not a metal mold. A writer, then, should be wary of using overworked allusions such as these: "Trojan horse," "sword of Damocles," "winning a Pyrrhic victory," "cutting the Gordian knot," "patience of Job," "voice in the wilderness," "mortal coil," "Waterloo," "Cassandra," "Don Juan," "Romeo," "Galahad," "Svengali." In the course of an essay, a very few such allusions may give pleasure if aptly used, but they will become tedious if multiplied.

Obscure, far-fetched, or merely decorative allusion is often distracting. The best allusions in modern prose at once drive home the point to be made and permit the reader to understand what is being said even if he does not recognize the allusion:

In France, the Court played at shepherds and shepherdesses while the peasants ate grass. Today we in America are the rich minority of world society. Are we any less prone than they to while away our most precious gift of time in pursuit of distractions fully as trivial as those of Le Trianon or Le Hameau? (References to the court of Louis XVI) [ADLAI STEVENSON]

In the movies, then, the leading adversaries of Christianity are represented as snivelling, grape-peeling, effeminate imbeciles. We are left wondering why the Roman Empire took so long to decline and fall. (A reference to Gibbon's *Decline and Fall of the Roman Empire*) [HENRY POPKIN]

The proponents of space travel seem to hold this truth self-evident, that it is somehow desirable for man to get away from the Earth. (A reference to The Declaration of Independence) [ROBERT PLANK]

Following is an example in which younger readers would probably miss the allusion but see the point of the statement. Mary McCarthy is reflecting on the possibly imminent end of American civilization along with the rest of the world:

Unfortunately, as things seem now, posterity is not around the corner.

She is echoing Herbert Hoover's often-repeated statement in the early years of the Depression: "Prosperity is just around the corner." If a reader picks up the echo, he is rewarded with enjoyment of the (rather acrid) joke; if not, he still sees what the writer is driving at.

Allusiveness can enrich the suggestiveness of prose, and it can help achieve economy of exposition. But to do either well it must be suitable to the subject and so arranged that it will not obscure the point to be made. A writer should be willing to ask himself, "Will the meaning of this statement be clear even if my allusion is not understood?" If the answer is "No," the writer should either give up the allusion or provide a paraphrase, as Van Wyck Brooks does in this instance:

In almost every one of Mark Twain's sallies he burns down the house in order to roast his pig—he destroys, that is to say, an entire complex of legitimate pretensions for the sake of puncturing a single sham. (A reference to Charles Lamb's "Dissertation Upon Roast Pig")

Euphemism

A euphemism is a more acceptable substitute for a word or phrase considered likely to cause pain, to offend polite ears, or to be disagreeably explicit. Its purpose is not necessarily to deceive, but to clothe ugly or inconvenient facts with attractive or at least decently vague connotations. It is always the result of an effort to displace a word that is considered to have ugly overtones.

Thus *antisocial* now appears alongside *criminal*, and *sex deviate* alongside *pervert*. *Insane asylums* become *mental hospitals*, and *prisons* become *reformatories* and then *rehabilitation centers*. *Alcoholic* and *drug addict* have almost universally replaced *drunkard* and *dope fiend*. When the change is complete, the newly established word is no longer felt to be a euphemism but is accepted as the neutral and proper designation for whatever it refers to. Thus the word ceases to be a euphemism, and the less condemnatory attitude originally behind it no longer necessarily attaches to the word. Lawbreakers are probably just as afraid of *reformatories* as they once were of *prisons*. One can speak with as much horror of *drug addicts* as of *dope fiends*. Typical is the fate of a recently invented euphemism in this accusation scrawled across the wall of a New York City building: "Lorraine is an under-achiever."

Most euphemisms provoke merriment (or anger) in those sufficiently alert to language to notice them:

Politics:

> to liberate—to conquer
> to pacify the population—mass murder of civilians
> the democratic faith—often, the American national interest as defined by the speaker
> the final solution of the Jewish problem (a Nazi phrase)—genocide
> people's democracy—police state dictatorship
> police action—war
> strategic withdrawal—retreat

Occupations:

> sanitation engineer—garbage collector
> extermination engineer—rat-catcher
> field representative—salesman
> custodian—janitor
> police informant—stool pigeon

Death, disease, and old age:

> passed on, passed away—died
> last repose, final sleep—death
> senior citizen—old man or woman
> terminal cancer patient—someone dying of cancer

The body:

> tummy—abdomen, stomach, or belly, whichever is meant
> halitosis—bad breath
> hips, derriere—buttocks
> bosom—breasts

Respectable modern prose avoids such expressions, for they smack of deception and the gushy language of advertising. Political euphemisms that clothe horrifying realities in bland words suggest a brutal cynicism in those who invent and use them. It is not "more polite" to call a stomach a "tummy"; it merely suggests a schoolgirl awkwardness. The sentimental overtones of "passed away" are as undignified as the coarse ones of "kicked the bucket." Even very formal writing, once so reticent, now calls things by their plain names.

Euphemism, however, is not always a vice of language that ought to be avoided. It makes the art of diplomacy possible, and it can prevent a good deal of needless bad feeling in ordinary controversy. The substitution of "emergent nation" for the blunter "backward country" has saved embarrassment at the United Nations and in foreign offices. To say at the end of unsuccessful negotiations that the participants were "unable to reach agreement" is less provocative than to say that they "quarreled the whole time." It is more tactful, and often more accurate, to say that someone is "under a misapprehension" than to call him a "liar." Such mild euphemisms can be conciliatory where harsh language would only provide another source of irritation.

Among writers of modern realistic fiction, there is often a conscious and even doctrinaire inversion of the euphemistic habit of speech. These writers always call mucus "snot"; all odors are "stinks"; their heroes are always kicking people in the "guts" rather than the abdomen. This systematically harsh language is effective in a certain range of fiction, but it has little place in the more temperate climate of discursive prose, which prefers the neutrality of "odor" and "abdomen" to the violence of "stink" and "guts."

Exotics: Archaisms, Briticisms, Borrowed Words

Archaisms, Briticisms, and foreign words all appear from time to time in good American English, but are felt to be somewhat apart from the rest of the American English vocabulary. They are visitors rather than permanent residents, and they require special treatment.

ARCHAISMS

Words labelled "obsolete" in a dictionary have passed out of use and present no problem to the writer. Archaic words are now passing out of the language and do sometimes present problems. Presumably no one in his right mind would now write "Eftsoons we partake of orts from yestereen" for "We often eat last night's leftovers." But writers in search of the comic, the quaint, or the poetic sometimes seize on archaic expressions. Descriptions of nature seem to present a special temptation:

It was a glorious *morn* when I arrived at Yellowstone Park.
We all gathered around the campfire at *eventide*.
The day was dark and *drear*.

Sometimes an inexperienced writer uses archaisms in a misguided effort to sound "literary":

Mark Twain often writes of the days of *yore* on the Mississippi.
In his old age Melville would often *tarry* by the docks, watching the ships come and go.

Such usages are usually labored and ineffective. Religious, poetic, and legal vocabularies have preserved a good many archaisms (*saith, thou, eve, morn, hereof, hereunder,* and so on), but ordinary prose usually avoids them. Only Charles Lamb in the last century and Winston Churchill in our own have been able to make antiquated language consistently viable in their prose. And even Churchill relies more on magnificently old-fashioned words than on truly archaic ones. Only an experienced writer should risk the use of archaic words.

Archaisms are now used chiefly for humorous purposes. Some young writers, thinking that "saith" and "quoth" are in themselves funny, use them at random. Or they engage in this kind of incongruity:

Since breaking off her engagement, my sister has been a *damsel* in distress.

When I saw the blood on the carpet, I thought I would fall into a *swoon*.

Such attempts at humor are feeble because nothing lies behind the purely verbal incongruity. A more adequately motivated use of archaism for humorous purposes sometimes succeeds, at least in journalistic prose. Sometimes a writer establishes a mocking contrast between a medieval-sounding vocabulary and a modern subject matter; he does not quite come out and say that his subject itself is an archaism, but the implication is plainly there:

Surrounded by the *serried ranks of his retainers*, the President this morning left by jet for the West Coast.

Dr. Peale seems to think that he can exorcise the bomb by crying, "*Avaunt!*"

Like the heavily armored knights *of old*, the Mayor finds it difficult to move around very fast in an emergency.

BRITICISMS

The standard English written in America and that written in Great Britain are largely the same, but there are minor differences of spelling and vocabulary. Occasionally, an American writer may decide that British spellings are more elegant than ours and come out with *labour, connexion, cheque,* or *programme* rather than our *labor, connection, check,* and *program.* No matter how much an American writer likes British spelling or vocabulary, he is wise to adhere to American practice. Otherwise he will almost certainly be set down as affected and snobbish by his readers. The sole exception occurs when an American writer is dealing with English life. Then, using *lift* for elevator, *lorry* for truck, and *cinema* for movies may help to evoke the characteristic atmosphere of English life.

BORROWED WORDS

English has always borrowed freely from other languages, especially French and Latin. Borrowed words that have been in use for some time are usually completely anglicized: they lose their foreign spellings, pronunciations, and plurals, and are assimilated to English forms. These words present no problem to the writer, who uses them without thinking of their origins. It has often been argued that words from Anglo-Saxon—the direct ancestor of modern English—are stronger and more direct than the equivalent words borrowed from other languages and therefore should be preferred. But only a handful of people know anything about the history of the words they use, so that most writers cannot make their word choices on the basis of etymology. Further, words of Anglo-Saxon origin are *not* always more forceful than others. Consider these pairs:

Anglo-Saxon Origin	*Old French Origin*
fearful	horrible
shove	push
take	seize
strong	powerful

Anglo-Saxon Origin	Old French Origin
wrath	rage
work	labor
waste	ravage
bold	brave
slay	murder

Surely the words of Anglo-Saxon origin are not perceptibly stronger or pithier than their companions from Old French. A competent writer judges the effectiveness of a word by its current use, not its ancestry.

Some words are in transition between their original foreign forms and anglicized forms. They have alternate spellings, pronunciations, and plurals; accents and other marks are retained by some users and dropped by others: éclair—eclair; façade—facade; cliché—cliche; crêpe —crepe; vertebrae—vertebras; formulae—formulas; nuclei—nucleuses; memoranda—memorandums; chateaux—chateaus. Both forms are correct in these examples, but a dictionary is indispensable in resolving doubts about words with alternate forms. Words that have a primarily literary or intellectual currency often retain their foreign spelling and pronunciation longer than more widely used foreign words: e.g., *coup d'état, fait accompli, laissez faire, lapsus linguae, nouvelle vague, parvenu, nouveau riche, Zeitgeist, Weltanschauung, Bildungsroman,* and *non sequitur.* Such words are underlined in copy and italicized in print. On the other hand, such widely used words as *cafe, phenomenon, finale, chauffeur,* and *fillet* are *not* underlined or italicized; they are no longer felt to be foreign words.

Occasionally meanings change in borrowed words that were initially used by the learned and then became more popular:

Alibi (Latin "elsewhere") was restricted to the proof that one was elsewhere when a crime was committed. Now general English uses it to mean any excuse or disproof of guilt.

Decimate was restricted to "reduce by one-tenth." It has come to mean "to ravage" or "to destroy in large part."

Dilemma meant to be faced with two (and only two) undesirable alternatives. General English now sometimes uses it to mean any problem or difficulty, no matter how many alternatives it presents, though this use is rare in careful prose.

Protagonist originally meant the chief actor in a drama. Now it can mean any one of the principals in a drama or an event, so that it is now possible to speak of protagonists.

Except for *decimate*, the most formal prose restricts itself to the narrower meanings, but most writing in general English uses the wider ones.

Until this century, many, perhaps most, British and American authors made copious use of foreign words and phrases, freely using *cum grano salis* instead of "with a grain of salt," *affaire du coeur* instead of "love affair," or *soupçon* instead of "pinch." Now such locutions are generally felt to be ostentatious. A contemporary writer who decorates his prose with foreign phrases is likely to seem irritatingly precious:

From May through September, *la saison pour la plage*, these docks are diving boards for husky ragamuffins. [TRUMAN CAPOTE]

Not that this is the Height's sole *maison de luxe*: we are blessed with several exponents of limousine life—but unarguably, Mrs. O. is *la regina di tutti* [CAPOTE]

Good modern practice is to use foreign words either when there is no fully satisfactory English equivalent or when they evoke relevant national or historical associations. English has no words, for instance, that have quite the same force as *coup d'état, nouvelle vague, téte-à-téte*, or *Weltanschauung*. In such cases, modern writers use foreign locutions freely, for they fill a gap in the English vocabulary.

Even when there is a readily available English word, foreign words are sometimes to be preferred because they carry with them associations that the English equivalent does not. In writing of France during the French Revolution, it is suitable to use such phrases as *canaille, emigrés, grand seigneur*, and *ancien régime*; they have historical connotations that are lacking in the English *rabble, refugees, great lord*, and *old order*. English *glory* lacks the overtones of General de Gaulle's *gloire*, and English *lightning war* and *substitute* do not have the force of Nazi Germany's *Blitzkreig* and *Ersatz*. In addition to evoking the life of a certain era or nation, foreign phrases can also evoke the atmosphere that surrounds some abstract ideas:

Presumably the crescent calf was considered, in the art schools, to approach more nearly to the Platonic Idea of the human leg than did the poor distorted Appearance of real life. Personally, I prefer my calves with the bulge at the top and a proper ankle at the bottom. But then I don't hold much with the *beau idéal*. [ALDOUS HUXLEY]

The most obvious example [of luxury art] is the art of eighteenth century France, where, however, the arrogant elaboration demanded by powerful patrons is sometimes sweetened, and given lasting value, by a reasonable belief in the *douceur de vivre*. [KENNETH CLARK]

If foreign words are used sparingly and strictly tested for their suitability to the context, they can add connotative richness to a writer's language. Frequently and loosely used, they only create clutter.

Synonyms

English is particularly rich in synonyms—that is, in groups of words with closely related meanings. It has thousands of word-clusters such as these:

> fear, dread, fright, alarm, dismay, consternation, panic, terror, horror, trepidation
>
> old, aged, ancient, venerable, antique, antiquated, archaic, obsolete
>
> pride, conceit, vanity, vainglory, self-esteem
>
> weak, feeble, frail, fragile, infirm, decrepit

Clearly, the words in such groups are seldom completely equivalent in meaning, or freely interchangeable. There is even some difference of connotation between "an old woman" and "an aged woman," where the denotation is the same. In most word groups, the differences are more pronounced. The statement "His pride had something of sublimity in it" is not at all the same as "His conceit had something of sublimity in it." Synonyms enrich our language and are a valuable resource for the writer, but he must respect their varying shades of meaning and connotation.

A writer usually begins to look for a synonym when he wants to avoid using the same word too often, or when he thinks that the word he has is too general or too specific, or has the wrong connotations.

Trying to find different names for the same thing in order to avoid repetition is hazardous. Some young writers are advised by handbooks never to use the same word twice in the same sentence (or the same paragraph). Like most purely mechanical rules about word choice, this one probably does more harm than good. Faithfully followed, it can lead to this kind of absurd variation:

Big lies, little falsehoods, untruths for the sake of gain, deceptions for their own worth—these are the stock in trade of the sensational journalist.

The repetition of "lies" is far more forceful:

Big lies, little lies, lies for the sake of gain, lies for their own sake—these are the stock in trade of the sensational journalist.

Some writers go far beyond trying to avoid repetition; they develop a taste for "elegant variation" and enjoy calling the same thing by as many different names as possible. This habit can lead to ludicrous vices of style. Here is the first paragraph of an essay on the humming-bird:

> The humming-bird is the tiniest *feathered creature* in all the world, one of the most brilliant in plumage, and the only *bird* that can fly straight up, down, sideways and backwards. This *faerie Titania of the airways* delicately feeds on the wing and sparklingly bathes in tiny ponds of dew caught on broad leaves—a *flying flower* fashioned by Nature in an inspired mood.

In the next three pages of this *Reader's Digest* article, the humming-bird is also called a "ruby-throat" (the name of a species), a "radiant wanderer," a "wee suitor," a "gnome-like champion," a "hummer," and a "tiny favorite of nature." This inventiveness is misplaced; it belongs to a "flowers of rhetoric" way of writing that now has only historical interest, and little enough of that. The writer would have done better to write "hummingbird" or "he" or "it" as often as he needed to, rather than weary the reader with laborious ingenuity.

There are two important situations, however, in which a writer needs to avoid repetition of the same word in the same neighborhood. In the first, a noun is too frequently repeated when pronouns would be equally clear and less obtrusive or a synonym could be used without artificiality:

> The *problem* of urban renewal is at last getting some attention from the federal government. But the solution of the *problem* still lies with the cities themselves, though they lack the resources to deal with the *problem* effectively.

The second sentence would be better if it read:

> But *its* solution still lies with the cities themselves, though they lack the resources for *large-scale urban renewal*.

In the second situation, the same word, or one of its derivatives, is used in two different senses in the same neighborhood:

> Officials estimate that renewing the Beloit Park *neighborhood* will cost somewhere in the *neighborhood* of fifty million dollars. ("In the neighborhood of" should be changed to "approximately.")

> Rather than *draw* on his last reserves, the general decided to *withdraw* and regroup his forces. ("Withdraw" should be changed to "retreat.")

A supply of synonyms is invaluable for achieving precision of denotation and for conveying shades of feeling. Since one of the worst faults of modern prose is its excessive generality, synonyms are most frequently useful in giving the writer a more specific word to replace the general one he has already hit upon. If a writer who had described someone as "expressing strange opinions in an angry style" recognized that his formulation was somewhat too general, he might change it to "stating eccentric opinions in a truculent style," thereby defining the quality of the strangeness and the anger. Or he might change "he does not deal with the points that his opponents have made" to "he evades the objections that his opponents have raised."

Synonyms are particularly useful for translating pompously formal abstract statements into plainer English:

> Three interrelated factors rendered the cessation of hostilities inevitable.
> (Three related events brought the fighting to a stop.)

> Interpersonal relationships within the primary societal group show a frequent tendency to deteriorate within an urban environment.
> (In cities, family ties are often weakened.)

> Mr. Smith exhibited aggressive behavior toward the Board of Directors.
> (Mr. Smith fought with the Board of Directors.)

Somewhat less often they help in rephrasing a statement that is too colloquial:

> The deal was finalized yesterday.
> (The contract was signed yesterday.)

> The mess has been cleared up.
> (The problem has been solved.)

> Mary Lou always has the wiggles during lectures.
> (Mary Lou is always restless during lectures.)

Synonyms are also useful to a writer who wants to make a statement either more forceful or softer:

> My impression (belief, conviction) is that you are misinformed (mistaken, wrong).

> Your statement is incorrect (untrue, false, a lie).

> Your arguments are inconsistent (incoherent, chaotic).

> Your generalizations are debatable (dubious, improbable, incredible).

The more a writer is aware of alternative possibilities in phrasing a statement, the greater his chances of hitting on the exact equivalent in words of his thought. College dictionaries and dictionaries of synonyms [3] can be helpful if used with discretion. They are *not* good places to look for new words to use; they *are* good places to remind one of the possibilities of choice among the words he already knows. They can give a useful jog to the memory, but they can be disastrously misleading if a writer decides to try a previously unknown word picked out of a list of synonyms.

Synonym-hunting can go too far and turn into a perverted search for the *mot juste*, the uniquely right or striking or colorful word. The result can be this kind of tortured preciosity:

Whether plenipotentiaries from the pearl-floored palace of Poseidon or mariners merely, Viking-tressed seamen out of the Gothic North languishing after a long and barberless voyage, they are included permanently in my memory's curio cabinet: an object to be revolved in the light that way and this, like those crystal lozenges with secretive carvings sealed inside. [TRUMAN CAPOTE] [4]

3 The most widely used dictionaries of synonyms are *Webster's Dictionary of Synonyms*, Fernald's *Standard Handbook of Synonyms, Antonyms, and Prepositions*, Soule's *A Dictionary of English Synonyms*, and Roget's *International Thesaurus*.

4 Since Capote is a talented writer, he is probably being playful here, or maybe he decided to sacrifice everything to alliteration. Even so, the search for novelty has gone too far.

13

LEVELS OF USAGE

MUCH of the connotation of words is determined by the "level of usage" to which they belong, by the cultural and social atmosphere in which they habitually appear. For example, *frightening* is standard English, *scary* is colloquial, and *creepy* is adolescent and slangy.

Everyone who speaks a language has some feeling for its levels of usage. "I'm a'fixin' to go down the road a piece" *sounds* like dialect. "He fingered her as a bag woman for the fuzz" would surely *sound* slangy even to someone who did not know that it meant "He accused her of being a collector of protection money for the police." "I reject the imputation" belongs recognizably to the sphere of formal (or stilted) English. The equivalent statements "I deny the charge," "It's a lie," and "That ain't so" represent a descending scale of formality. Further, the first two statements suggest public utterance, either spoken or written, the second two private conversation. Systematic classifications of levels of usage vary in detail, but there is wide agreement about three large (and loose) categories of usage.

General, Vulgate, and Formal English

The most inclusive is "general" English, which is the basis of most writing and talking. It includes all the ordinary words of the language —*do, be, make, in, out, and, since, red, green, man, woman*. It is the language almost everyone uses and agrees upon. It dominates the vocabulary of fiction, of radio and television speech, of business communications, of private conversation and personal letters. It is the part of the English language that is truly "our common speech" because it is so widely shared.

General English also has a large group of words that are more often heard than seen—the words most dictionaries call "colloquial." These words are by no means substandard or "illiterate." They simply belong more to conversation and private correspondence than to spoken or written public utterance. In refusing to join a friend for coffee, it is certainly all right to say, "I can't make it," but that is hardly the language one would use to decline a dinner invitation from the French Consul-General. Colloquial words imply familiarity and ease; they belong more to personal and domestic life than to the world of public affairs and intellectual discussion.

"Vulgate" or nonstandard English includes slang, the more recondite forms of profanity, dialect speech, localisms, and words restricted in use to groups that seldom express themselves in print or public speech—hoboes, thieves, policemen, mechanics, soldiers, sailors, truck drivers, factory workers, and so on. This speech seldom appears in print except as part of dramatic dialogue in fiction or in deliberately "local color" writing. By and large, it is the speech of the uneducated and, as far as the printed word goes, the inarticulate. Although some of this speech is wonderfully expressive, it makes only fleeting appearances in the vocabulary of the educated, usually in the form of an enlivening splash of profanity or slang.

If vulgate English is almost entirely a spoken language rather than a written one, something close to the opposite might be said of much formal English, the learned or bookish part of the language. It is used in ceremonial oratory and public lectures and in conversation on literary and scientific subjects. But its main use is in textbooks, in poetry, in literary essays, in scientific writing, in history, in philosophy, and in the other pursuits of high culture.

These three levels of usage—general, vulgate, and formal—obviously reflect our social and educational structure. Although there are dialect-speaking millionaires and erudite hoboes, people who know formal English are generally somewhere near the top of the social heap, and people who habitually speak vulgate English are generally somewhere near the bottom. This fact has led some writers on language to decry talk about "levels of usage" as snobbish and antidemocratic; they seem to think it somehow wicked to identify some words as "slang" or "dialect" and thus point out what social significance is generally attached to them. But this social aspect of words is as much a fact about them as their phonology and morphology. Good writers always have a discriminating sense of the level of usage they are drawing on for a particular word or phrase. Incompetent writers ignore distinctions among levels of usage at their peril. Everyone—including Tennessee mountaineers and Bronx housewives—would regard a serious discussion of the Geneva Disarmament Conference written in the dialect of the Tennessee hills or the *patois* of the Bronx as a very dubious performance.

In recent years, a few of the more headstrong students of linguistics have attacked the standards of acceptable usage set by editors, writers, and teachers—the people who spend much of their professional lives deciding what is or is not good English and who are in effect the arbiters of propriety in English prose. The linguists point out that no word or grammatical form is *inherently* better than any other; all are the products of historical changes that have gone on in the past and will continue in the future; "rules" of language are simply descriptive generalizations about usage and must change as usage changes. No one can reasonably quarrel with these assertions, but, as some linguists seem reluctant to add, it does not follow that "anything goes" in speech and writing. Not even the most emancipated professor of linguistics regularly uses "ain't" as a negative form of the linking verb in his lectures. Nor does he feel free, at least in print, to call his opponents "jerks" or "meatballs." When the occasion calls for relatively formal prose, the linguist, like everyone else, observes the conventions that go with such prose.

Many of the stern prohibitions in the older handbooks of English are the product of a false analogy between English and Latin; many contemporary pronouncements about correctness in language are no doubt the product of misinformation or irrational prejudice. But whatever their flaws, handbooks of English, editorial style sheets, and dictionary usage labels are an effort to record an educated consensus about the proprieties and conventions of English prose: they tell the prospective writer what kind of verbal behavior is appropriate.

Acceptable Levels of Prose

The language of normal nonfictional prose is a mixture of formal and general English, with an occasional spice of the vulgate. With its immense resources of vocabulary, it offers a good deal of freedom to the writer in choosing the level of usage he wishes to adopt. Sometimes it relies heavily on the bookish diction of formal English. Sometimes it comes close to the rhythms and locutions of popular speech. Here are three examples of different acceptable levels of modern English prose:

Yet when we have become acclimated to Joyce, when the charismatic legend becomes with familiarity not so fierce and the vatic paraphernalia of the style and method less intimidating, do we not find that we are involved in a conception of life that reiterates, in however different a tonality, the Wordsworthian vision? One of the striking things about *Ulysses* (to speak only of that work) is that the idea of evil plays so small a part in it; the conception of sin has but a tangential relevance to the book. The element of sexuality which plays so large a part in the story does not raise considerations of sin and evil. The character of Leopold Bloom, who figures in the life of Joyce's Poet much as the old men in Wordsworth figure in his life—met by chance and yet giving help of some transcendent yet essentially human kind—is conceived in Wordsworthian terms: in terms, that is, of his humbleness of spirit. [LIONEL TRILLING]

Among the words first taught to children by their doting parents are the terms for the parts of the human body. Pressing down the diminutive button-like protuberance which shows signs of one day becoming a full-blown human nose, mama asks beguilingly: "What is this?" The child, shrewd and skilled already in the enormous task of humoring grown-ups, but nevertheless somewhat confused by the rain of new terminology about him, looks up cooperatively and suggests with hope but little conviction: "Baby's ear." "Oh, no!" the mellifluous voice proceeds, while the pressure is still maintained, "Baby's nose. *Nose!*" And so the baffling epithet is learned, presumably for a lifetime. [MARGARET SCHLAUCH]

Since work was distasteful to Davy [Crockett] he became, in turn, a backwoods justice of the peace who boasted about his ignorance of the law; an unsuccessful politician; a hack writer, heavily dependent on some unidentified ghost; and—hear this Junior—a violinist. Whenever a steady job threatened, he took to the woods. He was never king of anything, except maybe the Tennessee Tall Tales and Bourbon Sampler's Association. When he claimed he had shot 105 bear in nine months, his fellow tipplers refused to believe a word of it, on the sensible grounds that Davy couldn't count that high. [JOHN FISCHER]

The first quotation relies heavily on words more often seen in print than heard in speech. *Charismatic, vatic, paraphernalia, tonality, tangential,* and *transcendent,* which are all borrowed from Latin or Greek, have made their way into formal written English but have never penetrated colloquial English. They are unabashedly "highbrow" words which indicate that the writer is attempting neither to simplify his subject nor to achieve a conversational tone. He consistently chooses more dignified and somewhat less familiar words where there appears to be a choice: *acclimated* instead of *used to; intimidating* instead of *frightening; reiterates* instead of *repeats; sexuality* instead of *sex.* To be sure, these choices are in part determined by the desire for greater precision of meaning: *intimidating,* for instance, means something more restricted than *frightening*, and has a different connotation. But they also give rise to an effect of dignified formality and seriousness. This stately and erudite language would be out of place in many contexts, but in literary criticism addressed to cultivated readers, it is well suited both to the subject and to the audience.

The second quotation is considerably less formal than the first. It was written by a linguist addressing a general audience, not her fellow experts. The writer is not afraid of bookish words, as witness *diminutive, protuberance, beguilingly, mellifluous, presumably,* and *epithet.* But she moves from the formal toward the colloquial in using *mama* and *baby* instead of *mother* and *infant;* also, *humoring* and *buttonlike* have a conversational ring. Although the essay from which this quotation is taken is about the linguistic process technically known as "metaphorical extension," the writer avoids the technical language of linguistic science. The norm of her language is general written English, with occasional modulations toward either the formal or the conversational. This is the language best suited to writing addressed to a general audience: all of its vocabulary is the shared property of educated people.

The third quotation, from a popular magazine, is deliberately breezy and colloquial in its vocabulary—*hack writer, ghost, took to the woods, steady job, maybe* (instead of *perhaps*), *claimed, tipplers,* and *couldn't* (instead of *could not*). Written at the peak of the Davy Crockett fad, the essay is a journalistic treatment of a not very serious topical subject. Its language is by and large that of general written English, and it avoids anything that is downright slangy. But it also avoids any hard words that belong primarily to formal written English, and it gains its characteristic tone from the use of old-fashioned colloquialisms, such as *claimed* and *tipplers,* that evoke the American rural past. This level of language is perhaps best suited, not to serious subjects, but to the light treatment of topical subjects.

The diction of all three passages is well within acceptable limits, despite marked variation. Each passage employs words that are difficult to imagine appearing in the other two, but the bulk of the vocabulary in all three is common property. Most of the words used could appear in anything from a philosophical treatise to a newspaper column without looking out of place. All three writers have adapted their language to their subject and to the audience they had in mind. Academic formality, journalistic breeziness, and the middle way between the two all have their appropriate occasions.

Each of these levels of usage also has characteristic vices. The most formal English can become pompous and unnecessarily abstruse, general English drab, and journalistic raciness vulgar and shrill.

Theodore Spencer's parody of contemporary literary criticism underlines the most prevalent vices of the formal style. He sets out to analyze the following well-known verses:

> Thirty days hath September,
> April, June, and November,
> All the rest have thirty-one,
> Excepting February alone,
> Which has only eight and a score
> Till leap year gives it one day more.

And begins:

The previous critics who have studied this poem, Coleridge among them, have failed to explain what we may describe as its fundamental *dynamic*. This I now propose to do. The first thing is to observe the order in which the names (or verbal constructs) of the months are presented. According to the prose meaning—what I shall henceforth call the prose-*demand* —"September" should not precede, it should follow, "April," as a glance at the calendar will show. . . . That is the only sequence consonant with prose logic.

Why, then, we ask ourselves, did the poet violate what educated readers know to be the facts? . . . It is here that the principle of dynamic analysis comes to our aid.

Dynamic analysis proves that the most successful poetry achieves its effect by producing an *expectation* in the reader's mind before his sensibility is fully prepared to receive the full impact of the poem. The reader makes a *proto-response* which preconditions him to the total response toward which his fully equilibrized organs of apperception tend. It is the proto-response which the poet has here so sensitively manipulated. . . . In his profound analysis of the two varieties of mensual time, he puts the *gentlest* month first. . . . It is the month in which vegetation first begins to fade, but which does not as yet give us a sense of tragic fatality. . . .

But the sensibility of the poet does not stop at this point. Having described what is true of *four* months, he disposes of *seven* more with masterly economy. In a series of pungent constructs his sensibility sums up their inexorable limitations: *All* (the capitalization should be noted) "have thirty-one." The poet's sensibility communicates a feeling to the sensibility of the reader so that the sensibility of both, with reference to their previous but independent sensibilities, is fused into that momentary communication of sensibility which is the final sensibilty of the poet and the sensibility of the reader. The texture and structure of the poem have erupted into a major reaction. The ambiguity of equilibrium is achieved.

The chief purpose of Spencer's parody is to ridicule a vice of thought rather than of language: the widespread practice of conjuring up a nonexistent problem and then subjecting it to solemn and painstaking analysis. But this failure of thought brings with it failures of style. Spencer pushes the disparity between language and subject to a comic extreme by employing the lofty language of literary criticism to discuss a verse meant to help people remember the number of days in each month. In doing so, he reveals one of the most frequent causes of collapse in formal style: incongruity between the triviality of the ideas expressed and the weightiness of the language. The formal style makes an implicit claim that its subject is serious and its thought scrupulous and cogent. If the thought is inconsequential and the subject matter no more than a quibble, the formal style will avenge itself by revealing the author's fatuity.

Spencer also parodies more specific failures of language to which formal prose is liable. There are the pseudotechnical terms thrown in to give a "scientific" flavoring to the discussion: "verbal constructs" for *names*; "prose demand" for *prose sense*; "proto-response" and "equilibrized organs of apperception" for God knows what. There is the repetition of intellectual fad words—*dynamic* and *sensibility*; by the time the author is through with them they have lost all meaning and are formulas of magical incantation. Stale adjective-noun combinations such as "full impact," "tragic fatality," "masterly economy," and "inexorable limitations" are balanced by one attempt at a striking phrase in "pungent constructs," which misfires. Finally, the sacrifice of meaning to intellectual pretension reaches a climax in the resounding nonsense of the last line: "The ambiguity of equilibrium is achieved."

Formal style fails when a writer tries to be too high-flown; very informal style often fails when the writer tries to be too breezy and slangy, when every sentence must have its "colorful" word and every point be made with a show of wit. Here is part of an article titled "Hipitaph" from *Time*:

The Beat Generation has finally got what it wanted—lost. Essentially the products of a public-relations campaign carried on by amateur flacks in stovepipe slacks, the untalented beats picked their own title and by noisy promotion tried to associate themselves with the talented expatriates of the '20s whom Gertrude Stein named the Lost Generation. With the help of eager squares, including some journalists, the beats even styled themselves a Movement—but it was one of the great stationary movements of all time, since nothing budges that is fueled by pretension and pot.

Now, after less than four years, the beats have all but vanished, leaving behind a curious footnote to the nation's night life: about the only durable mark that the beatniks made on American culture is the coffeehouses that flourish in a dozen cities—and the coffeehouses themselves have been largely responsible for the disappearance of the beats. With cover charges and minimums, they now discriminate actively against the vestigial beards.

Generally the coffeehouses need the tourist trade, and "There aren't enough tourists who can stand the creeps," as one Chicago host puts it. A Manhattan coffee bin has a sign over the door that says DOGS, BUT NO CATS. . . .

The beats are gone, man, gone. The bongo drums in Denver's Exodus lie unused and uncared-for. In San Francisco, where it all started, even the Co-Existence Bagel Shop has been closed since autumn. And in Chicago, when a newspaper wanted a "typical" picture of two beats in a coffeehouse, reporters had to comb the city for hours before they found two sad, sandaled shades and dragged them to the Oxford to be shot.

This is a very slick performance. Whoever wrote it is obviously lively and inventive, with a formidable mastery of his craft. The satirical treatment of a light and ephemeral subject no doubt admits of a certain verbal playfulness—puns, plays on words, slang, "colorful" language, alliteration and humorous metaphor. The play on "lost," "get lost," and "Lost Generation" is ingenious, as are the punning use of "movement," "vestigial," and "shot"; the slang is vivid and fits the contexts. But the language is so busy, so brash, so insistently clever, so smugly knowing in its use of contemporary slang and in its allusions to metropolitan fads that it soon becomes wearisome. The style seems always to be calling attention to the author, saying "See what a clever boy am I," or indirectly flattering the reader with the assumption that he too is a sophisticated man of the world looking down in amusement on the antics of lesser beings. The subject matter is simply raw material that can be converted into *Time*-speak. The writer of this brassy, flashy, relentlessly cute prose seems to know everything about turning a phrase except when to turn it off.

The following extract is neither too breezy nor too high-flown, but it pays a disastrously high price for its respectability:

A characteristic that the world should and will demand of youth today is a tremendous capacity for work. Even in the day-to-day task of earning a living there is much to be said for developing the habit of giving one's utmost. It is an expression of honesty and integrity that ultimately finds its reflection in everything we do, whatever the nature of the anticipated reward may be. Material or aesthetic, sustaining or uplifting, the reward comes out of giving over of one's total energies, not in performing half-heartedly and with a divided mind. And the pressure of hard work, faced unflinchingly, hardens physical and spiritual muscles alike, as the gruelling task or the humdrum assignment or the distasteful chore is met and conquered each day. University years, if they are truly to be fruitful according to the highest standard, will tax intellectually and physically as nothing else in previous experience. The burdens will be heavy and constant, the demands will be unrelenting and merciless, the expectations will often seem to be maddeningly unrealistic; but here are being shaped the patterns of thought and action to last all the rest of one's life, and only the best will serve unless one stands ready to compromise integrity. Ability to throw every ounce of strength into coping with the demands and pressures will leave the student triumphant and equipped with a hitherto-undreamed-of power.

At best, exhortations to hard work are likely to be depressing, but the gray, inert language in which this one is delivered makes it particularly dispiriting. Nowhere in the passage is there a concrete image or a novel turn of expression, a living metaphor, or a wholly unpredictable word. Its norm is the commonplace expression of commonplace ideas. Instead of direct points directly made, there is a shower of words. Thus, "A characteristic that the world should and will demand . . ." instead of "The world demands . . . ." Nouns and adjectives usually appear in unproductive pairs: "honesty and integrity," "heavy and constant," "demands and pressures," "unrelenting and merciless." By a slightly unfair game of questions and answers, it is easy to demonstrate how threadbare the language is. What is there much to be said for? "Giving one's utmost." How should one face hard work? "Unflinchingly." What should university years be? "Fruitful." What must be thrown into coping with demands? "Every ounce of strength." Such phrases have long since lost their ability to evoke either thought or feeling, and will persuade no one to mend his idle ways. The passage, then, commits the one really unforgivable literary sin: it is dull.

Profanity and Slang

Both profanity and slang are best avoided by writers who are not completely sure of their control over tone. Profanity has made its way into serious modern fiction and even into poetry (see, for example, the poetry of e. e. cummings); but there it usually appears in the speech of a character: that is, as a dramatic device. The essay, formal and informal, is still wary of so-called dirty words, but a good many accomplished modern essayists permit themselves an occasional "damn" or "hell" for emphasis:

We need more people who don't give a damn and can awaken responses in us. [ARTHUR SCHLESINGER, JR.]

A puzzled and irritated drama critic for *The New Yorker* recently wrote:

I didn't know whether I was looking at a noisy farce, a spook show, or another damned allegory, which it indeed turned out to be.

Even such relatively mild bits of profanity are, of course, only appropriate in informal essays, usually on topical subjects. It may be all right in a lightly ironic review to say of a contemporary novelist that he "lands the heroine in one hell of a pickle," but the phrase could not properly be used to describe Tolstoy's *Anna Karenina*. The formal essay avoids profanity altogether for the good reason that a writer who aspires to speak with the voice of pure reason can scarcely permit himself to begin swearing.

Much slang is vivid, witty, and tonically irreverent. It is often apt and expressive. For instance, the great jazz saxophonist Lester Young, in asking his drummer to accompany him only on the cymbal, not the bass drum, is reported to have said, "No bombs, man, just the tink-ti-boom." In the situation, the statement could not be better. Nevertheless, slang is a very minor resource for the essayist. Much of it is unintelligible outside a small group; much ages quickly and disappears after a few months or years; much becomes trite and shopworn through overuse in speech. In a formal essay, slang is, of course, avoided altogether. In an informal essay, two or three slang expressions may be enlivening, if they are particularly apt. More than that will almost inevitably suggest either adolescent chatter or journalistic flashiness. Even in the informal essay, the slang words chosen are usually not from the deep recesses of slang coinage, but from the region of slang that shades off into ordinary colloquial usage:

We hear of a girl who was loaded with furs and automobiles by a sharpie using absconded funds. Over the transatlantic wires they flash her confession: "I never knew he was in an illegal business. He told me he was a gambler." [ALISTAIR COOKE]

The college finds itself in possession of something which can have an important economic value, if it jazzes up the spectator-appeal element and gives the game a little professional flavor. [HUNTER GUTHRIE]

A reader whose erogenous zones are more temperate than the author's begins to feel either that he is a square (a guilty sentiment that he should not yield to) or that he is the captive of an addict. [MARY MCCARTHY]

You must be careful, generally, when thinking about Russian political life of the Provisional Government period, not to equate it with the relatively decorous and bloodless exercise that we know as politics in our English-speaking countries. There was no similarity. In Russia, politics was a mortal exercise—it was played for keeps. [G. F. KENNAN]

Technical Language and Intellectual Vogue Words

The twentieth century has seen an immense growth in technical language, sometimes unflatteringly described as *jargon*. For centuries, medicine, law, and theology have employed large technical vocabularies to describe their subject matters, and for centuries the jargon of these professions has been the butt of satire for its pedantry and mystification. In our own century, the natural sciences have had to coin thousands of new terms for new objects of study and new ideas. The social studies—economics, sociology, anthropology, and the like —have invented bulky technical vocabularies in an effort to give a scientifically precise account of their subjects. Even such traditionally humanistic (and therefore largely non-technical) studies as history and literary criticism have buttressed themselves with a new technical language that can be understood only by initiates. Indeed, almost every occupational group among the educated and the half-educated now bedecks itself with an impressive technical vocabulary. Social workers, professional educators, osteopaths, business administrators, embalmers, and advertising men, to name a few representative groups, now all have a special language that a novice must master before he is permitted to enter the temple.

Technical language is, of course, indispensable in any highly developed civilization whose very existence is based on specialized knowledge and skills. It provides a way of talking accurately and precisely about a multitude of processes, facts, and ideas that scarcely exist in the general consciousness and have no names in the general language. Technical language invents new words freely, usually by compounding Greek or Latin roots; it also draws on the general language for common words such as *work* or *mass* and, redefining them with greater rigor, sharpens loosely used common words into precise intellectual instruments. Without such word-making, highly specialized technical and scientific discourse would scarcely be possible.

Although no outsider can make an authoritative judgment about needs for technical language in any particular professional group, it is clear that technical language in general has been much inflated and much abused during the last thirty or forty years. Periodically, outraged scientists, doctors, lawyers, and government administrators try to clear away some of the verbal jungle of redundant, ambiguous, or laboriously roundabout expressions that have sprung up within their professions. In humanistic studies a fancy technical term is often introduced to denominate some perfectly familiar and commonplace idea. The way social scientists, psychologists, and educators can use jargon to dress up a dumbfoundingly pedestrian observation has become almost a national joke. Here is the *Review of Educational Research* saying that education trains the mind:

Given information about the pupil, the learning process, and the complexity of situational variables, the generalized outcome of education appears to be the development of the intellective process, including the so-called higher mental processes such as thinking, problem solving, and creative thinking.

Here is part of a report of "research" on the attitude of school teachers toward faculty meetings:

The results of this study seem to confirm some of the assumptions made concerning 1) the relationship that may exist between the nature of specific group interaction and the kinds of interpersonal perceptions and attitudes that may exist concurrently within an organization, 2) the effects on satisfaction with an experience when one's preferences in regard to what ought to happen are continually denied, and 3) the effect of size of group on apparent freedom to interact verbally. [*Journal of Educational Research*]

Although we do not know about the assumptions, and although the whole passage is puzzling, after prolonged thought, we decided that the passage probably means something like this: 1) The way teachers feel about faculty meetings reflects the way they feel about their school in general. 2) Nobody enjoys being thwarted all the time. 3) In large groups, real discussion is almost impossible.

Sentences like the following may account for the massive reluctance of the educated public to read the works of even some distinguished social thinkers who have something of weight to say:

It is needless to add that the movement of universalism and singularism shows close association with that of realism and nominalism, with the respective system of truth, with eternalism and temporalism, idealism and materialism, Ideational and Sensate art, and so on.

And so on, indeed! The thought that the list of -isms might be indefinitely extended staggers the mind. Even a sympathetic reader is likely to recoil.

Alongside the legitimate functional growth of technical language, there has been a spurious growth of jargon for its own sake. The prestige of science has led other disciplines and occupations to invent scientific-sounding terms in an effort to surround themselves with the glamor and intellectual authority of science. Pretentious and evasive words drive out plain ones. Thinness of content and muddle are concealed in verbal ornaments four syllables long. In addition, intellectual vogue words, sometimes called the journalese of the educated, are used to dignify commonplace observations. These words appear everywhere for a time and then, eroded by thoughtless use, disappear to be replaced by others equally transitory. Here are a few favorites of the moment which seem to be used more often for their powers of incantation than for their meaning: *alienation, ambiguous, ambivalent, archetypal, charismatic, deterministic, dynamic, existential* (probably the worst offender), *interplay, organic, perceptive, reductionist, simplistic, structure, tension, texture.*

A more serious writing problem among the intelligent young than those pitfalls of grammar and usage that preoccupy traditional handbooks is a taste for "flowers of rhetoric" plucked from jargon and intellectual vogue words. Like many of their elders, they fall prey to pedantry and deck their ideas in the most ostentatious language they can find. For them, a beginner is always a "neophyte"; an authoritative judgment is always "magisterial"; poverty is a "societal issue"; butterflies are "Lepidoptera"; an upsetting experience is a "trauma"; improving one's reputation is "enhancing one's image"; making more money is "maximizing profits"; quarrelsome brothers and sisters experience "sibling rivalry"; hungry infants make a "nutritional demand" when they cry, and experience an "environmental disequilibrium" when they wet the bed.

Such high, astounding terms may be justified in specialized writing addressed to fellow adepts in the mystery; at any rate, the various technical language groups must be left to set their own jargon in order. But in writing meant for a general audience, the rules suggested by common sense should be sufficient. Be wary of intellectual vogue words and be sure that you can assign a reasonably definite meaning to any one that you use. Never use technical language when there are words in general English to do the same job. Use a technical term only when you are certain that everyone will understand it, or when you are prepared to define it in nontechnical language. If you must, say to your professional colleagues, "Pre- and post-pubescent males who come from under-advantaged socioeconomic environments and have displayed antisocial tendencies reveal, with statistically significant frequency, hostile attitude-formations toward those individuals whose societal role is to exert directive authority over their life-activities." For the rest of the world, "Delinquent boys usually dislike school teachers and policemen" will suffice.

14

FUNCTIONAL VOCABULARY

A FUNCTIONAL vocabulary is one that fully accomplishes the task of communication without waste of words. Functional language is straightforward, preferring the succinct to the long-winded. It avoids ambiguity, vagueness, and padding—the use of expressions merely taking up space rather than adding to the substance of a discussion. It is as concrete and specific as the subject matter permits, because concrete and specific words give the reader something definite to grasp, enabling him to follow the writer's meaning more easily. In the widest sense, functional language is the successful adaptation of verbal means to a persuasive end, and everything in this book is in some way concerned with the functional use of language. Here we confine ourselves to methods for dealing with the various kinds of haziness and wordiness that often impede communication.

Though averse to waste of words, functional language need not always be terse and factual. It may be elaborate and colorful, and it may include such ornamental devices as word play, allusion, irony, and metaphor if these are likely to give pleasure to the reader. What functional language cannot be is empty: if it gives neither knowledge nor pleasure, if it affords neither elegance of expression nor solidity of communication, it is unfunctional—that is, useless.

Abstract and Concrete

Except for the proper nouns, almost all words are abstract in the sense that they do not denominate individual things but classes of things. Even such concrete words as *hat* and *umbrella* are abstract in this sense, for they are the names of a class rather than an individual object. A hat may be a man's funereal black bowler or a woman's spring hat with a red ribbon and a feather, but of both we might say, "What a hat!" The word *hat* ignores the differences in size, shape, and color and identifies the common property of the two objects—they are coverings for the head. This abstractness inherent in language does not impede communication but makes it possible: we understand the world largely through our ability to organize the flux of sensation and perception into entities and classes of entities. For instance, the familiar act of recognizing what something is usually involves the recognition of what *class* it belongs to: "Why, she's not carrying a basket of fruit on her head, she's wearing a hat." "That's an umbrella he's carrying, not a cane." This kind of abstractness presents no special practical difficulties for the writer.

But there is another, more restricted sense, in which words are abstract. Abstract words in this second sense are those that refer to something intangible—something that cannot be directly experienced by the senses. They are the opposite of concrete words, which refer to tangible things. *Book* is concrete, but *literature* is abstract; *the White House* is concrete, but *Presidential authority* is abstract; *judge* is concrete, but *law* is abstract. Even if abstractions refer to things that cannot be seen or touched, most of them have a fairly definite core of meaning: *opposition, opinion, hope, childhood, infancy, similarity,* and the like do not often cause difficulties of communication. The so-called "high-level abstractions," however, are a continual source of difficulty: *democracy, beauty, guilt, progress,* and *normality,* to take instances almost at random, are exceedingly difficult to use without equivocation because they mean so many different things and cannot be checked against a definite, tangible region of experience. The only way to cut down on the potential misunderstandings inherent in these words is to be alert to their dangers and to define them for oneself in the way suggested on pp. 141–42.

Aside from the confusion that surrounds high-level abstractions, abstract words have one other serious disadvantage for the writer: since they refer to intangibles, they present no images to the mind. They give the reader nothing he can visualize or grasp, and for that reason, highly abstract prose is often hard to follow. The reader is likely to feel that he is being led into a bloodless and bodiless realm where nothing has a recognizable shape or a resemblance to the ordinary world he sees and knows. A story told by the English lexicographer Eric Partridge illustrates this point:

The young lady home from school was explaining. "Take an egg," she said, "and make a perforation in the base and a corresponding one in the apex. Then apply the lips to the aperture and by forcibly inhaling the breath the shell is entirely discharged of its contents." An old lady who was listening exclaimed: "It beats all how folks do things nowadays. When I was a gal they made a hole in each end and sucked."

Described altogether by abstractions, even what is most familiar can become unrecognizable.

Necessarily, much of our discourse is about things that cannot be seen or touched, and abstract words make up a very important part of our vocabulary. Abstract language dominates in mathematics, philosophy, and science, and in any region where "pure" ideas rather than immediate experience are paramount. To read mathematics or philosophy, most people must undergo a special training to accustom themselves to move always at the level of the general and the abstract. Most people need the concrete to help them understand the abstract.

Fortunately, many abstract ideas can be stated with the help of concrete language that makes them more vivid and definite. Many words for mental events are borrowed from the realm of physical events, and a writer who exploits these parallels of language between the mental and the physical can make his subject more vivid to his readers. In the following example, William James uses concrete imagery to give tangibility to a highly abstract discussion of the instability of human ideals:

And yet if he be a true philosopher he must *see* that there is nothing final in any actually given *equilibrium* of human ideals, but that, as our present laws and customs have *fought* and *conquered* other past ones, so they will in their turn be *overthrown* by any newly discovered order which will *hush up the complaints* that they still give rise to, without producing others *louder* still. . . . And although a man always risks much when he *breaks away* from established rules and *strives* to realize a larger ideal whole than they permit, yet the philosopher must allow that it is at all times *open* to anyone to make the experiment, provided he fear not *to stake his life* and character *on the throw*. The *pinch* is always here. *Pent in* under every system of moral rules are innumerable persons whom it *weighs upon*, and good which it represses; and these are always *rumbling* and *grumbling* in the *background*, and ready for any issue by which they may get free.

The great advantage of concrete language is that it evokes images and sensations. It appeals directly to the senses and the feelings, calling up the familiar world we can all see and respond to. It adds flesh and blood to the skeleton of thought. Without the help of concrete language, abstractions remain vague and shapeless; they float in a void, eluding the reader's grasp.

A very useful way of rendering the abstract more concrete is to use synecdoche—a figure of speech in which the part signifies the whole. Sometimes it is used almost unconsciously, as in the expressions "*mouths* to feed," "farm *hands*," and "marching *feet*." Used purposively, this figure of speech can enliven expression by putting an image before the reader rather than an abstraction. The part used to signify the whole should be a significant one, and relevant to the point under discussion:

These latter did not fail to notice that the intellectuals of whom the Petrograd Soviet was exclusively composed had lily-white hands which had obviously never touched *lathe* or *plow*. [G. F. KENNAN]

They are willing, apparently, at least for a season, to endure the wretched Parisian *plumbing*, the *public baths*, the Paris *age*, and *dirt*. [JAMES BALDWIN]

The new "ruling class" of *car salesmen* and *sausage manufacturers* is adequately represented by Dr. Erhard, who in many respects resembles Stressemann, though he is decidedly less interesting. But then the *Bundesrepublik* with its *stagnant politics*, its *dreary journals*, and its increasingly *parochial universities*, is altogether not a very stimulating affair. [GEORGE LICHTHEIM]

Personally, I would rather leave my money for a newspaper than for a *cathedral*, a *gymnasium*, or even a *home for streetwalkers with fallen arches*, but I have seldom been able to assemble more than $4.17 at one time. [A. J. LIEBLING]

General and Specific

General and *specific* are relative terms. *Grain* is specific in relation to *food*, but general in relation to *wheat*, which in turn is general in relation to *Iowa winter wheat*. The most general words are universals such as *organism*, *time*, *space*, and *number*. The most specific are proper names: *Mrs. James Smith, Grand Central Station*. Most words can be fitted into a scale running from general to specific: for instance, organism, mammal, man, American, Northeasterner, New Yorker, Brooklynite, and so on down to Mr. James Smith, who lives on Flatbush Avenue. The usual way to make a word more specific is to attach qualifiers to it: American; white, Anglo-Saxon, Protestant American; white, Anglo-Saxon, Protestant American born and living just outside Providence, Rhode Island.

The writer's problem is to discover the exact degree of generality or specificity that suits his purpose. Sometimes, although rarely, a writer errs on the side of being too specific:

> 98.7% of all Shakespearean critics writing since 1920 agree that *Hamlet* is a better play than *Titus Andronicus*.

> Seurat's painting *La Grande Jatte* is composed of 16,423 separate dots of paint.

Such statements are only slightly exaggerated examples of what happens when a writer is more specific than the adequate treatment of the subject requires. They indicate a fussy pedantry and a mistaken belief that numerical accuracy is always relevant. The following would be more in keeping with the degree of precision called for by the subject:

> Everybody agrees that *Hamlet* is a better play than *Titus Andronicus*.

> Seurat's pointillist paintings are made up of thousands of separate dots of paint.

On occasion, a writer may decide to give "the facts and nothing but the facts" and confine himself exclusively to very specific statements. If he does so for very long, he will almost certainly become unintelligible, for without a general statement to interpret their significance, a collection of bare data is without order or direction.

The faults of being overly specific are negligible when they are compared to those of being too general, for probably the worst flaw in modern prose is that it is too general and abstract. Again and again, nebulous generalities drive out concrete, specific statements:

> Certain sections of personnel have made representations in regard to the heating system. (The girls in the stenographic pool have complained that the building is overheated and underventilated.)

> The faculty has reached a consensus that the syllabus for honors students must be made more comprehensive. (The faculty has agreed that honors students must be required to read more widely.)

> I would characterize that hotel as an undesirable place to stay. (That hotel is dirty and has bedbugs.)

> Economic considerations prevent the implementation of your program. (Your program is too expensive.)

> There is a trend toward certain kinds of foreign cars. (More people bought foreign sports cars this year than last.)

Statements like these blur the edges of meaning and envelop ideas in a haze of vagueness, a haze that is a constant threat to clarity, vigor, and precision.

Vagueness

In conversation, the things we know about the person who is speaking, his tone of voice, his facial expression and gestures, all help us to grasp the significance of what he is saying. If we do not understand him, we can stop him and ask questions. Between close friends, the sketchiest remarks may be fraught with meaning because the friends know the complex of ideas and feelings that lie behind the words. But in writing we have only the words on the page to guide us. If statements are vague and general, we cannot stop the writer and cross-examine him, nor, ordinarily, can we rely on what we know about him to supply missing parts of argument or exposition.

Vague writing is the failure to provide enough tangible details. It merely points in the direction of the idea or experience the writer is discussing and does little to set the subject directly before the reader. It relies on the general word rather than the specific one, the abstract rather than the concrete. It fails to give the reader the specific details, concrete images, and examples that make generalities come to life. Following are illustrations of vagueness in individual statements, along with suggested improvements.

Before the war I taught for a while.
(Before the Korean War, I taught mathematics at a small high school in the Middle West for six years.)

The trip was made difficult by poor weather.
(Heavy white fog settled down on the Turnpike just as we were crossing the Pennsylvania line, and after fifteen minutes it was so thick that we could hardly see cars fifty feet away.)

In the past, the labor unions were mostly organizations of workers in the higher brackets.
(Until well into the twentieth century, American labor unions were largely made up of highly skilled workers in such trades as printing.)

Imperialism in Africa influenced the situations that led up to World War I.
(The scramble of the European powers to divide Africa up among themselves intensified their rivalries at home and increased the growth of tension and suspicion in international relations that preceded World War I.)

Vagueness often arises from the use of a group of indispensable common words that might be called "thing-words" because by themselves, like pronouns, they have no definite meaning. Among the most frequently used are *area, aspect, case, consideration, data, factor, field, instance, manifestation*, and *phenomenon*. Properly used, they refer to some idea or fact given earlier. Without such reference, they merely encumber statements with meaningless phrases or baffle the reader, who would like to know the *name* of the mysterious "factor" or "aspect" under discussion.

When a reader can discover no reference to a meaning in one of the "thing-words," communication stops altogether. By itself, the statement, "This factor is manifest in many aspects of the phenomenon" conveys nothing. Even in a context which supplies information about what the "factor" and the "phenomenon" are, it is feeble and vague, forcing the reader to look back for too many referents at once.

Ambiguity

The Delphic Oracle of Greece is famous still for prophecies so ambiguously phrased that whatever happened the prophecy could be considered fulfilled. Herodotus reports these two answers to questions about who was to be victorious in war:

> Apollo says that the Greeks the Persians shall subdue.
> The king yet lives that Cyrus shall depose.

Ambiguous phraseology has helped out many a prophet, and is sometimes richly suggestive in poetry and drama. But in normal prose it seldom does more than block communication.

Ambiguity arises when two or more meanings are equally possible for the same word, phrase, or sentence. Many statements, taken by themselves, would be completely ambiguous, but ordinarily their context makes clear which meaning is the relevant one. Thus, in "I have been skating on very thin ice all winter," the "ice" may be either literal or metaphorical. If the next sentence reads, "I have been sick and out of work since November" the relevant sense of "thin ice" is established.

But sometimes context does not clear up ambiguity, or does so only after the reader has had the trouble of puzzling it out. Ambiguity most often arises in connection with problems of sentence structure and vocabulary that we have discussed elsewhere. Dangling and misplaced modifiers (see pp. 30, 40) create ambiguity:

Standing in the distance, David could see the mountains.
(Is David standing in the distance, or are the mountains, or are both?)

Heavily armed as he was, the detective had difficulty subduing the robber.
(Who has the gun?)

So may faulty pronoun reference (see p. 18):

Martha told Sara that she was sorry she could not come to the meeting.
(Which one cannot come to the meeting?)

Or faulty predication (see p. 48):

The denial of the accuracy of the report was rejected by the Chairman of the Armed Services Committee.
(After two or three readings, one may decide that the statement means "The Chairman of the Armed Services Committee denied that the report was inaccurate.")

Divided usage of words (see p. 139) can also be a source of ambiguity:

Jesperson made a very *fine* distinction between *junction* and *nexus*.
(A distinction the writer approves of heartily, or one that is subtly made?)

As can elegant variation (see p. 162):

Of all the distinctively modern ailments, *tension* seems to be the most widespread, if we are to trust the advertisers of pills and panaceas. *Anxiety* seems to pursue the contemporary American in every moment of his business and home life. *Worry* has become the new national disease. Continual *uneasiness* . . . (Is there one disorder, or are there four?)

Sometimes the most common words become ambiguous:

The lawyer asked the witness to give more relevant facts.
(Further facts? Facts more closely related to the issue at hand?)

I like Jim as well as Joe.
(As much as? In addition to?)

Sometimes ambiguity is deliberate, as in this answer to a memorandum:

We shall lose no time in considering your suggestions.

Unlike vagueness and wordiness, ambiguity (in the narrow sense that we have employed here) is comparatively rare. It will almost never appear in the work of a writer who is willing to go beyond asking himself, "Will the reader understand me?" to the more stringent question, "Is there anything here that a reader might possibly misunderstand?"

Verbiage

Even lively ideas and a potentially lively style can be dragged down into dullness if they are weighted with verbal deadwood—words and phrases that add nothing to the meaning, elegance, or formal structure of a statement. Besides conciseness of structure (see p. 115), conciseness of vocabulary is desirable. Useless phrases and meaningless repetitions are most likely to appear in first drafts, because the writer is so preoccupied with shaping his thought that he has little attention left over for economy of expression. One of the main tasks of revision is to clear away excess verbiage either by simply drawing a line through the offending expression or by rewording a sentence.

The italicized words in these sentences add nothing and should be struck out:

Many of Whistler's paintings are all gray and white *in color.*
The early reviews of James Joyce's masterpiece were usually vituperative *in nature.*

Superfluous prepositions are a waste of words:

Please refer *back* to the first chapter.
The book tries to penetrate *into* the mysteries of prehistoric times in New Mexico.
He descended *down* the garden path.
He continued *on* in the same familiar vein for more than an hour.
The murderer always returns *back* to the scene of the crime.
Where is the Post Office *at?*

Many writers habitually use long prepositions instead of short ones. The mere length of "according to," "in regard to," "by means of," and "in terms of" would not be troublesome if they were not used so often as substitutes for shorter, or more precise connectives:

We went to Washington *by means of* the train. (by)
Never judge *in terms of* appearances. (by)
We cannot reach a decision, *inasmuch as* none of the documents have arrived. (since)
In terms of the present outflow of gold, the government has changed its policy *in regard to* duty-free imports. (Because of, on)
Each plan must be judged *according to* its merits. (on)

Often the predication of a clause can profitably be shortened and made more direct:

These new discoveries *serve to show* the good effects of international cooperation in science.
(These new discoveries *show* . . .)

The heavy rains *have had the effect of causing* dangerous mud slides.
(The heavy rains *have caused* . . .)

Improvements in food storage methods *have been brought about* during the last ten years.
(There *have been* improvements . . .)

The Planning Commission *will give consideration to* all petitions.
(The Planning Commission *will consider* . . .)

A writer who feels that every noun must have its adjective and every verb and adjective its adverb is certain to clutter up his prose with verbiage. Many adjectives of intensification are overworked in the hope that they will strengthen the noun they modify: a *serious* emergency, an *acute* crisis, an *alarming* increase, a *stirring* speech, an *unprecedented* move, an *essential* condition, an *inevitable* consequence, a *definite* decision, and *past* history (all history is past). In the hope of being more forceful, some writers sprinkle about such adverbs of intensification as *extremely, exceedingly,* and *exceptionally:* an *extremely* detailed report, an *exceedingly* difficult decision, an *exceptionally* large number. *Very* has almost lost its meaning through overuse: a *very* harsh law, a *very* absolute denial. One soon expects to hear of diseases that are *very* fatal and of criminals who are found *very* guilty by the jury. *Literally* (that is, *in fact*) is sometimes illogically used as an intensifying adverb, apparently meaning *figuratively.*

The committee has *literally* dropped the whole appropriations mess into the President's lap.
Henry *literally* tore the other debating team to shreds.
In the middle of his speech, the Senator *literally* changed horses in mid-stream.
The new foreign exchange policy *literally* throws out the baby with the bath water.

A writer who always uses such means of emphasis, a writer for whom all crises are *acute* and all consequences *inevitable,* will have nothing left to say when a crisis *is* acute or a consequence inevitable. He has devalued his stock of emphatic words.

Some writers go beyond adorning every word with a modifier to operate on the principle that words are best in pairs. The belief that two words are better than one often leads to needless duplication:

Hobbes thought that life was nasty, *brutish, animalistic*, and short.
The demonstrations against the government appear to be *spontaneous* and *unplanned*.
She looked at the waiter with an *icy, frozen* stare.

In each pair of italicized words, two words are used to do the work of one: one of each pair should be struck out. Sometimes it is more effective to reorder a sentence to make the duplication meaningful:

Herodotus considered the troops of Xerxes *fearful* and *cowardly*.
(Herodotus considered the troops of Xerxes cowardly—equally fearful of the Greeks and of the sea.)

Her *notoriety* and *fame* soon spread from Chicago to the West.
(Her notoriety, her dishonorable fame, soon spread from Chicago to the West.)

As a final warning, consider what might happen if someone decided to say everything twice in every part of a sentence:

The plots and conspiracies of the rash, hot-headed revolutionaries who want to overthrow the present government and topple it from power have brought about and inspired more fear and panic in the big metropolitan cities than in the rural countryside.

Inflated vocabulary is often a source of verbiage: it dresses up plain ideas in fancy language, always prefers the long and sonorous word to the short, pithy one. Sometimes the process goes so far that meaning is quite buried under the rain of stately language. The slow march of Dr. Samuel Johnson's Latinate sentences still sometimes catches up a writer who wants to sound impressive. Here is an example quoted by the grammarian Otto Jesperson:

The proverbial oracles of our parsimonious ancestors have informed us that the fatal waste of our fortune is by small expenses, by the profusion of sums too little singly to alarm our caution, and which we never suffer ourselves to consider together.

The proverb, of course, is "Take care of the pennies and the pounds will take care of themselves." Eloquently used, this style may sometimes give an impression of solemn dignity, but more often it is merely long-winded.

Sometimes verbiage springs from excessive caution, a determination to be clear and explicit no matter how labored the language. This admirable motive can lead to an obscuring of the main point to be made. In the following passage, from a thoughtful and valuable book, the authors are trying to say that theories of personality are different from other psychological theories and also different from one another:

Let us turn now to some of the distinctive features of personality theory. Although this body of theory is manifestly a part of the broad field of psychology, still there are appreciable differences between personality theory and research and research and theory in other areas of psychology. These differences are particularly pronounced in regard to early development of personality theory, and exist in spite of a great deal of variation among personality theories themselves. The individual differences between personality theories imply that almost any statement that applies with detailed accuracy to one theory of personality will be somewhat inaccurate when applied to certain other theories. In spite of this, there are modal qualities or central tendencies which inhere in most personality theories, and it is upon these that we shall focus our discussion.

In their desire to be painstakingly accurate, the writers have sunk their central idea in a quagmire of words. The same desire for a "rigorous" use of language may account for the wordiness of this sentence written by a distinguished literary critic:

A fifth relation between theory and poems, that which will be the final focus of our argument, is that which obtains when in any historical era we can discern a specific affinity between theory as such and poems; that is, when what the theory says seems to be a specially appropriate description of what the poems are.

In the interests of economy and simplicity, the sentence might well be rewritten to read:

Finally, there is a fifth relation between theory and poems when in any historical era we find a close affinity between them: that is, when the theory seems to be a specially appropriate description of the poems.

Two Examples

Scattered bits of verbal deadwood are only a nuisance; but prose that is consistently wordy and vague, full of undefined abstractions and empty "thing-words" is simply not worth reading unless insights of genius are lurking somewhere beneath the surface. The passage following is typical of prose that fails because of vagueness and generality, threadbare abstraction, and lack of concreteness:

[1]Turning to still another element of consideration as the student surveys his world, he has the task of creating within himself a keen sensitivity to life in its many facets. [2]The kind of worldliness expected or even demanded of youth—and I use the word in its most positive sense —is one that requires each to be a person of taste. [3]If they are to see the important aspects of life in their true relationship, students will have to collect within themselves a richness of experience in all such aspects. [4]The degree of discrimination and selectivity developed as the arts and sciences are probed at higher and higher levels will help to establish deeper cultural appreciation for our civilization as a whole. [5]Every individual compromise with quality is a contribution to general retrogression and deterioration. [6]If he turns away from excellence, whether in literature or art or music or craftsmanship or even vocational skill, he strengthens the more callous and bestial parts of his nature and gives encouragement to the cynical and amoral forces opposing him. [7]If he concerns himself more and more with the search for what is true and good and beautiful, so does he build a bulwark against defeat, not only of the body but of the mind and spirit.

The writer wants to say that young people would do well to cultivate an interest in the arts and sciences, but instead of talking concretely about how, when, and where they may best do so, he raises the more difficult and nebulous question of *why* they should. The answer, so far as one can make it out, is threefold: 1) Every youth is now expected to be a "person of taste." 2) Cultural experiences help the young to understand life and "appreciate" their civilization. 3) If they do not cultivate excellence, civilization decays and the young themselves become more bestial and callous. The first proposition is self-evidently false: "persons of taste" are rarities, and always have been. The other two, if debatable, are certainly defensible.

But instead of forthright assertion, persuasive demonstration, and concrete illustration, we have a cloud of words, words that are less vehicles for meaning than substitutes for it. The author is attracted to thing-words such as *elements of consideration, facets,* and *aspects.* "Turning to another element of consideration as the student surveys his world . . ." means Next. In the third sentence, "the important aspects of life in their true relationship . . ." leaves us wondering what the writer thinks the most important aspects of life are and which of their relationships he takes to be true. Since "in all such aspects" refers to "the important aspects" we get nonmeaning raised to the second power.

Also, by purposeless inflation, the author loses the strength of simple verb forms. In the first sentence, "he has the task of creating within himself a keen sensitivity . . ." is less forceful than "he must develop a keen sensitivity . . ." (*Create* needs to be changed to *develop*, for sensitivity, like talent or intelligence, can be developed, but not created at will.) In the third sentence, "will have to collect within themselves . . ." is equivalent to *must acquire*. In the seventh sentence, "concerns himself more and more with the search for . . ." should be reduced to *searches for*.

One wonders what distinctions of meaning the author had in mind when he uses these pairs of words: "discrimination and selectivity" (sentence 4); "retrogression and deterioration" (sentence 5). They look suspiciously like duplicate words for single ideas.

In addition to being wordy, the author is inclined to toss about abstractions that are slippery enough even when used with care. *Sensitivity, worldliness, taste, experience,* and *excellence* all have a clear *direction* of meaning that can be made definite by an adequately developed context. For instance, the meaning of *worldliness* and *taste* could be filled out in some such way as this:

Modern youth is expected to be worldly, in the good sense of that term: to know about books and pictures and music, to be at home with ideas and suspicious of cant, to prefer elegance and style to commercial slickness; young people, in short, are expected to be persons of taste.

But *good, true,* and *beautiful* need more than a few phrases if their meaning is to be adequately stipulated. When they are thrown about for purposes of general exhortation, they are mere cries of approval, not words.

No doubt a defense of art or learning, or a plea for young people to cultivate their faculties is a dangerous occasion for a writer; it seems to invite piety rather than thought, resounding phrases rather than solid meanings. But is is possible to write with good sense, grace, and reasonable clarity on such an occasion. Consider the following paragraphs by the distinguished English novelist E. M. Forster, who is vindicating the claims of art:

I believe in art for art's sake. It is an unfashionable belief, and some of my statements must be of the nature of an apology. Fifty years ago I should have faced you with more confidence. A writer or speaker who chose "Art for Art's Sake" for his theme fifty years ago could be sure of

being in the swim, and could feel so confident of success that he sometimes dressed himself in esthetic costume suitable to the occasion—in an
embroidered dressing-gown perhaps, or a blue velvet suit with a Lord
Fauntleroy collar; or a toga, or a kimono, and carried a poppy or a lily or
a peacock's feather in his medieval hand. Times have changed. Not thus
can I present either myself or my theme today. My aim is to ask you
quietly to reconsider for a few minutes a phrase which has been much
misused and much abused, but which has, I believe, great importance
for us—has, indeed, eternal significance. . . .

   What does the phrase mean? Instead of generalizing, let us take a
specific instance—Shakespeare's *Macbeth*, for example, and pronounce
the words, "*Macbeth* for *Macbeth*'s sake." What does that mean? Well,
the play has several aspects—it is educational, it teaches us something
about legendary Scotland, something about Jacobean England, and a
good deal about human nature and its perils. We can study its origins,
and study and enjoy its dramatic technique and the music of its diction.
All that is true. But *Macbeth* is furthermore a world of its own, created
by Shakespeare and existing in virtue of its own poetry. It is in this aspect
Macbeth for *Macbeth*'s sake, and that is what I intend by the phrase
"art for art's sake." A work of art—whatever else it may be—is a self-
contained entity, with a life of its own imposed on it by its creator. It has
internal order. It may have external form. That is how we recognize it.

   It is to the conception of order that I would now turn. This is important to my argument, and I want to make a digression, and glance at order
in daily life, before I come to order in art.

Setting out to persuade his readers that art is important, Forster
redefines and defends a famous slogan of the late nineteenth century
Aesthetic Movement—a slogan much attacked in its own day, and
generally regarded in ours as outmoded and slightly silly. Forster's
tone is relaxed, and the prose is unobtrusive and seemingly casual.
But the skillful management of the diction is at least as important
as the explicitly developed arguments in bringing the reader into
sympathy with the attitude Forster wishes to recommend. First of
all, he uses words with more precision than might be suggested by
his easy tone:

   "Apology" is often used loosely for an expression of regret. Forster
uses it in the restricted and precise sense of "something written or
spoken in defense or justification of what appears to others to be
wrong," though still with a hint of the wider meaning.

   "Aspect" is frequently used without any meaning at all. Forster
specifies what it refers to and uses it as definitely as the word permits:
"a state or phase in which anything appears and may be regarded."

   "Educational" is often vaguely applied to whatever is regarded as harmless and somehow uplifting. Forster immediately reminds us that a thing is "educational" when it *teaches* us something.

"Eternal significance" is not a phrase of general approval only. It indicates "having a meaning not bounded by time."

"Of the nature of" is not an empty filler, but means "similar to, but not exactly the same as . . ."

When Forster offers us pairs of words closely related to one another in meaning, he is not engaged in meaningless duplication, but conveys genuine distinctions:

"Misused and abused" is not used as a set formula on the pattern of "upward and onward" or "betwixt and between," but sets down two distinct facts: one, that the slogan was misused by the Aesthetic Movement (the essay, after all, is an exercise in redefinition) and, two, that the slogan was abused by contemporaries as faddish and irresponsible.

"Something about legendary Scotland, something about Jacobean England" is not just a literary way of saying "Great Britain." It reminds us that *Macbeth* recounts a legend of prehistoric Scotland, but was written from the point of view of early seventeenth-century England.

"Study . . . and study and enjoy" distinguishes between the knowledge yielded by a study of the play's sources and the combination of knowledge and pleasure given by its technique and euphony.

The meanings of the words considered so far are all made clear by the way they are used in context; they require no set definitions. But when Forster comes to the central terms of his argument—"order" and "self-contained entity"—he can no longer rely on context to make his meaning plain, and he therefore shifts his method, spending most of the rest of his essay explaining directly his key terms. He nowhere makes a ponderous display of formal definition or of the fussiness about logical form that sometimes passes for intellectual rigor, but he always does whatever is necessary to keep the denotations of his words in control.

Forster also maintains remarkable control over tone and connotation in his diction. Since that control involves the writer's ability to shape to his purposes the most subtle nuances of language, a full explanation of Forster's methods would take forever. But perhaps a rather sketchy illustration of the connection between Forster's choice of words and his approach to his material and audience will suggest how he manages tone and connotation.

Forster's advocacy of "art for art's sake" springs from deep conviction, and he begins with a straightforward assertion of belief. Yet his tone is neither didactic nor insistent. He approaches his audience through the informal point of view of "you and I and all of us together" (see p. 99), and with a friendliness that never lapses into chumminess. He approaches his subject with a mixture of diffidence and mild authority, of genial irony and controlled intensity, of homeliness and dignity. Note how two unobtrusive words reflect this general attitude toward subject and audience.

Unfashionable. Some of the other possible ways of expressing the idea of "unfashionable" are "old-fashioned," "outmoded," "antiquated," "out of date," "obsolete," "old hat," and *"demodé."* Forster's choice of "unfashionable" avoids the pretentiousness of *"demodé"* and the excessive colloquialism of "old hat." It avoids the pejorative overtones of "outmoded," "antiquated," "out of date," and "obsolete" as well as the false assumption so often behind these four words that it is a significant objection to a belief that it is "out of date"; beliefs are objectionable when they are false, not when they are old. "Unfashionable" also avoids the slightly folksy suggestion of "something from the good old days" in "old-fashioned." "Unfashionable" is the most neutrally descriptive of all these words; it is neither too formal nor too familiar. And it carries the suggestion that Forster wants: it implies that the present disfavor of "art for art's sake" is as much a matter of arbitrary fashion as was its past vogue.

Aim. In the series of synonyms "intention," "purpose," "design," "aim," "end," "objective," and "goal," "aim" has several advantages for Forster's purpose. It suggests, though not very distinctly, the concrete image of taking aim at a mark. It has a homely and informal ring, with nothing of the intellectual loftiness which "intention" and "objective" often carry. It does not have the elegance and hint of irony of "design," an irony that springs from its use in such statements as "I have designs on you." "Aim" has neither the purely subjective emphasis of "intention" and "purpose" nor the exclusive emphasis of "objective" and "goal" on what is to be attained. "Aim" refers both to purpose and to desired result. "Purpose" would be too diffident, "goal" too strong, because of its overtones of struggle. "Aim" has just the degree of emphasis, concreteness, and unpretentiousness that expresses Forster's attitude toward what he is doing.

Of course, the author did not go through a cumbersome examination of all these alternatives in order to choose his words. He may well have hit upon them without any conscious deliberation at all. Sureness of taste and a fully developed individual style usually permit an author to dispense with such labor. But less accomplished writers need to sharpen their awareness that such choices are available and influence the quality of their prose. Having a feeling for the right word is in part a talent: it cannot be created by sheer will power and work. But it is also in part a skill that can be developed by the habit of paying disciplined attention to the alternatives presented by our English vocabulary.

Finally, Forster manages the balance between abstract and concrete, general and particular with great skill. He is not afraid of abstractions when he needs them: surely "art for art's sake" is one of the most equivocal abstractions ever invented, and Forster not only uses it but feels free to say that it has "eternal significance." He has not been cowed by modern arguments that all non-scientific and non-mathematical statements more general than "Martha Brady milked Farmer Smith's brown cow at 4:12 P.M." are meaningless. But he is willing to argue, define, and describe as concretely as his subject permits.

In the first paragraph, he presents the Aesthetic Movement, which nurtured "art for art's sake," entirely through references to the costumes and stage properties favored by the glittering aesthetes of the late nineteenth century. Thus the moral and intellectual atmosphere surrounding the phrase is presented entirely through concrete images —words that call to mind sensations. The contrast of these frivolous images with the solemn "eternal significance" at the end of the paragraph carries the point of Forster's first argument: that whatever the affectation and self-dramatization once connected with it, the phrase has a permanent importance.

In the second paragraph, the author explicitly shifts the argument from general to specific by converting "art for art's sake" into "*Macbeth* for *Macbeth's* sake," and by so doing gives his readers something they can envisage more easily than "art" in general. At the end of the quotation he is preparing to convey the idea of order in art through comparison with the more tangible notion of order in daily life. When he uses a vague word like "aspect" he follows it by an enumeration of particulars. In short, he does whatever can be done to convert abstract into concrete statements and to specify what he means by his generalities.

The passage as a whole reveals the writer's willingness to go to some trouble to make his subject agreeable and intelligible to his readers. One of his chief means of doing so is to use language that is accurate, consistent in tone, and rich in concrete suggestion.

15

OBLIQUE LANGUAGE

M OST statements make straightforward assertions about actions, qualities and equivalencies: "The dog bit the postman"; "Jane's hair is red"; "Mr. Smith is a tax accountant." "If these statements are adequately formulated, there is, so to speak, no gap between what is said and what is meant; we take the words at their face value. But consider the proverbs "A rolling stone gathers no moss" and "Still waters run deep." We immediately recognize that these are not observations about the natural world, but about human nature: they are not meant to tell us about stones and water, but about people always on the move and people who remain quiet. The two proverbs exploit the power of language to make statements obliquely rather than directly. Such statements, like Polonius, "by indirections find directions out." Oblique language is so pervasive that no writer can avoid using it; if he uses it purposely, it can be a source of richness and strength in his prose.

Figurative Language

Many people think of figurative language as something found almost exclusively in poetry, and it is true that poetry uses metaphor in a more powerfully concentrated way than prose does. But metaphor-making is one of the most basic of all linguistic activities; our ordinary speaking and writing is full of "dead metaphors"—that is, expressions whose figurative basis is no longer consciously recognized. For instance, the names for parts of human and animal bodies are often extended to parts of inanimate objects. We speak of the *leg* of a table, the *foot* of the stairs, the *mouth* of a cave or river, the *elbow* of a pipe, the *nose* of an airplane, the *eye* of a needle, the *ears* of a pitcher, the *waist* of a ship, the *neck* of a bottle, the *arm* of a chair, and so on. Or consider the way in which the names of animals are used to indicate certain human qualities: one may call someone a mouse, a rat, a cat, a cow, a pig, a bull, a lion, a fox, a wolf, an ox, a snake, and so on.

All these expressions are based on some perception of resemblances between things not ordinarily considered to be of the same kind: cats and women, the bottom of the stairs and the foot of a man, the cone of an airplane and the nose of a man. Figurative speech, then, always involves comparison. The statement "Henry is a large, awkward boy" is a *literal* assertion of the equivalency of "Henry" and "large, awkward boy." The statement "Henry is a moose," which has the same syntactical form, is a *figurative* assertion that there are points of resemblance between "Henry" and a "moose." In the same way, "The argument is difficult to understand" is a literal statement; "The argument is slippery and hard to grasp" is figurative.

In prose, at least, most metaphor is not put in the form A *is* B: that is, it is not made the point of the main predication. Rather it appears in lesser structures: "The story *hurries* to a close"; "*hair-splitting* arguments"; "a *brassy* singer"; "an admission *hedged* with qualifications"; "a *mountainously* fat woman"; "The cushions of the seat *melted* beneath me." Such half-submerged metaphors do not call attention to themselves, but they add to the vividness of prose. In the following passage from F. Scott Fitzgerald much of the effect comes from the unobtrusively metaphorical turns of expression:

Now the standard cure for one who is *sunk* is to consider those in actual destitution or physical suffering—this is an *all-weather beatitude* for *gloom* in general and fairly salutary *day-time* advice for everyone. But at three o'clock in the morning, *a forgotten package has the same tragic importance as a death sentence,* and the cure doesn't work—and in a real *dark night* of the soul, *it is always three o'clock in the morning,* day after day. At that hour the tendency is to refuse *to face things* as long as possible by *retiring into an infantile dream*—but one is continually startled out of this by various contacts with the world. One meets these occasions as quickly and carelessly as possible and *retires* back once more *into the dream,* hoping that things will adjust themselves by some great material or spiritual *bonanza.* But as the *withdrawal* persists there is less and less chance of the *bonanza*—one is not waiting for the *fadeout* of a single sorrow, but rather being *an unwilling witness of an execution,* the disintegration of one's own personality.

Such writing hovers on the borderline between literal and figurative statement, its metaphorical texture giving it richness, and its literalness giving it solidity.

More explicit metaphors stand out from their surroundings and call attention to themselves. They are meant to be striking and to underline the point they are making:

Bards of old sat in the shade of sacred trees for inspiration. Those who sing the epic of today sit in the vast shadow cast by the toadstool of Hiroshima. [ROBERT PLANK]

There is no good arguing with the inevitable. The only argument available with an east wind is to put on your overcoat. [JAMES RUSSELL LOWELL]

The pursuit turned out to be long and tortuous, leading at last into the vast forests of scholastic science. [HENRY ADAMS]

I also note, to my relief, a weakening of the whimsical forms *oke, oke-doke, oky-doky,* and *oky-dory,* the last probably a love child of O.K. and *hunky-dory.* [H. L. MENCKEN]

Since metaphors like these make a special claim on the reader's attention, they are most effective when they emphasize an important rather than a trivial point and when they fit in with the general tone of a passage. A special temptation is to use a metaphor that is too violent for the context:

> In the second movement of the sonata, Maestro Fromaggio chewed up the music and spewed it all over the auditorium.

> The jungle of American politics houses more buzzards and rats than lions and tigers.

> My Latin teacher chopped all the students' heads off with great regularity.

The most explicit kind of metaphor is the simile, which connects the terms compared with "like" or "as." "Mildred's hat is like mine" is not a simile; but the statement "Mildred's hat is like a pineapple" is. Here are some examples of effective similes. All but one compare something abstract or relatively unfamiliar with something concrete or something more familiar:

The highballs, the red and white wines, the champagne, the cognac were gurgling inside me like a sewer. [HENRY MILLER]

Her mind lay open and orderly, like a notebook ready for impressions. It was not long, however, before she shut it up with a snap. [MARY MC CARTHY]

One generation abandons the enterprises of another like stranded vessels. [THOREAU]

Some lands are flat and grass-covered, and smile so evenly up at the sun that they seem forever youthful, untouched by man or time. Some are torn, ravaged and convulsed like the features of profane old age. [LOREN EISELEY]

Bentham is like an engineer in a community smitten by an epidemic, who while one agitator recommends the overthrow of the government and another recommends a reform of religion, quietly suggests a repair of the drains. [D. C. SOMERVELL]

The last two examples here are almost analogies—extended figures of speech which express several points of resemblance rather than just one or two. Though analogy can never legitimately be offered as a piece of *evidence* for or against anything, it is sometimes invaluable as a means of *explanation*. Sometimes an analogy may occupy several paragraphs, or even run to several pages. In the passage given below, the author not only describes the resemblances between the mysterious processes of radiation and the familiar action of water-ripples in a pond; he also carefully limits the application of the analogy by showing where the resemblances end:

Disturb the surface of a pond with a stick and a series of ripples starts from the stick and travels, in a series of ever-expanding circles, over the surface of the pond. As the water resists the motion of the stick, we have to work to keep the pond in a state of agitation. The energy of this work is transformed, in part at least, into the energy of the ripples. We can see that the ripples carry energy about with them, because they cause a floating cork or a toy boat to rise up against the earth's gravitational pull. Thus the ripples provide a mechanism for distributing over the surface of the pond the energy that we put into the pond through the medium of the moving stick.

Light and all other forms of radiation are analogous to water-ripples or waves, in that they distribute energy from a central source. The sun's radiation distributes through space the vast amount of energy which is generated inside the sun. We hardly know whether there is any actual wave-motion in light or not, but we know that light, as well as other types of radiation, are propagated in such a form that they have some of the properties of a succession of waves. [SIR JAMES JEANS]

Extended metaphor is not always used primarily to explain something. In the following example the historian C. Vann Woodward is elaborating the traditional comparison between the course of history and the course of a river to give his exposition more pictorially interesting movement:

Southern history, on the other hand, took a different turn in the nine-teenth century. At intervals the even bed gave way under the stream, which sometimes plunged over falls or swirled through rapids. These breaks in the course of Southern history go by the names of slavery and secession, independence and defeat, emancipation and reconstruction, redemption and reunion. Some are more precipitous and dramatic than others. Some result in sheer drops and falls, others in narrows and rapids The distance between them, and thus the extent of smooth sailing and stability, varies a great deal.

Another figurative use of language is personification: the treatment of institutions, ideas, objects, and classes as if they were persons. Often personifications are merely a neutral device that permits economy of statement. The following are colorless formulas that call no particular attention to themselves:

> The White House announced today . . .
> The Kremlin replied . . .
> The unions have called for . . .
> The University today mourned the death of . . .

At other times, however, personification can be memorable because of the striking way in which it puts an abstract idea vividly and concretely:

Art is the accomplice of love. [REMY DE GOURMONT]

Puritanism, believing itself quick with the seed of religious liberty, laid, without knowing it, the egg of democracy. [JAMES RUSSELL LOWELL]

Opportunity is the great bawd. [BENJAMIN FRANKLIN]

Public opinion is a vulgar, impertinent, anonymous tyrant who deliber-ately makes life unpleasant for anyone who is not content to be the average man. [DEAN INGE]

Personification is a powerful instrument both of confusion and persuasion in polemical writing. The confusion arises when the writer forgets that a personification is a mental convenience, not a reality, and his personified idea begins to lead a life of its own, dis-tinct from the facts for which it stands. Both the confusion and the power are evident in the first paragraph of *The Communist Manifesto*:

The bourgeoisie, historically, has played a most revolutionary part. The bourgeoisie, whenever it has got the upper hand, has put an end to all feudal, patriarchal, idyllic relations. It has pitilessly torn asunder the motley feudal ties that bound man to his "natural superiors," and has left remaining no other nexus between man and man than naked self-interest, than callous "cash payment." It has drowned the most heavenly ecstasies of religious fervor, of chivalrous enthusiasm, of philistine sentimentalism, in the icy water of egoistic calculation.

The fact that Marx and Engels cast the bourgeoisie as a villain in a historical melodrama contributes to the dramatic power of the manifesto, but it also provokes mistrust from the empirically minded, who must wonder whether that sprawling, shapeless, long-lived, complex entity "the bourgeoisie" could really have acted in so conveniently dramatic a fashion. Personification can be a powerful way of making abstractions live, but when they behave too much like characters in a well-made play, they invite the reader's suspicion.

An occasional problem that besets all kinds of figurative expression is mixed figure or mixed metaphor. Poetry and impassioned prose often mingle logically incompatible figures of speech with powerful effect, as in Hamlet's "taking arms against a sea of troubles." A writer of temperate prose may change his metaphors as often as he likes, but he will make sure that one is securely out of the way before he introduces another, so that there is no blending of incongruous figures of speech. Probably the most common source of inadvertently mixed metaphor is the meeting of two figurative expressions that, separately, have a much weakened metaphorical force. Not exactly "dead" metaphors, they are enough enfeebled so that the writer overlooks the metaphorical sense of what he is saying:

> The hand of the Red Cross keeps watch over the health of the nation.

> The tidal wave of new paperback books has fired the imagination of America's educators.

> By dissecting with surgical skill the conventional assumptions of modern economics, Dr. Smithers has exploded some of its most venerable myths.

> The enthusiasm of the audience was much dampened by the dry manner of the speaker.

Clichés and Trite Expressions

Clichés are metaphors gone to seed; they are formulas of expression that have been over-worked until they have lost their original freshness and force. Clichés are tolerable in conversation, for in talk we accept a certain banality of expression, but in writing they indicate a thoughtless willingness to use the first locution that comes to mind. Thousands of formulas are used constantly, but do not become clichés: "a nice day," "mashed potatoes and gravy," "how do you do," "he said." Such expressions are neutral and colorless; they do not call attention to themselves and do not wear out. Most clichés, however, were probably once novel and striking turns of expression; they have been ruined by success, becoming tiresomely familiar through repetition. They are neither neutral enough to pass unnoticed, nor vivid enough to have any power of evocation.

These similes, and many more like them, are too battered to appear in good prose, except perhaps rarely for irony or for a folksy flavor:

brave as a lion	heavy as lead
(like a) bull in a china shop	honest as the day is long
caught like a rat in a trap	light as a feather
cheap as dirt	meek as a lamb
cold as a fish	a memory like a sieve
collapse like a house of cards	old as the hills
cool as a cucumber	pretty as a picture
drunk as a lord	silent as the grave
dying like flies	sober as a judge
fighting like cats and dogs	thick as thieves
good as gold	ugly as sin
hate like poison	

Noun-adjective combinations in which the adjective once had metaphorical force often become clichés:

budding poet (or novelist)	piercing stare
cast-iron constitution	ruby lips
foolproof alibi	sickening thud (or dull, sickening thud)
golden voice	vagrant thoughts
iron will	unholy mess
iron-clad contract	witching hour
mortal remains	wolfish appetite

In general, neutral language is to be preferred to these faded novelties; it is at least inoffensive and straightforward.

Overlapping with clichés are trite expressions in general. These prefabricated phrases have to a large extent lost both their denotative meaning and their suggestion of metaphor. They have become mere emotional cries or displays of hollow pomp. A writer given to trite expressions not only deadens his prose (or makes it ridiculous); he also paralyzes, or prevents, thought. A writer who calls any bumbling mediocrity in public life an "elder statesman" after he has reached a certain age is either cynical, ignorant, or indifferent to what he says. The advertising copy writers who describe films as "colossal," "stupendous," "breath-taking," "sizzling," "heart-warming," "light-hearted," "raw," "shocking," or "spell-binding," are simply making hopeful noises.

Although every aspect of modern life has a supply of shopworn expressions, politics is probably the richest of all sources of the trite. The explanation probably lies in the exigencies of impromptu speaking, a large part of any politician's professional life, where a stock of ready-made statements is indispensable. Still, expressions such as these appear in carefully prepared public statements:

> _____ must be the watchword.
> agonizing reappraisal of current thinking
> bastion of democracy (or citadel of freedom)
> campaign of vilification
> carry aloft the torch of liberty
> champion of the rights of the people
> dedicated public servant
> face the future with confidence
> fuzzy-minded liberal (or mindless conservative)
> grim specter
> hard core
> put our house in order
> put our shoulders to the wheel
> rise in wrath against their oppressors
> sapping the moral fiber
> seething discontent
> a standard-bearer who will carry the banner of the party to victory
> staunch defender
> toiling masses
> undying faith

Such expressions are worse than irritating; they are dangerous because they encourage deception and self-righteousness. Anyone who speaks habitually of "our sacred institutions" is likely to think that *all* our institutions, including the Post Office and the oil depletion allowance, are sacred. He will cry out against any change as if it were sacrilege. Someone who speaks habitually of "the downtrodden masses" is likely to find the existence of masses who are *not* downtrodden inconceivable and be unable to think clearly about their problems or view of life.

The intelligent reader may be either cynically amused or repelled by trite, cliché-ridden prose, but he will certainly not be persuaded by it. The writer does well to reject the too familiar metaphor and the prefabricated phrase.

Irony

Like other abstractions with a multitude of referents, *irony* is hard to define because it covers so much territory. It includes the tragic irony of Shakespeare and the Greek dramatists; the philosophical irony of Socrates; the brilliant farce of Don Quixote's tilting at windmills; the simple "trick" endings of O. Henry's short stories. More than that, irony is a way of looking at life—a general attitude toward experience. The essential feature of all irony is the perception of incongruity. The ironic man is the opposite of the fanatic, who sees the world by the light of a single overmastering idea. The ironic man is skeptical and flexible, willing to entertain alternative ideas, to see more than one side of things. Whether with amusement, sorrow, or detachment, his imagination is attracted by incongruity: between desire and its frequently unsatisfactory fulfillment; between what appears to be and what is; between what is and what ought to be; between what might be expected to happen and what does actually happen; between high moral professions and low conduct; between what is said and what is meant.

Verbal irony, which is our immediate concern, shows this same delight in the incongruous, in unexpected juxtapositions and contrasts that are deliberately chosen to reveal a hidden meaning or to cast a new light on a subject. The ironic writer may overstate or understate his point; he may treat a trivial subject with poker-faced seriousness, or, more rarely, he may treat a serious subject very lightly. He may say the reverse of what he means, as Antony does in *Julius Caesar* when he says of Caesar's murderers, "So are they all, all honorable men." Or he may slip in a phrase here and there that jars with the general tone of a passage and thereby reveals his ironic attitude toward what he is saying. Whatever his strategy, the ironic writer must be in secure control of his language and keep the point he wants to make always before him. The language of irony easily disintegrates into crude sarcasm or spluttering, and random incongruities with nothing behind them are worthless.

Perhaps the most common form of verbal irony is to say the reverse of what is meant:

We may find ourselves insensibly succumbing to one of the most insidious vices of the human mind: what the Germans *in their terse and sparkling way* called the hypostatization of methodological categories, or the habit of treating a mental convenience as if it were an objective thing. [G. M. YOUNG italics added]

Sometimes a writer sets up an ironic discord between the usual connotations of a word and the context in which it appears:

Many Germans and many Nazis—probably an overwhelming majority of them—must have been tempted *not* to murder, *not* to rob, *not* to let their neighbors go off to their doom, and *not* to become accomplices of all these crimes by benefiting from them. But, God knows, they had learned how to resist temptation. [HANNAH ARENDT]

Normally, all temptations are toward evil (as in the Lord's Prayer: "Lead us not into temptation, but deliver us from evil."); here the temptation is to refuse to commit the worst crimes of which human beings are capable. The irony is not a random play on words: Hannah Arendt is underlining the dilemma of conscience under a totalitarian regime where murder and robbery are legally approved and humane feeling is outlawed.

An ironic writer may quietly emphasize whatever is inappropriate in attitude or behavior. E. M. Forster describes what happened after the great eighteenth-century writer Voltaire and his mistress, Madame du Châtelet, submitted scientific papers in a competition:

Neither he nor she obtained the prize for the Nature and Propagation of Fire. The judges complimented him on being a poet and her on being a lady, but appear to have been slightly shocked by the number of facts they mentioned, and divided the prize between three other competitors who confined themselves to theory.

The ironic comedy springs from the somewhat topsy-turvy behavior of the men of science who were the judges. They praise two aspiring scientists for being, respectively, a poet and a lady, and they are "slightly shocked" by an accumulation of facts. The judges are made to appear mad, in a dignified sort of way, and Voltaire and Madame du Châtelet are scored off by being offered artistic and social recognition rather than the scientific recognition they want.

Similarly, the historian D. W. Brogan:

Matthew Arnold, in his high aesthetic fashion, thought that the Civil War, and especially the assassination of Lincoln to the tune of a Latin motto, *Sic semper tyrannis*, made American history quite respectable.

Although Brogan himself is considering American history from the point of view of its dramatic and artistic quality, he is aware that history cannot quite be judged as if it were a play or a novel. His ironic observation about Matthew Arnold's finding the Civil War aesthetically "respectable" reveals his own sense that raising the question of the aesthetic merit of a historical event may be, if pushed very far, preposterous.

The degree of explicitness with which irony is presented varies greatly. Sometimes irony is a quietly dropped hint that the author is skeptical of what he is saying. In these two sentences from Gibbon's *Decline and Fall of the Roman Empire*, only the phrases "advantageous offer," "supine inattention," and "innumerable prodigies" indicate that Gibbon is describing the spread of Christianity with a sardonic smile:

When the promise of eternal happiness was proposed to mankind on condition of adopting the faith and observing the precepts of the gospel, it is no wonder that so advantageous an offer should have been accepted by great numbers of every religion, of every rank, and of every province in the Roman Empire.

But how shall we excuse the supine inattention of the pagan and philosophic world to those evidences which were presented by the hand of Omnipotence, not to their reason, but to their senses? During the age of Christ, of his apostles, and of their first disciples, the doctrine which they preached was confirmed by innumerable prodigies.

"Advantageous offer" reduces the offer of salvation to an ordinary commercial transaction; the linkage of "supine inattention" and "innumerable prodigies" quietly hints that if the miracles of early Christianity had actually happened they would not have gone so entirely unnoticed in the pagan world. The subtly ironic flavoring of Gibbon's phrases, sometimes overlooked by his readers, represents a limit of unobtrusiveness beyond which an ironic writer is unwise to go. An irony yet more quiet and unemphatic than Gibbon's would probably be missed altogether by its audience and remain a private joke of the author's.

Indeed, irony far more pronounced than Gibbon's is sometimes misunderstood, as a recent literary controversy demonstrates. The distinguished political philosopher Hannah Arendt, in her recent book on the Eichmann trial in Jerusalem, analyzed its appalling revelations with a cool and measured irony, avoiding all direct expressions of horror. Apparently she agreed with Gaboriau's maxim, "Calmness and irony are the only weapons worthy of the strong." The reviewer for *The New York Times* missed the irony and denounced the book violently for sympathizing with Eichmann and other Nazis. In later controversy the reviewer pounced on the concluding sentence of the author's analysis of Eichmann's statement that he had nothing personally against all the Jews he had helped to kill: "Alas, nobody believed him." "Is not that sympathizing?" cried the reviewer. Such are the risks of irony, if the reader is obtuse and the author subtle.

At the other end of the scale from these subdued ironies is the controlled violence of the following passage from Jonathan Swift's *An Argument Against the Abolishment of Christianity:*

> Another advantage proposed by the abolishing of Christianity is the clear gain of one day in seven, which is now entirely lost, and consequently the kingdom one seventh less considerable in trade, business and pleasure . . .
> I hope I shall be forgiven a hard word, if I call this a perfect *cavil.* I readily own there hath been an old custom, time out of mind, for people to assemble in churches every Sunday, and that shops are still frequently shut in order, as it is conceived, to preserve the memory of that ancient practice, but how this can prove a hindrance to business or pleasure, is hard to imagine. What if men of pleasure are forced, one day in the week, to game at home instead of the chocolate house? Are not the taverns and coffee-houses open? Can there be a more convenient season for taking a dose of physic? Are fewer claps got upon Sundays than other days? Is not that the chief day for traders to sum up accounts of the week, and for lawyers to prepare their briefs? But I would fain know how it can be pretended that the churches are misapplied? Where are more appointments and rendezvous of gallantry? Where more care to appear in the foremost box with greater advantage of dress? Where more meetings for business? Where more bargains driven of all sorts? And where so many conveniences and incitements to sleep?

The power of Swift's irony springs largely from the fusing of a passionate indignation at human vice and folly with a sober and incisive prose. The denunciation is strong, but the language is severely restrained and concise. If it is not to degenerate into rant, irony requires economy and constraint. Compare the following heavy-handed example with Swift's brief, "And where more conveniences and incitements to sleep?":

One would think that any person after a day's work would be able to sleep peacefully, but apparently Americans have even lost the art of sleeping. In fact, so keyed up are they that I, a minister with ample opportunity to test the matter, must report that the American people are so nervous and high-strung that now it is almost next to impossible to put them to sleep with a sermon. It has been years since I have seen anyone asleep in church. And that is a sad situation.

The famous preacher gains by the back-handed compliment to the fascination exercised by his sermons, but he loses his irony by diffuseness.

Requiring both delicacy and power, irony is difficult to handle well and often falls flat in inexperienced hands. Unseasonable or labored irony is offensive enough to justify Thomas Carlyle's dictum: "It may be said that an ironic man, especially an ironic young man, is a pest to society." But there is nothing quite as telling as irony when it is well used. The reader is given the intellectual pleasure of discovering incongruity along with the delight of pithy expression.

Overstatement and Understatement

Overstatement and understatement are closely related to irony, and are often used for ironic purposes. Overstatement is a form of exaggeration; it uses highly emphatic or even extravagant language to delineate its subject. Used irresponsibly (and often ineffectively), it is all too familiar in advertising and in travel literature:

For sheer natural beauty and variety of scenery, Cedar Rapids is unparalleled. A sportsman's paradise as well as a brilliant cultural center, Cedar Rapids offers gracious living and elegant cuisine to the many holiday-makers who flock there every year.

This kind of puffery will succeed only with the most naive, for overstatement as a selling device is almost universally suspect.

Overstatement, however, can be a respectable and useful rhetorical device. To state an idea or perception in a somewhat exaggerated way may make it easier for the reader to grasp. An example is the comment of the eminent art historian Heinrich Wölfflin on Michelangelo's famous statue of David:

What does Michelangelo put forth as his ideal of youthful beauty? A gigantic hobbledehoy, no longer a boy and not yet a man, at the age when the body stretches, when the size of the limbs does not appear to match the enormous hands and feet. Michelangelo's sense of realism must have been satisfied for once. He shrank from no consequences, he even ventured to enlarge the uncouth model into the colossal. Then we have the unpleasant attitude, hard and angular, and the hideous triangle between the legs. Not a single concession has been made to the line of beauty. The figure shows a reproduction of nature, which on this scale approaches the marvellous. It is astonishing in every detail, and causes renewed surprise from the elasticity of the body as a whole, but, frankly speaking, it is absolutely ugly.

In order to point up the element of the grotesque in the statue, Wölfflin quite legitimately overstates his description to throw into relief the characteristics he wants made prominent.

Overstatement is most frequently used for humorous purposes. It is the basis of the tall tale, which piles exaggeration on exaggeration, and it can often enliven critical or polemical writing if it is inventive and reasonably good-natured. Here is Samuel Clemens on "Fenimore Cooper's Literary Offences":

> In his little box of stage properties he kept six or eight cunning devices, tricks, artifices for his savages and woodsmen to deceive and circumvent each other with, and he was never so happy as when he was working these innocent things and seeing them go. A favorite one was to make a moccasined person tread in the tracks of the moccasined enemy, and thus hide his own trail. Cooper wore out barrels and barrels of moccasins in working that trick. Another stage property that he pulled out of his box pretty frequently was his broken twig. . . . It is a restful chapter in any book of his when somebody doesn't step on a dry twig and alarm the reds and whites for two hundred yards around. Every time a Cooper person is in peril, and absolute silence is worth four dollars a minute, he is sure to step on a dry twig. There may be a hundred handier things to step on, but that wouldn't satisfy Cooper. Cooper requires him to turn out and find a dry twig; and if he can't do it, go and borrow one. In fact, the Leatherstocking Series ought to have been called the Broken Twig Series.

A specialized form of overstatement is invective—abusive name-calling elevated to a literary device. It is not much used in modern prose, though it has a long and distinguished history in English and American literature. Invective is still useful to a writer who feels that he is confronting something absolutely outrageous, something that can only be described in the language of abuse. Good invective is both resourceful in insult and at least moderately plausible:

A Whig is properly what is called a Trimmer—that is, a coward on both sides of a question, who dare not be a knave or an honest man, but is a sort of whiffling, shuffling, silly, contemptible, unmeaning negation of the two. [WILLIAM HAZLITT]

The American, if he has a spark of national feeling, will be humiliated by the very prospect of a foreigner's visit to Congress—these, for the most part, illiterate hacks whose fancy vests are spotted with gravy and whose speeches, hypocritical, unctuous, and slovenly, are spotted also with the gravy of political patronage, these persons are a reflection on the democratic process rather than of it; they expose it in its underwear. [MARY MC CARTHY]

Understatement, the reverse of exaggeration, puts an idea in less strong language than might be expected, or states it negatively (litotes). The quotations given earlier from Gibbon and Hannah Arendt illustrate ironic uses of understatement, and we here illustrate its somewhat more specialized uses. Stating an idea negatively may sometimes give it additional force:

Mrs. Higgins' new Civil War romance is almost as long as the Manhattan telephone directory, but not so interesting.

South Africa is not very popular with the other African states.

The Bible is not without its uses to us the clergy [SAMUEL BUTLER]

Stalin was not what you would call a nice man. [G. F. KENNAN]

Understatement can be an effective means of anticlimax. Often statements are anticlimactic because of the writer's ineptitude (see p. 59), but anticlimax is also a classic form of humor, a kind of verbal pratfall: an extravagant rhetorical buildup is punctured at the end by a flat understatement:

By far the most tremendous stage entries I ever saw were those of Mr. Wilson Barrett. I remember particularly a first night of his at which I happened to be sitting next to a clever but not very successful and rather sardonic old actor. I forget just what great historic or mythic personage Mr. Barrett was to represent, but I know that the earlier scenes of the play resounded with rumours of him—accounts of the great deeds he had done, and of the yet greater deeds that were expected of him. And at length there was a procession: white-bearded priests bearing wands; maidens playing upon the sackbut; guards in full armour; a pell-mell of unofficial citizens ever prancing along the edge of the pageant, huzzaing and hosannaing, mostly looking over their shoulders and shading their eyes; maidens strewing rose-leaves; and at last the orchestra crashing to a climax in the nick of which my neighbor turned to me and, with the assumption of innocent enthusiasm, whispered, "I shouldn't *wonder* if this were Barrett." [MAX BEERBOHM]

Although understatement is usually thought of as belonging primarily to humor and irony, it can be used effectively in the most serious contexts. When the subject itself is overpowering, when one writes about death, poverty, extreme suffering, mass destruction or harsh injustice, a flat, understated language that neutrally records the facts can often be more effective than any rhetorical amplification. Here is an extract from a description of living conditions in Chicago during the thirties:

One widow with a child of nine, who had formerly made $18 a week in a factory and who has since been living on $4 a week relief and two or three hours' work a day at fifty cents an hour, has tried to get along without garbage but has had to fall back on it frequently during a period of three years. Another widow, who used to do housework and laundry but who was finally left without any work, fed herself and her fourteen-year-old son on garbage. Before she picked up the meat, she would always take off her glasses so that she would not be able to see the maggots; but it sometimes made the boy so sick to look at this offal and smell it that he could not bring himself to eat. He weighed only eighty-two pounds. [EDMUND WILSON]

Facts like these do not need the support of overwrought language in order to make an impression.

PART FOUR

ORGANIZATION
AND DEVELOPMENT

16
MAKING A BEGINNING

In the words they share, writing and ordinary speech are much alike. In syntax, there is a marked contrast: speech is full of half-sentences, exclamations, silences, detached words and phrases, sentences that change direction in the middle; writing depends on complete, internally consistent syntactical units. In organization and development of ideas, the contrast between writing and conversation is even more pronounced. Conversation flows along from one subject to another, progressing casually by successive digressions. An idea emerges in fragments here and there, intertwined with half a dozen other ideas; it is mentioned, drops out, reappears, is passionately argued until it is swept away by some new topic. Conversation is made up as we go along, and it depends on the ability of the speakers to improvise. In short, conversation is a pretty disorderly affair.

Even in private talk, however, the sequence of ideas is not altogether dreamlike. When you recount a personal experience, you try to arrange the story in chronological order. When you tell somebody how to do something, you have to explain step by step. When you describe a scene, you have to decide where to begin, what to emphasize, and what to leave out. When you want to argue a point, you must make some effort to match up evidence and generalizations. Even if you only want to compare two movies or baseball teams, or explain how to bake a cake or change a tire, you must do some rudimentary work of organization if you are to be understood.

In good writing, organization is not rudimentary or intermittent, but fully worked out and consistent. Most writing, even the most conversational in tone, tries to do away with the fragmentary, unsequential aspects of conversation. Instead of gleaming through fitfully from time to time, an important idea is brought to the foreground and kept there, secondary matter is relegated to the background, and irrelevant matter is excluded. The sequence in which points are to be made is carefully planned. The relationship among ideas is made explicit by transitions and connectives. Concrete details fit in with one another and with the generalizations they support, ideas follow one another in logical order, and everything serves to reveal something about the central topic. Good prose serves ideals of unity, relevance, and effective sequence.

Gathering Material

Everyone who sits down to write is going to write *about* something, and presumably he knows what it is, at least in a general way. He knows that he wants to say something about Freud, or *War and Peace*, or the World Series, or the next election. But he may have no clear idea of exactly what he wants to say, what parts of his subject are important or unimportant, or what his central point is. He must first gather material for his discussion, and then subject it to a process of selection and arrangement.

Of the two main ways of gathering material for a subject, the first is dignified by the name "research": it involves consulting bibliographies and reference books, reading books and articles, interviewing people, taking systematic notes—in short, starting more or less from scratch to acquire a systematic body of knowledge about something. No long essay or book would be possible without this process of gathering and sifting a considerable mass of information. The second, less laborious, process is often sufficient for shorter pieces. Most people know more than they think they do about subjects they want to write on; what they need is to take an inventory of their ideas and information on the subject. An interior dialogue of questions and answers about the subject will bring to light bits of information and half-formulated ideas. Forgotten facts will emerge, new lines of argument will suggest themselves, and unnoticed connections between ideas will become apparent.

Jotting down all these random ideas and facts is helpful. It gives the writer an inventory of his resources for dealing with a subject. Suppose that you were composing an essay or a report on the proposed expansion of a small liberal arts college, Greenacres, and you wanted to mull over all aspects of the problem before sitting down to write a connected first draft. Here are some of the points that might come to mind:

1. Availability of money.
2. Number of applicants for admission (how many qualified applicants?).
3. Quality versus quantity.

4. Availability of suitable faculty.
5. Residence halls.
6. Effect of increased numbers on intellectual life.
7. New buildings.
8. Larger variety of courses.
9. Fragmentation of learning.
10. Loss of individual identity of students.
11. Increased demand for higher education.
12. Effect of increased numbers on intellectual life.

Under each point you would set down pertinent details and opinions as they occurred to you, accumulating all the raw materials for your final picture of the subject, and making a tentative outline.

Organizing

When this process is complete, you have before you the mass of material that constitutes a *subject*. The next problem is to convert that subject into a thesis. By "thesis" we mean a fully defined point of view toward the material—a clear idea of the leading points you want to make.

Your thesis determines which of the points you jotted down would appear in the first draft and which would be excluded as irrelevant. Suppose this is your leading idea: "Expansion of the college would inevitably lead to a lowering of the intellectual quality of the student body and the faculty." Then points 5 and 7 become irrelevant: residence halls and new buildings have no bearing. The topic also determines which ideas are primary and which are secondary. In this instance, points 2, 3, 4, and 6 would dominate the discussion, and the rest would be secondary. Further, the topic determines the way you deal with each individual point. For instance, you have to acknowledge the increased demand for higher education. Since your main point is that the demand cannot properly be met by Greenacres College, you might do well to describe the pressure for more higher education in your introductory paragraph. The rest of your paper would be an explanation of why a small liberal arts college cannot meet the demand. In discussing the availability of suitable faculty, you would not be so much concerned about the total number of Ph.D.'s turned out each year by American universities as with the rarity of the peculiar combination of qualities needed by a member of the Greenacres College faculty. An adequately formulated topic, then, determines the overall structure of a paper and also the kind of emphasis given to each of its parts.

Converting a subject into a thesis involves a narrowing down from a general subject to a more specific one. Beginning writers are usually tempted by all-inclusive subjects: "The Influence of the Eighteenth Century on the Nineteenth Century," "Fascism and Democracy," or "The Rise of Science." Such subjects as these are suitable for seasoned writers who plan to devote a number of years to them; in the hands of the young and inexperienced, they are not likely to lead to much besides empty, second-hand generalities. Someone who thinks himself qualified to write on the influence of the eighteenth century on the nineteenth most likely knows little about either century. Otherwise he would not be deluded into thinking that he could treat so vast a subject meaningfully—to him it is not vast because his knowledge of it is so slight.

Narrowing down a subject involves adding qualifications to it and at the same time beginning to formulate the leading question that the essay will attempt to answer. Thus the subject "Tragedy" might be narrowed to "English Tragedy," then to "Shakespearean Tragedy," then to *Hamlet*, and then finally (if the essay were to be brief) to "*Hamlet*, Act I, Scene 1." The writer now has a subject that has been cut down to a manageable size, but he does not have a thesis—there is no point of view, no motive for writing. The writer would still have to decide what questions he wanted to ask and answer about the material before him. Suppose he had been much struck by the way in which the opening scenes of great tragedies establish mood and foreshadow events to come. He might then be able to formulate his leading question: "In what ways does Act I, Scene 1 of *Hamlet* set the mood of the play and foreshadow events to come?" His subject would then have a thesis, and discussion would be motivated.

The thesis of an essay usually has to be revised and refined in the course of writing, but there is little point in beginning to organize and develop a paper before you know what its center and main direction are going to be. The nature of the thesis largely determines the form of the organization.

Organizing an essay is in part a somewhat mechanical business of fitting individual arguments and pieces of information into sentences and paragraphs, and then fitting sentences and paragraphs into an overall pattern, rather like fitting together the pieces of a jigsaw puzzle. But fitting together the parts of an essay is harder than fitting together the pieces of a jigsaw puzzle; the writer has to *invent* the final picture that he wants to give, for it will not emerge of itself as he fits the pieces together. Every essay has a beginning, a middle and an end, and every writer will conform to that very general shape. But there are no standardized patterns of organization that can be followed like recipes in a cook book. Like everything else in writing, the pattern of organization should flow out of the nature of the material, the purpose of the writer, and the character of the prospective audience. Thus the suggestions about organization that follow are necessarily rather general. The writer will have to adjust them to meet the needs of his individual subject and purpose.

Outlining

Organization is a way of sorting out material into different groups, of devising categories and arranging material within them. The random jottings made at the beginning are arranged in groups, and an order of precedence is established within each group. At this point, many writers find the formal outline a help. Though a few find it a hindrance and should avoid it, and others use it as a kind of sacred preliminary ceremony having nothing to do with the actual writing of the paper, yet an outline can provide a blueprint that will save costly expenditures of time and energy.

The most common types of outlines are the topic outline, the sentence outline and the paragraph outline. The paragraph outline simply states the main points to be made in each paragraph in the order they will follow in the final paper; it is primarily useful for short papers or individual sections of longer papers:

PARAGRAPH OUTLINE:

"The Philosophies of Bacon and Plato"

THESIS: The aim of the Baconian philosophy is to provide men with what they need while they remain ordinary men, but the aim of the Platonic philosophy is to raise men far above their ordinary needs.

1. Plato did not much favor the invention of the alphabet because it is a crutch for the memory and intellect; it weakens the power of memory, engraving knowledge on pieces of paper rather than the soul.

2. Bacon valued the invention of writing highly, in large part because it made strenuous feats of memory unnecessary.

3. Plato thought that the science of medicine was at best only to be tolerated because it could cure acute disorders, but he disapproved of the

arts that keep men alive after their powers of thought and action have declined.

4. Bacon found medicine the most interesting of all sciences, and thought that anything which ministered to the comfort of an invalid was a valuable invention.

5. Plato treats men as though they should be gods; Baconian philosophy deals with men as they actually are.

The sentence and topic outlines provide a more detailed blueprint, and differ from one another only in details of form, the sentence outline being written out in grammatically complete sentences, the topic outline being written out in phrases that are all parallel in their grammatical structure. The sentence outline, most detailed of the three, has the advantage that sentences from it can sometimes be used without modification in the final form of the essay.

TOPIC OUTLINE:

"THE PHILOSOPHIES OF BACON AND PLATO"

THESIS: The aim of the Baconian philosophy is to provide men with what they need while they remain ordinary men, but the aim of the Platonic philosophy is to raise men far above their ordinary needs.

I. Plato's attitude toward writing:
   A. Writing a deceptive aid to the intellect.
      1. Similar to a go-cart in learning to walk or corks in learning to swim.
      2. Vigorous intellectual exertion made first unnecessary and then impossible.
   B. Advantages that would follow from the absence of writing:
      1. Strenuous exercise of memory and understanding.
      2. Imprint of knowledge on the soul rather than on a piece of paper.
   C. Result of writing: knowledge of where information and ideas may be found, ignorance of information and ideas themselves.
II. Bacon's attitude toward writing:
   A. Writing far more useful in forwarding any science than unaided memory.
   B. Value of a highly developed memory:
      1. Usefulness of memory largely superseded by written records.
      2. Prodigious feats of memory no more valuable than exhibitions by rope dancers and tumblers.

III. Plato's attitude toward medicine:
   A. Medicine desirable as a cure for acute disorders or injuries to the healthy.
   B. Medicine undesirable as a means of keeping others alive:
      1. Those with constitutions ruined by debauchery.
      2. Those with feeble constitutions.
      3. Those with chronic diseases.
   C. Assumption that men should live only as long as they can be useful to the commonwealth.
   D. Appeal to mythical authorities.
IV. Bacon's attitude toward medicine:
   A. Assumption that all men should be made as healthy and comfortable as possible.
   B. Assumption that philosophy, the commonwealth, and medicine should all be at the service of mankind.
   C. Tolerant attitude toward invalidism and weakness of mind.
      1. Value of palliative medicines and treatments.
      2. Value of innocent recreations and comforts.
   D. Appeal to the example of Christ.

CONCLUSION: Plato wanted to make men into gods; Bacon accepted men as they were and tried to help them.

SENTENCE OUTLINE

The sentence outline is much like the topic outline, but often includes more concrete detail and is always written out in complete sentences, as in the following example:

I. Bacon took a great interest in medicine.
   A. He wanted to increase human comfort and decrease human pain.
   B. He thought knowledge and science were means to the end of human betterment.
   C. His thought was influenced by ideas of Christian beneficence.
II. Bacon was tolerant and helpful in his attitude toward human weakness.
   A. He felt no hostility toward the weak-mindedness and self-indulgence of valetudinarians.
   B. He thought any contrivance that would help the weak and sickly was worthwhile.
III. Bacon appealed to the example of Christ as a great healer of physical as well as spiritual ailments.

Now that you have looked at three types of outline, read the following excerpt from the *Essay on Lord Bacon* by Thomas Babington Macaulay, on which the outlines are based. Consider especially the way he knits together and fills out the individual points listed in the outlines:

On the greatest and most useful of all human inventions, the invention of alphabetical writing, Plato did not look with much complacency. He seems to have thought that the use of letters had operated on the human mind as the use of the go-cart in learning to walk, or of corks in learning to swim, is said to operate on the human body. It was a support which, in his opinion, soon became indispensable to those who used it, which made vigorous exertion first unnecessary and then impossible. The powers of the intellect would, he conceived, have been fully developed without this delusive aid. Men would have been compelled to exercise the understanding and the memory, and, by deep and assiduous meditation, to make truth thoroughly their own. Now, on the contrary, much knowledge is traced on paper, but little is engraved in the soul. A man is certain that he can find information at a moment's notice when he wants it. He therefore suffers it to fade from his mind. Such a man cannot in strictness be said to know anything. He has the show without the reality of wisdom. These opinions Plato has put into the mouth of an ancient king of Egypt. But it is evident from the context that they were his own; and so they were understood to be by Quinctilian. Indeed, they are in perfect accordance with the whole Platonic system.

Bacon's views, as may easily be supposed, were widely different. The powers of the memory, he observed, without the help of writing, can do little toward the advancement of any useful science. He acknowledges that the memory may be disciplined to such a point as to be able to perform very extraordinary feats. But on such feats he sets little value. The habits of his mind, he tells us, are such that he is not disposed to rate highly any accomplishment, however rare, which is of no practical use to mankind. As to these prodigious achievements of memory, he ranks them with the exhibitions of rope-dancers and tumblers. "These two performances," he says, "are much of the same sort. The one is an abuse of the powers of the body; the other is an abuse of the powers of the mind. Both may perhaps excite our wonder; but neither is entitled to our respect."

To Plato, the science of medicine appeared to be of very disputable advantage. He did not indeed object to quick cures for acute disorders, or for injuries produced by accidents. But the art which resists the slow sap of a chronic disease, which repairs frames enervated by lust, swollen by gluttony, or inflamed by wine, which encourages sensuality by mitigating the natural punishment of the sensualist, and prolongs existence when the intellect has ceased to retain its entire energy, had no share of his esteem. A life protracted by medical skill he pronounced to be a long death. The exercise of the art of medicine ought, he said, to be tolerated, so far as that art may serve to cure the occasional distempers of men whose constitutions are good. As to those who have bad constitutions, let them die; and the sooner the better. Such men are unfit for war, for magistracy, for the management of their domestic affairs, for severe study and speculation. If they engage in any vigorous mental exercise, they are troubled with giddiness and fulness of the head, all which they lay to the account of philosophy. The best thing that can happen to such wretches is to have done with life at once. He quotes mythical authorities in support of this doctrine; and reminds his disciples that the practice of the sons of Aesculapius, as described by Homer, extended only to the cure of external injuries.

Far different was the philosophy of Bacon. Of all the sciences, that which he seems to have regarded with the greatest interest was the science which, in Plato's opinion, would not be tolerated in a well-regulated community. To make men perfect was no part of Bacon's plan. His humble aim was to make imperfect men comfortable. The beneficence of his philosophy resembled the beneficence of the common Father, whose sun rises on the evil and the good, whose rain descends for the just and the unjust. In Plato's opinion man was made for philosophy; in Bacon's opinion philosophy was made for man; it was a means to an end; and that end was to increase the pleasures and mitigate the pains of millions who are not and cannot be philosophers. That a valetudinarian who took great pleasure in being wheeled along his terrace, who relished his boiled chicken and his weak wine and water, and who enjoyed a hearty laugh over the Queen of Navarre's tales, should be treated as a *caput lupinum* because he could not read the *Timaeus* without a headache, was a notion which the humane spirit of the English schools of wisdom altogether rejected. Bacon would not have thought it beneath the dignity of a philosopher to contrive an improved garden chair for such a valetudinarian, to devise some way of rendering his medicines more palatable, to invent repasts which he might enjoy, and pillows on which he might sleep soundly; and this though there might not be the smallest hope that the mind of the poor invalid would ever rise to the contemplation of the ideal beautiful and the ideal good. As Plato had cited the religious legends of Greece to justify his contempt for the more recondite parts of the art of healing, Bacon vindicated the dignity of that art by appealing to the example of Christ, and reminded men that the great Physician of the soul did not disdain to be also the physician of the body.

To sum up the whole, we should say that the aim of the Platonic philosophy was to exalt man into a god. The aim of the Baconian philosophy was to provide man with what he requires while he continues to be a man. The aim of the Platonic philosophy was to raise us far above vulgar wants. The aim of the Baconian philosophy was to supply our vulgar wants. The former aim was noble; but the latter was attainable.

Plato drew a good bow; but, like Acestes in Virgil, he aimed at the stars; and therefore, though there was no want of strength or skill, the shot was thrown away. His arrow was indeed followed by a track of dazzling radiance, but it struck nothing. Bacon fixed his eye on a mark which was placed on the earth, and within bow-shot, and hit it in the white. The philosophy of Plato began in words and ended in words, noble words indeed, words such as were to be expected from the finest of human intellects exercising boundless dominion over the finest of human languages. The philosophy of Bacon began in observations and ended in arts.

Some writers find it almost impossible to work from an outline; their thought refuses to move along the lines they have laid down for it. Such writers are unfortunate, for they must ordinarily suffer through a chaotic first, second, or even third draft before some order begins to emerge from their materials. The writer who can lay out a plan in advance and then proceed to give the flesh and blood of detail, concrete imagery, and specific argument to this skeleton of thought has all the advantage in rapidity and clarity of execution once he begins to write. He begins with order rather than struggling through a morass of disorderly scraps and pieces to find it.

Titles

Although titles come first of all in an essay, they are very often written last. From the very beginning, the writer needs a working title—an accurate label for his subject: "The Danger of Pesticides," "Migrant Farm Labor in Southern California 1945–1963," "John Donne's Pulpit Oratory." Such titles are certainly adequate; they tell the reader exactly what is to be discussed. They are usually final titles as well as working titles if the articles they head are government reports, essays for learned journals, or scientific reports. In writing of that kind, readers do not expect to find eye-catching titles.

The only really unacceptable title is one that is not even a clear label of the subject. Beginning writers who attempt the personal essay are especially prone to write empty titles: "My Vacation," "A Memory," "A Trip to Paris," "An Embarrassing Moment." Such titles are both trite and uninformative, and the writer should try to make them more meaningful by making them more concrete: "A Summer in the Maine Woods," "Memories of an Ohio Childhood," "Yet Another American in Paris," "A Misstep at the Waldorf." These titles may not bring a gleam of expectation to the reader's eye, but they will not depress him as the first group will. Sometimes, in an effort to arouse the reader's interest, a writer will abandon dignity and decorum and use a title that is sensational, cute, or speciously mystifying: "I Was a Teen-Age Pusher," "Hi There! A Salute to Our Latin American Neighbors," "Shades Among the Shadows."

Not all good titles must confine themselves to being precise labels for their subjects, however. Some titles can be allusive, resonant, and aesthetically attractive without becoming irrelevant to the subject or playing tricks on the reader. The following are good titles:

"Is Ivy Necessary?" (Henry Steele Commager) An argument in favor of urban universities.

"Four Years in a Shed" (Eve Curie) An essay about her parents' famous radium experiments.

"The Patient's Right to Die" (Joseph Fletcher) An argument against prolonging the suffering of the hopelessly ill.

The Earl of Louisiana (A. J. Liebling) About Governor Earl Long of Louisiana.

Virgin Land (Henry Nash Smith) About the American West.

To the Finland Station (Edmund Wilson) A historical study that ends with the arrival of Lenin at the Finland Station in St. Petersburg.

Introductions

The most emphatic positions in an essay are the beginning and the end; therefore they deserve particular care. Introductory paragraphs are notoriously difficult to write. In general, it is best to write a working introduction that states, no matter how flat-footedly, what the essay will be about; later, this paragraph can be rewritten, or, better yet, thrown out and replaced by something livelier and more cogent. If the great historian and stylist Gibbon found it necessary to labor for many hours over the first sentence of his *Decline and Fall of the Roman Empire*, lesser writers need not be surprised or discouraged by the difficulty of getting under way.

The kind of introduction you write will depend on the kind of essay and audience you envision. A writer for a mass circulation magazine usually tries for a very catchy beginning. A writer for a more limited (and more serious) audience will eschew such tactics, beginning with a terse indication of his subject and his point of view toward it.

There are only two "rules" which always apply to the beginning of an essay. The beginning should be interesting, and it should lead naturally into what follows. The first few sentences determine whether the reader wants to go on or to lay the essay aside. Such a vapid introductory statement as "The subject of racial integration has been a matter of bitter controversy during the last ten years" is not promising. It does not even have the advantage of showing what the focus of the paper will be—it may be a history of the controversy, or a discussion of integration issues themselves, or almost anything else.

Aside from empty, uninteresting beginnings, beginnings that are irrelevant to the subject are also ineffective. The politician's joke about a "funny thing that happened on the way to the auditorium" may catch the attention of the audience, but it does nothing to prepare for the ensuing discussion or to insure that the attention of the audience will be transferred from the joke to the substance of the speech.

Another ineffective beginning is to go too far away from the immediate subject—to preface a discussion of the French Revolution with a rapid review of the rise of feudalism in the Middle Ages, or to open a critical essay on Henry Fielding's *Tom Jones* with an elaborate statement about The Novel. A reliable rule of thumb is that the shorter the essay, the closer you must stick to the immediate issue. In a book, a writer can afford to come up to his subject by leisurely stages; someone writing a thousand or fifteen hundred words must go to the heart of his subject at once or lose his opportunity to say anything significant about it.

Within the general requirements of interest and relevance, good writers begin in a wide variety of ways. There being no set introduction that is suitable for all purposes, the writer should be aware that there are alternatives open to him. The most common ways of beginning are illustrated below.

1. Sometimes a writer begins by describing the received view of his subject, which the body of his essay will demolish. In this quotation, Arthur M. Schlesinger, Jr. marshalls all the stock epithets that are commonly bestowed on Andrew Jackson; then he goes on to show how poorly they fit Jackson's true character:

Andrew Jackson has long been the symbol of fighting democracy in American political life. On the lips of Democratic spellbinders his name is a call-to-arms: Jefferson, the sage of Monticello, is the serene philosopher of democracy, but Jackson is its militant champion, rude, brawling and irresistible. Schoolbook history adds the photo-montage: backwoods

Andy Jackson, rough, tough, lusty, hard as nails and irascible as a bumble-bee, defying successively the British, the Indians, the Eastern aristocrats, the United States Bank, the Supreme Court—all in the name of the common people, the unpolished, uncouth, good-hearted rabble, clad in buckskin and flourishing bowie knives, who stormed the White House on the day of his inaugural.

It is a good story, and it ought to be, for enough talents of diverse kinds went into inventing and perpetuating it.

2. A writer may begin with an analysis of the way a key term is used. Note that in addition to talking about how the word "revolu-tion" is used, Crane Brinton is also arguing that the events of 1832 in England deserve to be classed with other members of the category "revolution," thus giving his definition concreteness and argumenta-tive point.

There is hardly a better example of the imprecision of sociological terms than the word revolution. To apply it to the inventions of Watt and Cartwright, to the summoning of the Estates General in 1789, to the first performance of *Hernani*, to the flight of Charles I, and to the latest South American *coup d'etat* is almost to deprive it of meaning. In a narrower and purely political sense, it does denote an extra-legal and unusually violent change in the existing government. But even here the word revolution, as contrasted with *coup d'etat*, implies a change affect-ing the lives of quite ordinary citizens. Now England underwent in the first third of the nineteenth century industrial and artistic changes which all are agreed in calling revolutionary. A justifiable pride in the fact that the political changes of the time were achieved without violence, and a less justifiable desire to emphasize that Englishmen are not as Frenchmen are, have prevented our applying the word revolutionary to these political changes. Yet if revolution means in politics, as it does in art, morals, and industry, a real and only comparatively rapid alteration of our fundamental ways of doing things, the term should be used of the transfer of power symbolized in the Act of 1832.

3. A writer may begin with a quotation that leads directly to some important aspect of his subject. Germaine Brée begins with the first sentence of Proust's *Remembrance of Things Past*, and shows how it foreshadows the whole ambiguous, dreamlike atmosphere of the novel:

"I have long had the habit of going to bed early." From this first sentence of Proust's novel the reader is carried along in search of he knows not what, bewitched by the voice of the "I," which lures him along the strange meanders of an inner Lethe. The whole of *A la recherche du temps perdu* is projected through the long, monotonous, almost muffled soliloquy of the "I." The narrator first presents himself in his secluded bedroom shrouded in obscurity, an "amphibious man" emerging from the wavering borderland which lies between sleeping and wakefulness. The brilliant, brittle society which his tale evokes will always be bathed in that obscurity. Occasionally, out of the depths of sleep, the narrator summons up an image or a feeling which seems to come from the distant past. From this nocturnal birth on the borderland of sleep, the Proustian world retains the unreal atmosphere, vaguely disquieting and menacing, of those magic gardens and palaces which in fairy tales spring up from the heart of darkness or from some strange forest.

4. A writer may plunge the reader into the midst of an incident and then later go back to an earlier point to pick up the thread of exposition. George Orwell begins an essay on poverty in Marrakech with this incident:

As the corpse went past the flies left the restaurant table in a cloud and rushed after it, but they came back a few minutes later.

The little crowd of mourners—all men and boys, no women—threaded their way across the market-place between the piles of pomegranates and the taxis and the camels, wailing a short chant over and over again. What really appeals to the flies is that the corpses here are never put into coffins, they are merely wrapped in a piece of rag and carried on a rough wooden bier on the shoulders of four friends. When the friends get to the burying-ground they hack an oblong hole a foot or two deep, dump the body in it and fling over it a little of the dried-up, lumpy earth, which is like broken brick.

5. A writer may begin with an aphorism or familiar saying and then illustrate it concretely. Here Bergen Evans drives home the point of his aphorism by piling example on example, unloosing an avalanche of "psychic phenomena" on the reader:

Superstitions, as Bacon said, like bats, fly best in twilight, and the twilight of a confused liberalism seems particularly favorable to them. Certainly we are suffering, or enjoying, a period of unusual supernatural activity. Mysterious writings and rappings, rocking chairs that keep on rocking, wild rushings of the sun about the sky, roses that never fade, barrels that never run dry, coffee pots ditto, pictures that grow leaves, statues that sweat and weep, abominable snowmen, corpses that stay fresh and fragrant for fifty years, horses that answer three questions for a dollar, flat tires that repair themselves, monsters and sea serpents, half-ton stones that drag themselves across deserts, ghostly hitchhikers who suddenly disappear and are later discovered to have been persons long dead—in news stories, in table talk, in radio and television interviews, from pulpit, press, rostrum, forum, microphone, street corner, classroom, bar, and parlor, these stories descend on us in an uninterrupted stream.

6. A writer may begin by asking questions that are to be answered in the course of the essay:

Let us assume that you own one of the biggest gambling establishments in America, but still itch for expansion. How would you expand?

Let's say further that you've done enough research to discover that you can make the fattest profits by soliciting the enormous middle-class market. Then how would you induce large numbers of people of modest means to travel long distances and toss part of the family savings onto your green baize tables? [KEITH MONROE]

7. A writer may begin by justifying himself for raising a familiar subject once more on the grounds that it has not yet been treated satisfactorily. Philip Reiff sketches the popular conception of a "new" campus politics before going on to question whether this newness actually exists:

Once again we are hearing a good deal about the "politics of college youth'"—not only in this country but abroad. Magazine articles solemnly report "new" currents—new conservatism, new radicalism, new enthusiasms for working overseas and demonstrating at home. Few campus phenomena seem to be so widely reported and, at the same time, so oddly distorted for there has been very little careful analysis of what, precisely, is new about the present student activity, and even less concerning the ways in which it is, and is not, political.

8. A writer may begin by making a set of distinctions that throw light on his material. James Agee's description of the four grades of laughter is preliminary to a contrast between the boffo-filled silent comedies and the much thinner comic fare in more recent movies:

In the language of screen comedians four of the main grades of laugh are the titter, the yowl, the bellylaugh, and the boffo. The titter is just a titter. The yowl is a runaway titter. Anyone who has ever had the pleasure knows all about a bellylaugh. The boffo is the laugh that kills. An ideally good gag, perfectly constructed and played, would bring the victim up this ladder of laughs by cruelly controlled degrees to the top rung, and would then proceed to wobble, shake, wave and brandish the ladder until he groaned for mercy. Then, after the shortest time possible out for recuperation, he would feel the first tickling of the comedian's whip once more and start up a new ladder.

The reader can get a fair enough idea of the current state of screen comedy by asking himself how long it has been since he has had that treatment.

9. A writer may simply announce his subject and give some indication of the spirit and point of view that will govern the discussion, as do James Bradstreet Greenough and George Lyman Kittridge in this quotation:

A peculiar kind of vagabond language, always hanging on the outskirts of legitimate speech, but continually straying or forcing its way into the most respectable company, is what we call *slang*. The prejudice against this form of speech is to be encouraged, though it usually rests on a misconception. There is nothing abnormal about slang. In making it, men proceed in precisely the same manner as in making language, and under the same natural laws. The motive, however, is somewhat different, for slang is not meant simply to express one's thoughts. Its coinage and circulation come rather from the wish of the individual to distinguish himself by oddity or grotesque humor. Hence slang is seldom controlled by any regard for propriety, and it bids deliberate defiance to all considerations of good taste.

Not all these ways of beginning are suitable for all occasions, and none of them will work on any occasion if used ineptly or mechanically. But the writer perplexed about how to begin should bear in mind the range of possibilities that they suggest.

17

PRINCIPLES
OF EXPOSITION

E XPOSITORY writing is a mixture of argument, description and
narration; its main purpose is to explain something to a reader.
Unlike pure description and narration, it appeals primarily to the
understanding rather than to the feelings and senses. Unlike argumentative writing, it seeks to persuade primarily through clear explanation rather than through refutation and strict proof. In expository
writing, which is the appropriate vehicle for most discussions, argument, narration, and description are intermingled so that argument
is supported by description and narration—that is, by concrete images
and examples—and the significance of description and narration is
made clear by the general statements that compose the argument.

Outside mathematics and technical philosophy, almost all writing
consists of a mixture of specific details and general statements. An
essay with nothing but generalizations would be so abstract that the
reader would have difficulty seeing what the generalizations were
about; it would also be a set of dogmatic assertions demanding accept-
ance without explanation. An essay made up entirely of specific
details would fall apart into unrelated fragments because of the lack
of general statements to hold them together and explain their significance.

Effective balance between generalization and supporting detail
cannot be achieved by the mechanical application of rules, for it
changes from subject to subject and audience to audience. A philosopher writing for other philosophers might not need to give a single
concrete instance to illustrate his argument. A commercial writer
embroidering on the theme "people are funny" might do little more
than string together anecdotes that exhibit human foibles. In the
mass of writing between these two poles, the writer has to use his
judgment to determine when a generalization is needed to explain a

group of details and when details are necessary to make a generalization convincing. If a writer says, "When Jane walked into the office this morning, her hands were shaking and she looked pale and drawn," there is no need to add the more general remark, "She was feeling ill." On the other hand, if a writer says, "Fear of atomic warfare is world wide," there is no need to enumerate instances of this fear in the United States, Russia, India, and Ceylon. In the first example, generalization is unnecessary; in the second, supporting detail would be superfluous.

Paragraphs

The paragraph is the basic unit of expository writing: it is a group of interrelated statements that deal with a single aspect of the main thesis. It is a unit of thought, a way of showing that certain statements belong together. A well developed paragraph is very much like an essay in miniature, with a clearly defined thesis (a topic sentence) backed by supporting material that is arranged in a definite pattern. Every detail bears on the topic sentence, which in turn is directly relevant to the main thesis of the essay. A good paragraph, like a good essay, has unity and internal consistency.

There is no firm rule about paragraph length, but a good rule of thumb is that a paragraph is more than a single sentence and less than a page. Although newspaper paragraphs are usually less than a hundred words, and paragraphs in scholarly books may run for two or three closely printed pages, most paragraphs fall between these extremes, running between one hundred and three hundred words. The length of paragraphs within an essay will vary considerably because some parts of the subject require fuller treatment than others. Also, the total length of a piece of writing influences the average length of the paragraphs; a thousand-word book review usually has shorter paragraphs than a twenty-page article.

Whatever the length, there are always the same basic elements of the paragraph—generalizations and supporting details.

Generalizations

There is an element of generalization in every statement that goes beyond the assertion of an individual fact. In the following series of statements there is an increasing degree of generalization:

During the last month, there have been five automobile accidents at the intersection of Elm and Grape Streets. (A summary of five separate accidents.)

There is an accident almost every week at the corner of Elm and Grape. (The first statement simply says what has happened during the last month; the second implies that accidents will continue to occur at roughly the same rate.)

Elm and Grape is a dangerous intersection where there are frequent accidents. ("Five accidents in a month" has been translated into "frequent accidents," and the interpretation "dangerous" given to the Elm and Grape intersection.)

Traffic intersections are a source of danger to both motorists and pedestrians. (Elm and Grape have disappeared, and the assertion applies to all intersections.)

Traffic safety engineers are not devoting enough attention to making intersections safe for motorists and pedestrians.
(A wide inference is drawn, and, unlike the four preceding statements, this one requires a good deal of concrete support if it is to be made persuasive. If traffic safety experts are to be convinced that they should work harder on intersection traffic problems, they will have to be shown *why*.)

Only wide generalizations such as the last present serious problems in formulation for the writer. They must be based on an adequate body of evidence, not isolated instances plucked out arbitrarily to support a thesis. They must be capable of illustration and demonstration.

A writer should always be ready to show how a generality can be applied to individual cases, but sometimes this is very difficult to do, particularly in literary and historical studies, where often the material is an almost unmanageable tangle of conflicting evidence. The truth does not always come in the form of clear and distinct ideas, and a writer's material may demand rather loose or even hazy generalizations that are difficult to apply firmly and comprehensively. Nevertheless, it is an evasion of intellectual responsibility to avoid this problematic region of ideas, and it is no crime to indicate that a generalization is a tentative instrument of exploration rather than a conclusive assertion.

A writer should never be afraid to indicate the degree of credibility that attaches to a statement. "Possibly," "probably," "usually," "it may be that . . . ," "apparently," and similar locutions show the reader that he is expected to entertain the idea advanced, but not necessarily give full assent to it. If every general statement is preceded by this kind of qualification, the writer will appear wishy-washy and his argument will be tenuous. Still, if an assertion does not warrant positive conviction, the writer should warn the reader, and if a generalization applies to the subject only in a loose and incomplete way, the writer should make some acknowledgment of that fact.

Some generalizations *have* to be shaky because they deal in uncertainties. But most shaky generalizations arise because of imprecise formulation. Take, for example, these assertions:

The artist is an unusually sensitive, isolated, alienated man, cut off from society.

The poets of the Romantic Movement were fascinated by the exotic and the remote.

The first statement is, as it stands, untrue. Some artists in some periods of history have no doubt been sensitive, isolated, alienated men; but it would be easy to draw up a list of great artists from Aristophanes to Jane Austen who were nothing of the sort. The writer needs to acknowledge that his observation applies only to some artists at a certain period in modern history. Similarly, if a writer wants his reader to accept the second assertion he should at once acknowledge Wordsworth as an exception to his rule. The first generalization can be saved by an acknowledgment of its limited application, the second by admitting exceptions. Often a simple qualifier will convert a weak generalization into an adequately formulated one: such phrases as "often," "sometimes," "usually," "between 1940 and 1960," "in Southern California," "among composers of the second rank," "under ideal conditions" can tighten up a loose generalization sufficiently to make it a usable instrument of argument. A generalization stated in wider terms than the material warrants can often be cured of its ills by the simple addition of qualifiers that define the area to which the generalization applies.

Topic Sentences

Relatively abstract generalizations of the kind we have been discussing usually appear as topic sentences of paragraphs. A topic sentence is a general statement of what a paragraph is about, an assertion of its main point. Since a paragraph is a unit of thought dealing with some aspect of the main subject, that aspect needs to be named and defined somewhere in the paragraph. Nine times out of ten, the topic sentence occurs as the beginning of the paragraph, as in the following example:

One of the most interesting and engaging characteristics of island species is their extraordinary tameness—a lack of sophistication in dealings with the human race, which even the bitter teachings of experience do not quickly alter. When Robert Cushman Murphy visited the island of South Trinidad in 1913 with a party from the brig Daisy, terns alighted on the heads of the men in the whaleboat and peered inquiringly into their faces. Albatrosses on Laysan, whose habits include wonderful ceremonial dances, allowed naturalists to walk among their colonies and responded with a grave bow to similar polite greetings from the visitors. When the British ornithologist David Lack visited the Galapagos Islands, a century after Darwin, he found that the hawks allowed themselves to be touched, and the flycatchers tried to remove hair from the heads of the men for nesting material. "It is a curious pleasure," he wrote, "to have the birds of the wilderness settling upon one's shoulders, and the pleasure could be much less rare were man less destructive." [RACHEL CARSON]

Sometimes the topic sentence is not at the very beginning, but follows immediately after transitional material that links the paragraph to the preceding one. The paragraph quoted below is preceded by one that discusses the variety of city slums:

While there is great variety in our city slums, most of them have one thing in common: *they are eating away at the heart of the cities, especially the downtown areas.* The slums would, in fact, be much easier for the cities to endure if they were off in fringe areas. But in Chicago, Cleveland, St. Louis, Detroit—indeed, in almost every major metropolitan city —the slums envelop and squeeze the core of the city like a Spanish boot. If you start in the middle of almost any big city's main center of municipal government, or its main shopping district, and walk about ten blocks, you will be in a slum. The reason is that these core areas are the oldest areas; the housing around them is likely to be fifty or even a hundred years old and therefore especially prone to slum formation. The same may be said of the housing around the cities' great railroad terminals or port areas, which were also located and built up in other centuries. A visitor getting off a train, or debarking from a ship, almost always sees the seamy side of the city first. [DANIEL SELIGMAN]

Sometimes a topic sentence takes the form of a question which is answered by what follows. This device permits the writer to name his topic without defining his point of view at the very beginning:

What was it that cut the insects off from progress? The answer appears
to lie in their breathing mechanism. The land arthropods have adopted
the methods of air-tubes or tracheae, branching to microscopic size and
conveying gases directly to and from the tissues instead of using the dual
mechanism of lungs and bloodstream. The laws of gaseous diffusion are
such that respiration by tracheae is extremely efficient for very small
animals, but becomes rapidly less efficient with increase of size, until it
ceases to be of use at a bulk below that of a house mouse. It is for this
reason that no insect has ever become, by vertebrate standards, even
moderately large.

It is for the same reason that no insect has ever become even moderately intelligent. The fixed pathways of instinct, however elaborate, require far fewer nerve-cells than the multiple switchboards that underlie
intelligence. It appears to be impossible to build a brain mechanism for
flexible behavior with less than a quite large minimum of neurones; and
no insect has reached a size to provide this minimum. [JULIAN HUXLEY]

Infrequently, the topic is either unstated or submerged unobtrusively in a phrase or dependent clause. This method is suitable only
where the main drift of the author's meaning is so plain that it does
not need to be stated with any emphasis:

Few of the people who take these tests give much thought to *where
they come from.* For the most part, they are not made up by the schools
and other organizations that administer them. They are bought or rented.
Test-making has developed into a large, lucrative, and increasingly com-
petitive business—some of the test publishers employ travelling salesmen
to promote their wares. If you have a valid reason for giving a test, you
can probably find an appropriate one already in stock. Or you can commission a test-making organization to construct one to suit your special
needs—although the cost may run to many thousands of dollars. [BANESH
HOFFMAN]

Sometimes a writer puts the topic sentence at the end of a paragraph, so that it serves as a climax to the development of an idea
rather than as an introduction to a demonstration that follows:

There have been several composers, Campion, Hugo Wolf, Benjamin
Britten, for example, whose musical imagination has been stimulated by
poetry of a high order. The question remains, however, whether the lis-
tener hears the sung words as words in a poem, or, as I am inclined to
believe, only as sung syllables. A Cambridge psychologist, P. E. Vernon,
once performed the experiment of having a Campion song sung with
nonsense verses of equivalent syllabic value substituted for the original;
only six per cent of his test audience noticed that something was wrong.

It is precisely because I believe that, in listening to song (as distinct from chant), we hear, not words, but syllables, that I am not generally in favor of the performances of operas in translation. Wagner or Strauss in English sounds intolerable, and would still sound so if the poetic merits of the translation were greater than those of the original, because the new syllables have no apt relation to the pitch and tempo of the notes with which they are associated. The poetic value of the words may provoke a composer's imagination, but it is their syllabic values which determine the kind of vocal line he writes. *In song, poetry is expendable, syllables are not.* [w. h. auden]

Topic sentences are not a mere mechanical device, nor are they something used by amateurs and abandoned by professionals. All expository writers use them constantly, and they are a chief means of interpreting material and guiding the reader to the central point of each paragraph or section of an essay.

Supporting Detail

How much supporting detail? The disappointingly vague answer has to be, "Enough to accomplish your purpose." Commonplaces and universally acknowledged truths can stand by themselves without the addition of illustrative detail. Assumptions that are likely to be shared by the writer and his audience need only a few details to remind the reader of the actualities behind the generalization. Novel or controversial assertions, assertions which the reader must be actively persuaded to accept, require a lot of discussion and supporting evidence. To most audiences you can say, "Communism inspires fear of expropriation among property owners" without needing to go further to prove your point, but if you say something such as "The United States is now one of the most conservative countries in the world" you will need to do a lot of explaining to be convincing.

Many beginning writers think that when they have made a bare assertion, they have done: they see no need to give the flesh and blood of detailed discussion to the bare bones of their argument. Such writers need to remind themselves that assertion is not argument, and that abstractions need to be clothed in a body of concrete detail if they are to be meaningful. Other writers—particularly graduate students—suffer from the reverse problem. Unwilling to give up a scrap of the evidence they have so laboriously gathered, they unloose an avalanche of detail on the reader, never stopping when they have done enough to establish their point. The beginning writer usually needs to find more support for his generalizations; the apprentice scholar usually needs to prune the luxuriance of his evidence.

Effective supporting material need not be facts alone. Images, anecdotes, hypothetical examples, metaphors, analogies, subsidiary generalizations and lines of argument, allusions, even jokes and old saws can be useful. There are many routes to the effective development of ideas. Perhaps most useful of all, no matter what the subject, is to translate abstractions into visual or tactile terms when that can be done without distortion of the material. Sensory equivalents for ideas give life to ideas and make them more accessible to the understanding and imagination. Notice how William James uses sense imagery in his discussion of the moral ideals of poverty:

The opposition between the men who have and the men who are is immemorial. Though the gentleman, in the old-fashioned sense of the man who is well born, has usually in point of fact been predaceous and *reveled in lands and goods*, yet he has never identified his essence with these possessions, but rather with personal superiorities, the courage, generosity, and pride supposed to be his birthright. To certain huckstering kinds of considerations he *thanked God* he was forever *inaccessible*, and if in life's vicissitudes he should become destitute through their lack, he was glad to think that with his *sheer* valor he was all the freer to work out his salvation. . . . This ideal of the well-born man without possessions was embodied in knight-errantry and templardom; and, hideously corrupted as it has always been, it still dominates sentimentally, if not practically, the military and aristocratic *view* of life. We glorify the soldier as the man absolutely *unencumbered*. Owning nothing but his *bare* life, and willing *to toss that up* at any moment when the cause commands him, he is the representative of *unhampered* freedom in ideal directions. The laborer who *pays with his person day by day*, and has no rights invested in the future, offers also much of this ideal detachment. *Like the savage*, he may *make his bed wherever his right arm can support him*, and from his simple and *athletic attitude of observation*, the property-owner seems *buried* and *smothered* in ignoble externalities and *trammels*, "*wading in straw and rubbish to his knees.*" The claims which things make are corruptors of manhood, mortgages on the soul, and a *drag anchor on our progress toward the empyrean*.

18
PATTERNS OF EXPOSITION

Just as there are many kinds of material that can be used to support an idea, so there are many patterns of organization into which material can be arranged. These patterns are not arbitrary, but grow out of the nature of the subject and the purpose of the writer: they provide a design for what he has to say, and they lay out the lines along which his thought develops. Most single paragraphs and all essays combine many different patterns of organization; but, for the sake of clarity, it is useful to examine one at a time the most common patterns of organization and development.

Enumeration of Particulars

This is the simplest kind of organization, for it sometimes comes close to being a list of particulars—so much so that the chief danger of relying too heavily on enumeration is that the essay will disintegrate into a mere aggregation of disjointed remarks. But sometimes even a random order of enumeration gives exactly the effect a writer wants. In the following passage, Mark Twain gives the impression of Fenimore Cooper's flood of misused words by heaping up detail in a mass rather than arranging it in groups—nouns, verbs, and adjectives, say. A purposeful disorder can constitute a kind of order:

Cooper's word sense was singularly dull. When a person has a poor ear for music he will flat and sharp right along without knowing it. He keeps near the tune, but it is *not* the tune. When a person has a poor ear for words, the result is a literary flatting and sharping; you may perceive what he is intending to say, but you also perceive that he doesn't *say* it. This is Cooper. He was not a word musician. His ear was satisfied with the *approximate* word. I will furnish some circumstantial evidence in support of this charge. My instances are gathered from half a dozen pages of the tale called *Deerslayer*. He uses "verbal" for "oral"; "precision" for "facility"; "unsophisticated" for "primitive"; "preparation" for "expectancy"; "rebuked" for "subdued"; "dependent on" for "resulting from"; "fact" for "condition"; "fact" for "conjecture"; "precaution" for "caution"; "explain" for "determine"; "mortified" for "disappointed"; "meretricious" for "factitious"; "materially" for "considerably"; "decreasing" for "deepening"; "increasing" for "disappearing"; "embedded" for "enclosed"; "treacherous" for "hostile"; "stood" for "stooped"; "softened" for "replaced"; "rejoined" for "remarked"; "situation" for "condition"; "different" for "differing"; "insensible' for "unsentient"; "brevity" for "celerity"; "distrusted" for "suspicious"; "mental imbecility" for "imbecility"; "eyes" for "sight"; "counteracting" for "opposing"; "funeral obsequies" for "obsequies."

More often, the items to be enumerated are arranged in some kind of sequence. Suppose you were explaining what equipment, plants, and fish are needed to set up a home aquarium. You would not simply set down each item as it occurred to you. You would arrange the items in the sequence in which purchaser would buy them, beginning with the tank and ending with the various kinds of fish; you would impose a chronological order on the enumeration of particulars. Or suppose that you wanted to enumerate possible ways of travelling from New York to Athens. You would have to decide whether to begin with the worst way and work up to the best, or the reverse: in any case, the order would not be a random one, dependent on the order in which various means of travel popped into your head. Two useful ways of structuring an enumeration of particulars are either to arrange them in chronological series, if possible, or to arrange the particulars in an order of ascending or descending importance.

Explanation of a Process

Explaining a process involves writing a narrative about how something is done. The material may be as simple as a recipe for flapjacks, or as complicated as an account of how a synthetic fiber is produced, but the organizational outline will be basically a simple one. The writer need only be sure that he includes all the relevant steps, gets them in the right chronological order, and shows the connections between each of the steps. Here is Hilaire Belloc describing how to whet a scythe:

To mow a field well, you must start with a sharp scythe. There is an art in the sharpening of a scythe, and it is worth describing carefully. Your blade must be dry, and that is why you will see men rubbing the scythe-blade with grass before they whet it. Then also your rubber must be quite dry, and on this account it is a good thing to lay it on your coat and keep it there during all your day's mowing. The scythe you stand upright, with the blade pointing away from you, and you put your left hand firmly on the back of the blade, grasping it; then you pass the rubber first down one side of the blade-edge and then down the other, beginning near the handle and going on to the point and working quickly and hard. When you first do this you will, perhaps, cut your hand; but it is only at first that such an accident will happen to you.

Frederick Lewis Allen is describing how to start a Model T Ford:

If Mr. Smith's car is one of the high, hideous, but efficient model T Fords of the day, let us watch him for a minute. He climbs in by the right-hand door (for there is no left hand door by the front seat), reaches over to the wheel, and sets the spark and throttle levers in a position like that of the hands of a clock at ten minutes to three. Then, unless he has paid extra for a self-starter, he gets out to crank. Seizing the crank in his right hand (carefully, for a friend of his once broke his arm cranking), he slips his left forefinger through a loop of wire that controls the choke. He pulls the loop of wire, he revolves the crank mightily, and as the engine at last roars, he leaps to the trembling running board, leans in, and moves the spark and throttle to twenty-five minutes of two. Perhaps he reaches the throttle before the engine falters into silence, but if it is a cold morning perhaps he does not. Mr. Smith wishes Mrs. Smith would come out and sit in the driver's seat and pull that spark lever down before the engine has time to die.

Causes and Effects

Exposition may either begin with effects and then move backwards to causes, or go in the opposite direction, moving from causes to effects. Since effects are often more familiar than causes, they are usually the best place to begin, at least for an audience of nonspecialists. Thus, George Gamow moves from a familiar effect—volcanic eruptions—to the less well-known cause—the cooling and the shrinking of the globe:

Besides the terrific outbursts of volcanic activity, which eject thousands of tons of flaming lava and quantities of volcanic ash that can bury entire cities (remember the sad fate of Pompeii), the subterranean disturbances often take the form of vigorous oscillations of the crust felt all over the world. We learn from history that the cities of Lisbon and Messina were shaken into fragments by violent earthquakes, and Hollywood movies remind us vividly of the tragedy of San Francisco. During the past few years the newspapers have carried reports of major earth-

quake catastrophes in Chile, Turkey, and Rumania, while the name of
Japan is associated with an almost continuous sequence of quakes.
Remembering that all these, and a number of other major catastrophes
of the same kind, occurred during a period of time that is only a wink
compared with the entire life span of our planet, we become aware that
the crust of the Earth is actually very far from being the "safe solid
ground" it seems at first sight.

*The primary cause of all these tectonic phenomena, as they are called
in geology, lies in the steady cooling and shrinking of our globe.*

Comparison and Contrast

Comparison and contrast present more problems of organization than
the patterns discussed earlier. (Comparison emphasizes similarities;
contrast emphasizes differences.) First, obviously, the two things to
be compared must be comparable. On the face of it, a comparison of
the climates of Spitzbergen and Leopoldville would seem to have
little point. The differences are too obvious, and the writer could
arouse interest only by finding striking and unexpected similarities in
the midst of so much difference. Probably the most illuminating
comparisons are between things that seem very much alike, but, on
examination, reveal significant differences; or between things which
seem very different but turn out to have important similarities.

There are two basic patterns for organizing comparisons. If you
were going to compare the theater in New York and London, you
could write a sketch of New York theater, then a sketch of London
theater, and conclude with a section pointing out the similarities and
differences revealed by the two descriptions. An outline for a paper
so organized would look something like this:

    I. New York theater
       A. Number of plays produced
       B. Price and availability of seats
       C. Quality of the plays produced
          1. musicals
          2. "legitimate" plays
          3. classic drama
       D. Acting and production
    II. London theater
       A. Number of plays produced
       B. Price and availability of seats
       C. Quality of plays produced
          1. musicals

      2. "legitimate" plays
      3. classic drama
   D. Acting and production
III. Explicit comparison and conclusion

In this method of organization, each point in the first description has a parallel point in the second, and the sequence of topics is the same in both. This method works well in a comparatively short essay, less well in long ones. In an essay of more than ten pages or so, the third section would involve a good deal of wasteful back-tracking to remind the reader of what had already been said. The advantage of this pattern is that the writer can provide a complete picture of A and then a complete picture of B, thus giving the reader a more vivid sense of the two entities than in this pattern:

    I. Number of plays produced
      A. New York
      B. London
   II. Price and availability of seats
      A. New York
      B. London
 III. Quality of the plays produced
      A. Musicals
         1. New York
         2. London
      B. "Legitimate" plays
         1. New York
         2. London
      C. Classic drama
         1. New York
         2. London
 IV. Acting and production
         1. New York
         2. London
  V. Concluding evaluation

The advantage of this second pattern is that the comparison is explicitly made, point by point, as the writer goes along, and there is no need to go back over earlier ground. The disadvantage is that switching back and forth from London to New York may be somewhat dizzying and may destroy the unity of the impression given of the two theaters.

Sometimes the point-by-point comparison of two things is thought to be equivalent to having a point to make. But unmotivated comparisons are futile, and the writer must know what his main interest is—what he wants to accomplish by drawing the comparison. If the writer were primarily interested in revealing the deficiencies of the Broadway theater by contrasting it with the West End theater of London, he would put American theater in the foreground and bring in the London theater only to illuminate American theater. Simply choosing an organizational pattern for a comparison does not settle the problems of organization: a thesis still has to govern the movement of ideas.

Here are two examples of effective comparison. In the first, Lewis Mumford is comparing two kinds of city planners; in the second, J. F. Powers is comparing the contiguous cities of Minneapolis and St. Paul:

One of the things that have bedeviled city planning and housing in New York is the people who are concerned with these arts. They seem to know no middle ground between congestion and sprawl. Working within the city, they usually accept the fact that it is crowded and cluttered, and they think they have accomplished all that can be expected if they leave a little space between their buildings, and plant a little patch of park or asphalt a little strip of playground, without fundamentally alleviating the congestion and the brutal lack of intimacy in the architecture. Working in Westchester or Long Island, they often pretend that each house in a project is a mansion on a big estate, a veritable annex of Arcadia, though the houses may be so close together that you can't look out a side window without seeing your neighbor brush his teeth or quarrel with his wife. In general, the field has been divided between the conscious and unconscious disciples of Le Corbusier, who believes that even a village should be a skyscraper on stilts, and the disciples of Frank Lloyd Wright, who believes that cities should be abolished and that everyone should have at least an acre of land to live on. Neither school is producing the sort of city we all seem to have forgotten, the city in which it is a pleasure and a convenience to live.

Both cities are doomed by climate and circumstance not to realize the bright promise of their beginnings. St. Paul lives in retirement and grows old gracefully. Minneapolis will very likely collapse all at once like a noisy salesman from a heart attack. Doubtless St. Paul, the smaller twin (now), is more conscious of the war between the cities, having lost.

Minneapolis can assume a galling indifference to the struggle and get away with it, but the old meanness still crops out. On a street car in Minneapolis recently, I heard a passenger say as a colored woman rose to get off: "Look at that poor girl coming back from St. Paul," a reference to St. Paul's alleged dinginess and still no tribute to her industry.

However, we find ways to get back. At Lexington Park, home of the
St. Paul baseball club, a good thing to say when a Minneapolis Miller
flubs the ball a few feet is: "That woulda been a home run at Nicollet,"
a dig at Minneapolis-cracker-box ball park. (Alas, they are building a new
one that will be bigger than ours!) When I first came to St. Paul I heard
the audience at a neighborhood theater boo when a selected short of the
Minneapolis Aquatennial flashed on the screen. (I was puzzled then,
but now I boo with them: I just can't get enough of this heady chau-
vinism.)

Definition

Often a paragraph, and sometimes an essay or a whole book, is a kind
of extended definition (see pp. 142–48); the central concern is to
explain the meaning of a key term, and in very formal prose writers
usually begin by stating the definition abstractly and then filling in
with more concrete material and secondary terms that are components
of the main definition. Here is Stuart Hampshire defining what
Spinoza means by the "power of perfection of any finite thing":

A finite mode, such as a human being, has a greater power and perfection in so far as its successive states or modifications are less the effects of
external causes and are more the effects of preceding changes within itself.
Thus a human being, conceived as a finite mode of thought, has greater
power or perfection in so far as the succession of ideas which constitute
his mind are linked together as causes to effects; he is active and not
passive, in so far as the succession of ideas is a logical one (for Spinoza
does not, and cannot, distinguish between the 'cause of an idea' and the
'logical ground' of an idea); he has less power or perfection as a thinking
being in so far as this autonomous process of thought is interrupted by
ideas which are the effects of external causes on him, and in so far as his
present ideas are not explicable as the logical consequences of previous
ideas in his mind. In an absolutely powerful and perfect thinking being,
there would simply be an infinite sequence of ideas each one of which
would be logically related to its predecessor. . . . Most human minds
consist of a comparatively random sequence of ideas, random, not in the
sense that they are not the effect of causes of some kind, but in the sense
that the causes are external to the sequence; the sequence is therefore
not in itself intelligible as a self-contained sequence. The power and
perfection of an individual mind is increased in proportion as it becomes
less passive and more active and self-contained in the production of ideas.

Stuart Hampshire's method of analyzing a highly abstract idea into
its components and then showing how these components work to-

gether is more highly patterned and demanding on the reader's attention than the mass of definitions, which rely on giving examples, and showing how something differs from other things similar to it. Thus George Orwell on "dying metaphors" shows how they differ from "live" and "dead" metaphors, and then exemplifies:

A newly invented metaphor assists thought by evoking a visual image, while on the other hand a metaphor that is technically "dead" (e.g., *iron resolution*) has in effect reverted to be an ordinary word and can generally be used without loss of vividness. But in between these two classes there is a huge dump of worn-out metaphors which have lost all evocative power and are merely used because they save people the trouble of inventing phrases for themselves. Examples are: *Ring the changes on, take up the cudgels for, toe the line, ride roughshod over, stand shoulder to shoulder with, play into the hands of, no axe to gind, grist to the mill, fishing in troubled waters, on the order of the day, Achilles' heel, swan song, hotbed.*

Analysis

Sometimes an author develops his thought by dividing his material into its component parts, a process analogous to definition, but with the emphasis on a subject rather than a word. Often this process begins with making a distinction between two aspects of a single subject. In this example, R. G. Collingwood is making a distinction between the "inside" and the "outside" of the past:

The historian, investigating any event in the past, makes a distinction between what may be called the outside and the inside of an event. By the outside of the event I mean everything belonging to it which can be described in terms of bodies and their movements: the passage of Caesar accompanied by certain men, across a river called the Rubicon at one date, or the spilling of his blood on the floor in the senate-house at another. By the inside of the event I mean that in it which can only be described in terms of thought: Caesar's defiance of Republican law, or the clash of constitutional policy between himself and his assassins. The historian is never concerned with either of these to the exclusion of the other. He is investigating not mere events (where by a mere event I mean one which has only an outside and no inside), but actions, and an action is the unity of the outside and inside of an event. He is interested in the crossing of the Rubicon only in its relation to Republican law, and in the spilling of Caesar's blood only in relation to a constitutional conflict. His work may begin by discovering the outside of an event, but it can never end there; he must always remember that the event was an action, and that his main task is to think himself into this action, to discern the thought of its agent.

Another common form of analysis is to divide the parts of a subject according to their origins, as Sumner Ives does in this review of a dictionary:

The entries in *Webster's Third New International Dictionary* are based on three major sources. One, which is used by every reputable lexicographer, is the *Oxford English Dictionary*, an historical record of the English language which occupies about four feet of shelf space. It was compiled from over four million quotations illustrating the use of English words since the language was first written. The second major source is earlier Merriam-Webster dictionaries, especially the *Second Edition*. The third and most important source is a file of about four and a half million quotations from recent and contemporary writing and speech, each one illustrating some use of some word. If the word is rare, the collection of citations will be small; but if it is a very common one, the collection of citations may be several inches thick.

Analogy

Analogy is useful particularly in defining something unfamiliar or abstract by comparing it with something more familiar. Arguments developed by analogy are shaky (see p. 271), and no one can expect to refute or prove through the use of analogy. But where the writer wishes primarily to explain rather than to argue, the kind of extended metaphor that we call analogy is a useful device for restating the complex in simple terms or comparing something mysterious and unknown with something more familiar:

In the internal combustion engine, such as a gasoline-powered automobile, power is produced by the expansion of hot gases in the piston chamber. These hot gases produced by the ignition of a gasoline-air mixture push against the piston forcing it down and thus turning the drive shaft of the engine. This power is then transmitted to the rear wheels of the car by means of gears. Comparing this power conversion with the atomic engine we note that the power produced is also heat but it cannot be used as in an internal combustion engine. The heat must be removed from the core of the nuclear reactor by means of some coolant which circulates through it; this liquid is heated and may then be passed through what is called a heat exchanger. In the latter, steam can be produced and this can be used to drive a turbine which in turn may generate electricity. [RALPH E. LAPP]

Illustrations

The effective use of illustrations is perhaps the most important single means of developing ideas. The cardinal rule, of course, is that the illustration must really illustrate the point the writer is making. A writer will sometimes fail to realize that his illustration is working against his point rather than for it:

> Blanco City is one of the most progressive little cities in America. In four out of the last six years our high school football team has carried off all the regional trophies, and our marching band and drum majorette corps have won wide acclaim. The Prune Festival in June draws visitors from all over to join in the fun when the whole town goes on a spree for three days, and our new pleasure craft marina is crowded with boats from all up and down the coast. Four new drive-in movies have sprung up in Blanco City in recent years. (The implication of these examples is that Blanco City is pleasure-mad, but hardly "progressive.")

An example or illustration should also be interesting in itself. No matter how relevant an example is, if it is colorless and dull it will do little to develop an idea. Further, an illustration should be pruned of all the circumstantial elements that do not bear on the issue at hand. Writers, like speakers, sometimes set out to tell an illustrative story, forget that its purpose is to underline a point, and introduce all sorts of irrelevant matter. In a fully developed example that runs on for some length, every important idea in the general statement should be represented by an equivalent in the narrative; that is one of the chief virtues of the famous example given by T. H. Huxley in his essay, "The Scientific Method":

> Probably there is not one here who has not in the course of the day had occasion to set in motion a complex train of reasoning, of the very same kind, though differing of course in degree, as that which a scientific man goes through in tracing the causes of natural phenomena.
>
> A very trivial circumstance will serve to exemplify this. Suppose you go into a fruiterer's shop, wanting an apple—you take up one, and on biting it, you find it is sour, you look at it, and see that it is hard and green. You take up another one and that too is hard, green, and sour. The shopman offers you a third; but, before biting it, you examine it, and find that it is hard and green, and you immediately say that you will not have it, as it must be sour, like those that you have already tried.
>
> Nothing can be more simple than that, you think; but if you will take the trouble to analyse and trace out into its logical elements what has

been done by the mind, you will be greatly surprised. In the first place you have performed the operation of induction. You found that, in two experiences, hardness and greenness in apples went together with sourness. It was so in the first case, and it was confirmed by the second. True, it is a very small basis, but still it is enough to find sourness in apples where you get hardness and greenness. You found upon that a general law that all hard and green apples are sour, and that, so far as it goes, is a perfect induction. Well, having got your natural law in this way, when you are offered another apple which you find is hard and green, you say, "All hard and green apples are sour; this apple is hard and green; therefore this apple is sour." That train of reasoning is what logicians call a syllogism, and has all its various parts and terms—its major premiss, its minor premiss, and its conclusion. And, by the help of further reasoning, which, if drawn out, would have to be exhibited in two or three other syllogisms, you arrive at your final determination, "I will not have that apple." So that, you see, you have, in the first place, established a law by induction, and upon that you have founded a deduction, and reasoned out the special particular case. Well now, suppose, having got your conclusion of the law, that at some time afterwards you are discussing the qualities of apples with a friend: you will say to him, "It is a very curious thing, but I find that all hard and green apples are sour!" Your friend says to you, "But how do you know that?" You at once reply, "Oh, because I have tried them over and over again, and have always found them to be so." Well, if we were talking science instead of common sense, we should call that an experimental verification. And, if still opposed, you go further, and say, "I have heard from the people in Somersetshire and Devonshire, where a large number of apples are grown, that they have observed the same thing. It is also found to be the case in Normandy, and in North America. In short, I find it to be the universal experience of mankind wherever attention has been directed to the subject." Whereupon, your friend, unless he is a very unreasonable man, agrees with you, and is convinced that you are quite right in the conclusion you have drawn.

Huxley recounts a commonplace, although fictitious, incident which illustrates each characteristic of scientific method that he is concerned with. He develops the narrative in some detail because he wants to show the correspondence between the thought processes of ordinary life and the thought processes of science. Such fully developed narratives used as illustrations are probably less common than brief citations of illustrations that support a point. Huxley is writing a fully worked out little parable to illustrate the workings of the scientific mind; in the following example J. S. Mill masses brief illustrative references to refute an argument:

The dictum that truth always triumphs over persecution is one of those pleasant falsehoods which men repeat after one another till they pass into commonplaces, but which all experience refutes. History teems with instances of truth put down by persecution. If not suppressed for ever, it may be thrown back for centuries. To speak only of religious opinions: the Reformation broke out at least twenty times before Luther, and was put down. Arnold of Brescia was put down. Fra Dolcino was put down. Savonarola was put down. The Albigeois were put down. The Vaudois were put down. The Lollards were put down. The Hussites were put down. Even after the era of Luther, wherever persecution was persisted in, it was successful. In Spain, Italy, Flanders, the Austrian empire, Protestantism was rooted out; and, most likely, would have been so in England, had Queen Mary lived, or Queen Elizabeth died. Persecution has always succeeded, save where the heretics were too strong a party to be effectually persecuted. No reasonable person can doubt that Christianity might have been extirpated in the Roman Empire. It spread, and became predominant, because the persecutions were only occasional, lasting but a short time, and separated by long intervals of almost undisturbed propagandism. It is a piece of idle sentimentality that truth, merely as truth, has any inherent power denied to error, of prevailing against the dungeon and the stake.

Mill's historical illustrations involve only mentioning instances, with no development or description. His purpose calls for a mass of evidence, not for any fully developed account of it: Huxley's purpose calls for a single incident fully developed. The degree to which an illustration is developed, filled out, is determined by the author's overall plan, and by the kind of illustration he is using.

Mill's illustrations are historical facts; Huxley's a fictitious narrative. The different ways the two kinds are treated suggests some of the differences in presenting real and imaginary illustrations. In presenting real illustrations, the writer must, of course, stick to the facts, eliminate parts of the narrative that have no bearing, and place clear emphasis on the correspondence of illustration and generalization. In dealing with factual examples or illustrations, the writer is free to choose extreme instances or typical ones, as best suits his purpose. William James, for example, in his *Varieties of Religious Experience* chose almost all his wealth of illustrative material from the most extreme and dramatic forms of religious experience—sudden conversion, mystical visions, astonishing feats of asceticism—because he believed that such extreme instances brought into clearer relief the underlying nature of religious experience. In dealing with fictitious examples, the writer must be more cautious; he cannot freely invent unlikely examples. Facts do not have to be probable, but fictions do, if they are to be convincing. Notice how closely J. K. Galbraith keeps to probability in these hypothetical illustrations:

The opportunity for product differentiation—for associating monopoly power with the brand of personality of a particular seller—is almost uniquely the result of opulence. A hungry man could never be persuaded that bread that is softened, sliced, wrapped and enriched is worth more than a cheaper and larger loaf that will fill his stomach. A southern cropper will not, as a result of advertising, develop a preference for one brand of cooked, spiced and canned ham over another. He will buy plain sidemeat. No one would advertise the sound-effects of processed breakfast foods striking the milk to Scottish crofters who have only the resources to buy oatmeal. In such communities all the commercial advantages lie with the producers of plain bread, sidemeat and oatmeal.

19

DESCRIPTION

Taken in the widest sense, the term *description* covers the bulk of all expository writing: a definition is a description of an idea, a comparison a description of similarities. More narrowly, description is writing that gives a picture to the senses and imagination. It differs from narrative in that it does not deal primarily with action: it is still rather than moving. It differs from argument in being directed less to the understanding or the logical faculty than to the eye and the sensibility. Pure description is uncommon in expository writing, usually being intermingled with narrative and argument, providing a setting for action or visual images for ideas.

Two types of description come up most frequently in exposition: one is the picture of some physical object in the external world—a building, a mountain, a meadow, a machine. The problem is to render the way a thing *looks*, and therefore the writer must pick out its salient visual aspects and render them in some kind of order. This order is in large part determined by the point of view—by the angle of vision from which the writer sees his picture. Here is G. M. Trevelyan taking a bird's eye view of prehistoric Britain, as if he were looking down upon it from far above:

For many centuries after Britain became an island the untamed forest was king. Its moist and mossy floor was hidden from heaven's eye by a close-drawn curtain woven of innumerable tree-tops, which shivered in the breezes of summer dawn and broke into wild music of millions upon millions of wakening birds; the concert was prolonged from bough to bough with scarcely a break for hundreds of miles over hill and plain and mountain, unheard by man save where, at rarest intervals, a troop of skin-clad hunters, stone-axes in hand, moved furtively over the ground beneath, ignorant that they lived upon an island, not dreaming that there could be other parts of the world besides this damp green woodland with its meres and marshes, wherein they hunted, a terror to its four-footed inhabitants and themselves afraid.

Then he takes a sweeping circular view of the island:

A glance at any physical map will show how Britain has always thrust out towards the continent of Europe a low coast with an undulating plain behind, easy of access through many havens and navigable rivers. It was only westward and northward, against the Atlantic, that the island presented a mountainous and iron-bound coast—though even there the mouths of Severn, Dee, Mersey, Clyde and other lesser inlets held the makings of future history. But, from the earliest ages the flat south and east coastlines with the plains and low ridges behind them presented, so long as they were unguarded by a fleet, a standing temptation to the migratory tribes, pirates, plunderers and traders roaming along the continental shores.

The reverse of this all-encompassing view from a great distance, designed to give general outlines, is the microscopic view, which has a very narrow angle of vision, as close as the eye can get to the object:

The lens takes soundings for us in the depths of optical dimensions. There is no shock, for the young mind with a bent for science, like the first look through a microscope. I am not likely to forget the moment when I saw the green world of the algae come alive—delicate twisted bands of color in the glassy cell walls, diatoms like bits of carven glass, desmids like a trembling green lace, the hexagonal meshes of the water-net like the work of bobbins, and *Oscillatoria,* that plant that swims with a slow eel-like motion. Under the lens I witnessed life's crucial event, when I saw the whip tailed male cells escape from the sack of a sea kelp and assault the great, inert egg cell, like meteors raining upon a ponderous planet. Under that purposeful attack the planet cell began to roll with a great, a gentle, but an irresistible momentum, until one dart, predestined, broke through the surface tensions, dropped to the nuclear core like a solid thing descending through a gas, and then the conquered planet ceased its rolling and the rejected meteors dropped away. Life had begun again. [DONALD CULROSS PEATTIE]

Most description, of course, is between these extremes; its angle of vision is that of a normal human sight. The steps in description, then, usually correspond to the way something is actually seen in reality. Thus a writer may begin a description by giving a general impression or outline of what is before him and then filling in with successively finer details:

The Guggenheim Museum is a formidable, ponderous, closed-in concrete structure of almost indescribable individuality; the main element, the art gallery, might be called an inverted ziggurat that tapers toward the bottom—not the Mesopotamian kind, which stood on a square base, but Brueghel's round version in his "Tower of Babel." Functionally, this museum, which occupies a whole block front on Fifth Avenue, from Eighty-eighth to Eighty-ninth Street, divides into two parts—at the south end a low, telescoped tower (the ziggurat) crowned by a wired-glass dome visible solely from the air, and at the north end an attached administration building only half its height, a combination of rectangular and circular forms, with portholes for windows, opening on viewless balconies with solid parapets. The ground floor of the tower is recessed under the overhanging second floor to create a deep shadow, so that the tower appears to be set on a strong horizontal base formed by the continuous concrete band of the second-floor wall, which seems, because of the shadow, to float in space. [LEWIS MUMFORD]

The writer may describe literally how he himself sees something, combining a picture of the object with an account of his own reactions. In a famous passage from her *Journals* Dorothy Wordsworth moves closer and closer to the objects of description, showing how they change shape and appearance as the viewer approaches, and how the whole experience grows in beauty and unity:

When we were in the woods beyond Gowbarrow Park we saw a few daffodils close to the waterside. We fancied that the lake had floated the seeds ashore, and that the little colony had so sprung up. But as we went along there were more and yet more; and at last, under the boughs of the trees, we saw that there was a long belt of them along the shore, about the breadth of a country turnpike road. I never saw daffodils so beautiful. They grew among the mossy stones and about them; some rested their heads upon these stones as on a pillow for weariness; and the rest tossed and reeled and danced, and seemed as if they verily laughed with the wind, that blew upon them over the lake; they looked so gay, ever glancing, ever changing. The wind blew directly over the lake to them. There was here and there a little knot, and a few stragglers a few yards higher up, but they were so few as not to disturb the simplicity, unity, and life of that one busy highway.

A deliberate alteration of this normal sequence of observation can be useful in guiding the reader's perception to a particular point. Usually when we look at a painting, we see first the central figure, from which the eye moves out to the edges of the painting or to the background. Erwin Panofsky reverses the sequence in this description of a painting by Piero di Cosimo in order to use the central figure as the climax of his paragraph:

The scene is laid in a flowery meadow. The stretch of water appearing in the left background is merely a "landscape-motif" quite unrelated to the main incident. The six maidens show no amorous excitement whatever. They seem to have been suddenly interrupted in the peaceful occupation of gathering flowers and walking with their little dog; so sudden is the interruption that the two on the right have dropped the flowers they were carrying in their billowing draperies. Of these six maidens, the one on the left halts her step with a gesture of surprise, the one on the right looks rather amused in spite of the loss of her flowers, her neighbor points to the boy with an expression of supercilious pity. Finally, the central figure with motherly protectiveness helps the youth to his feet.

When a writer wishes to describe a typical rather than an individual object, he must select the salient characteristics that all members of the group share and create a generalized rather than a particularized picture. Usually, his description will make a less vivid pictorial impression than a description of an individual object, but it may have the virtue of suggestiveness. William G. Carleton fits his generalized description into the expository framework of question, definition, multiplied illustrations, and summarizing generalization:

Now, what is a bughouse square? A bughouse square is a public street, intersection or mall or park in a large city where gregarious, imaginative, exhibitionistic, and auto-compulsive "ism" peddlers, agitators, soapboxers, folk evangelists, teachers, showmen, faddists, cultists, cranks, crackpots, dreamers, and self-proclaimed messiahs congregate to impress one another and to display their wares. These performers attract a large number of disciples, camp followers, hecklers, "wise-guys," honest inquirers, and humble seekers. There is always present a large number of the skeptical and the disputatious. And there is invariably a sprinkling of unemployed, hobos, punks, pimps, faggots, fey proletariat, strumpets, beatniks, and the more robustious and less fastidious of the Bohemians. In short, a really first-class bughouse square is a bit of skid row, carnival, revival, poor man's town hall, and people's university rolled into one.

At the other extreme from this expository framework, James Agee sets about his generalized description of an ordinary evening in Knoxville, Tennessee, in the summer of 1915 in the manner of an impressionist painter, first suffusing his picture with evening lights and then sketching in the human figures in their customary attitudes:

Supper was at six and was over by half past. There was still daylight, shining softly and with a tarnish, like the lining of a shell; and the carbon lamps lifted at the corners were on in the light, and locusts were started, and fireflies were out, and a few frogs were flopping in the dewy grass, by the time the fathers and the children came out. The children ran out first hell bent and yelling those names by which they were known; then the fathers sank out leisurely in crossed suspenders, their collars removed and their necks looking tall and shy. The mothers stayed back in the kitchen washing and drying, putting things away, recrossing their traceless footsteps like the lifetime journeys of bees, measuring out the dry cocoa for breakfast. When they came out they had taken off their aprons and their skirts were dampened and they sat in rockers on their porches quietly.

The other most common kind of descriptive passage that appears in expository writing is the character sketch. To succeed, a character sketch, either of an individual or a type, must give a unity of impression. It must focus its detail on leading characteristics. In the following passage F. W. Dupee weaves together quoted phrases, summarized narrative, a list of attitudes and characteristic activities around the central ideas—the "spontaneity" and innocence of Minny Temple and the pathos of her early death:

Like all these Anglo-Saxon girls she was thought admirable because she was a rare thing in the modern world—a case of the free spirit, an incarnation of gratuitous impulse; and, as we shall see, she was doomed. "With all that ethereal brightness of presence that was peculiarly her own," Minny dominated the little circle without ever trying or caring. Spontaneity was so much her way that, unlike the Jameses, she couldn't communicate very well in writing. The animation of her surviving letters is charming because so frankly standard. "Sich is life," she sighs, and "My dearest Harry what a charming tale is Gabrielle de Bergerac! *Just* as pretty as ever it can be." A great reader, especially of George Eliot, she had opinions without being opinionated. *The Spanish Gypsy* was good but not so good as *The Mill on the Floss*. She wouldn't admit that she was really disappointed by Phillips Brooks, whom she had travelled to Philadelphia to hear preach, and yet "he doesn't, or didn't, touch the real difficulties at all." She studied German, attended the opera in New York, burned to visit Europe, cultivated intense friendships with other girls, preferred to dance at balls with experienced older men, and judged the boys of her own age candidly if quite cheerfully. And she died young— that was what finally confirmed her sacredness for Henry James—died at 24 of a lingering tubercular illness which kept her from ever getting to Europe and made her last years a nightmare of attempted cures, abandoned journeys, sudden collapses, and unpredictable hemorrhages. "Death, at the last, was dreadful to her," James was to write, "who would have given anything to live."

20

NARRATION

Narration is the ancient and subtle art of story-telling. It is only distinguishable from description insofar as one thinks of description as presenting a static picture and narrative as an account of events, whether a single incident or a long sequence of actions; more often than not, description and narrative are closely interwoven. History and biography are predominantly narration: their purpose is to give information about events, to tell what has happened in the life of a person or nation. Since all the available information can only very rarely be reported, the historian must exercise considerable selectivity: he must choose which events to recount fully, which merely to mention, which to ignore altogether. What distinguishes history from chronicle, exposition from cataloguing, is purposeful selection and organization of the events to be described. The historian does not report incidents simply because they are interesting or titillating in themselves but because they develop and support his view of the process described. Narration is at the service of ideas.

In the following brief excerpt from Carl Sandburg's biography of Lincoln, the author has chosen, among many possibilities, those events that focus on and lead up to Lincoln's mute anguish and loneliness:

To the homes of the settlers came chills and fever of malaria. Lincoln had been down, and up, and down again with aching bones, taking large spoons of Peruvian bark, boneset tea, jalap, and calomel. One and another of his friends had died; for some, he had helped nail together the burial boxes.

Ann Rutledge lay fever-burned. Days passed; help arrived and was helpless. Moans came from her for the one man of her thoughts. They sent for him. He rode out from New Salem to the Sand Ridge farm. They let him in; they left the two together and alone a last hour in the log house, with slants of light on her face from an open clapboard door. It was two days later that death came.

There was what they called a funeral, a decent burial of the body in the Concord burying ground seven miles away. And Lincoln sat for hours with no words for those who asked to speak to him. They went away from him knowing he would be alone whether they stayed or went away.

Sandburg does not have to tell us what the point of the narration is; it is clearly implied by his selection of events.

To move on to more strictly expository writing, let us consider a passage of narrative from a study of what the author calls "the sweet science" of boxing:

> Both came out for the third very gay, as Egan would have said, Marciano had been hit and cut, so he felt acclimated, and Moore was so mad at himself for not having knocked Marciano out that he almost displayed animosity toward him. He may have thought that perhaps he had not hit Marciano just right; the true artist is always prone to self-reproach. He would try again. A minute's attention from his squires had raised his spirits and slaked down his hair. At this point, Marciano set about him. He waddled in, hurling his fists with a sublime disregard of probabilities, content to hit an elbow, a biceps, a shoulder, the top of a head—the last supposed to be the least profitable target in the business, since, as every beginner learns, "the head is the hardest part of the human body," and a boxer will only break his hands on it. Many boxers make systematic presentation of the cranium part of their defensive scheme. The crowd, basically anti-intellectual, screamed encouragement. There was Moore, riding punches, picking them off, slipping them, rolling with them, ducking them, coming gracefully out of his defensive efforts with sharp, patterned blows—and just about holding this parody even on points. His face, emerging an instant from under the storm of arms—his own and Rocky's—looked like that of a swimming walrus. When the round ended, I could see that he was thinking deeply. Marciano came back to his corner at a kind of suppressed dogtrot. He didn't have a worry in the world. [A. J. LIEBLING]

All the details here are highly selective and purposive; they are not presented for their own sake. The passage is dramatic, but it is not meant to picture the mere spectacle of the prize fight. Had that been Liebling's purpose, he would have shown us much more of the crowd, the seconds, the lighting and noise of the auditorium, etc. Here he confines himself to a very satisfying pun on the word "anti-intellectual" (exactly relevant to his purpose) and to the word "screams" to suggest the nature of the audience. His subject is, rather, boxing itself. The actions and attitudes of the boxers in this account of a single round are presented to illustrate the confrontation of skill and brute strength in modern professional boxing.

The great virtue of narration, evident in both the preceding quotations, is its vividness, its dramatic immediacy. We can see what is
happening; we can feel as well as conceptualize events. Sandburg
might have reported simply, "Lincoln was greatly distressed by the
death of Ann Rutledge"; the difference of impact between the mere
statement and its dramatic realization attests to the rhetorical value
of narration. But its value rests entirely on its close relevance to the
idea or mood it is meant to embody. Gratuitously introduced anecdotes, however delightful or moving or intriguing in themselves,
undermine the writer's purpose.

Here are three examples of the effective use of anecdote to give a
sense of reality and immediacy to ideas. In the first, much of what
the writer wants to say of the mind and spirit of George Eliot is
revealed in her dying words:

> Hysteria, the effect of the exorbitant straining of their wills, the Vic-
> torians did, alas, too often achieve. George Eliot somehow escapes it.
> She is too level-headed. One pictures her, in life, moralising instead of
> making a scene. There is no hysteria in *Middlemarch;* perhaps there are
> no depths because there is so much determination. But there is a humane
> breadth and resolution in this novel which offers neither hope nor despair
> to mankind but simply the necessity of fashioning a moral life. George
> Eliot's last words on her deathbed might, one irreverently feels, be placed
> on the title-page of her collected works: "Tell them," she is reported to
> have said, "the pain is on the left side." Informative to the last and
> knowing better than the doctor, the self-made positivist dies. [v. s.
> PRITCHETT]

An anecdote about the great philosopher Immanuel Kant vividly
introduces a discussion of humanism from an historical point of view:

> Nine days before his death Immanual Kant was visited by his physician.
> Old, ill and nearly blind, he rose from his chair and stood trembling
> with weakness and muttering unintelligible words. Finally his faithful
> companion realized that he would not sit down again until the visitor
> had taken a seat. This he did, and Kant then permitted himself to be
> helped to his chair and, having regained some of his strength, said *"Das
> Gefühl für Humanität hat mich noch nicht verlassen"*—"The sense of
> humanity has not left me." The two men were moved almost to tears.
> For, though the word *Humanität* had come, in the eighteenth century,
> to mean little more than politeness or civility, it had, for Kant, a much
> deeper significance, which the circumstances of the moment served to
> emphasize man's proud and tragic consciousness of self-approved and
> self-imposed principles, contrasting with his utter subjection to illness,
> decay, and all that is implied in the word "mortality." [ERWIN PANOFSKY]

Sigmund Freud tells a simple story to show how unconscious motives influence the little accidents and slips of everyday life:

> My inkstand is made out of a flat piece of Untersberg marble which is hollowed out to receive the glass inkpot; and the inkpot has a cover with a knob made of the same stone. Behind this inkstand there is a ring of bronze statuettes and terra cotta figures. I sat down at the desk to write, and then moved the hand that was holding the pen-holder forward in a remarkably clumsy way, sweeping on the floor the inkpot cover which was lying on the desk at the time.
>
> The explanation was not hard to find. Some hours before, my sister had been in the room to inspect some new acquistions. She admired them very much, and then remarked: "Your writing table looks really attractive now; only the inkstand doesn't match. You must get a nicer one." I went out with my sister and did not return for some hours. But when I did I carried out, so it seems, the execution of the condemned inkstand.

All these examples of anecdotal narrative succeed because they bring home to the reader the points the writers are making. All are exactly relevant and economically presented.

The problem of selection looms particularly large when it is necessary to condense a series of events into brief compass. And necessary it very often is, especially in historical writing and in any kind of commentary on events which must be summarized before the commentary can be made. The passage quoted above from Sandburg is obviously a very condensed account; he makes no attempt at a moment-by-moment narration, but combines very general statements ("Days passed") with a few vivid, concrete details that seem most relevant and telling for his purpose. That is the way summarized narration is prevented from becoming a dull abstract or précis—by giving enough concrete detail to keep the account alive. It is not, then, the simple mechanical process it is sometimes thought to be; it requires more than the bare outline of events; it should give the reader some feeling for its subject as well as an abstract understanding. Edmund Wilson is one of the most masterful summarizers now writing in English. Here he is at the difficult task of reducing the events of the last section of James Joyce's *Ulysses* to the form of summarized narrative:

> [Bloom] has gotten into the habit in the past of cooking breakfast for Molly in the morning and bringing it to her in bed—it is the first thing we have seen him doing at the beginning of the day; but tonight,

before he goes to sleep, he gives her to understand that he expects her to get breakfast next morning and to bring it up to him. This amazes and disconcerts Mrs. Bloom, and the rest of the book is the record of her meditations as she lies awake thinking over Bloom's homecoming. She has been mystified by his recent behavior, and her attitude toward him now is at first a mixture of jealousy and resentment. She congratulates herself upon the fact that, if Bloom neglects her nowadays, her needs are ably supplied by Blazes Boylan. But as she begins to ruminate on the possibility of Stephen Dedalus's coming to live with them, the idea of Blazes Boylan's coarseness becomes intolerable to her: the thought of Stephen has made her fastidious, and, rapidly becoming very tender about him, she prefigures a relation between them of an ambiguous but intimate character, half-amorous, half-maternal. Yet it is Bloom himself who has primarily been the cause of this revolution in Molly's mind: in telling her about Stephen, he has imposed upon her again his own values; in staying away from the house all day and coming back very late at night, and in asking for his breakfast in bed, he has reasserted his own will. And she goes back in her mind over her experience of Bloom—their courtship and married life. She remembers how, when she had promised to marry him, it had been his intelligence and sympathetic nature, that touch of imagination which distinguished him from other men, which had influenced her in his favor—"because he understood or felt what a woman is and I knew I could always get around him"; and on the day when he had first kissed her, he had called her "a flower on the mountain." It is in the mind of his Penelope that this Ulysses has slain the suitors who have been disputing his place.

A final type of narration, with its own special problems, is that of typical or generalized action. It very often has as its chief actor some abstract personage such as "the consumer," "the American college girl," "the Soviet diplomat," or "the comedian." These are type figures which do not correspond to real people, but represent a cluster of traits assumed to be characteristic of most members of a group. Narratives about them relate typical actions, not individual ones. These "model" persons and the generalized narratives about them are an indispensable part of modern writing in sociology, politics, economics, history, and even literary study, where constant reference is made to "the critic," "the reader," "the thinker," and so on. As long as the writer and reader keep clearly in mind the difference between these models and concrete reality, they are an important convenience of thought; if they are confused with concrete actuality, they at once become worse than useless. In some instances, the "model" and the concrete actuality are obviously very close together:

The driver of the old Model T was a man enthroned. The car, with top up, stood seven feet high. The driver sat on top of the gas tank, brooding it with his body. When he wanted gasoline, he alighted along with everything else in the front seat; the seat was pulled off, the metal cap unscrewed, and a wooden stick thrust down to sound the liquid in the well. There were always a couple of these sounding sticks kicking around in the ratty subcushion regions of a flivver. Refuelling was more of a social function then, because the driver had to unbend, whether he wanted to or not. Directly in front of the driver was the windshield—high, uncompromisingly erect. Nobody talked about air resistance, and the four cylinders pushed the car through the atmosphere with a simple disregard of physical law. [LEE STROUT WHITE]

In the following passage, the type-figures—the architects, office workers, workingmen—are serviceable representations of an average cluster of characteristics, but both reader and writer are aware that there are many architects, workingmen and typists who could not be made to fit the model:

While this architect may be regarded by his family and neighbors as a "professional man," he himself is all too sharply aware that he is doing nothing more than the most dull and deadening draftsman's work in a vault ranked with his similars, who know him to be nothing more than they are—all-but-anonymous units in the firm's labor force. In short, it is painful for him to be confronted with the evidence that the difference between him and the factory worker may be only one of degree. It is a pun that can hurt. . . . .

The hidden bonds of boredom and frustration that link the lives—if they only knew it—of the professional man and the workingman are close to the surface in the working pattern of the burgeoning millions of clericals and technicians, which is so similar to that of the numerically declining working-class. The typist in the clattering cavern of a typical insurance office, indistinguishable from her sisters who tap the machines at their serried desks, the file clerk punching her Hollerith cards under the fluorescents in any of a dozen labyrinthine bureaucracies, the stock clerk running off labels in the automated shipping department of a rationalized department store—all these may have their half-attentive ears filled all day with Strauss waltzes piped in by solicitous employers, their mouths filled with coffee piped in twice a day at the insistence of their union or their personnel supervisors. But what are their minds filled with? Year by year, day by day, what they do becomes increasingly routinized in the interest of production and efficiency, just as does the labor of the assembly-line worker. [HARVEY SWADOS]

21
ARGUMENTATION

ARGUMENTATIVE writing is a special kind of exposition because of the relationship it assumes between the writer and the reader. Most expository writing has some argumentative elements, but assumes that the reader and writer are more or less in accord—that the reader, at least for the time being, is willing to suspend disbelief and adopt the writer's point of view. The primary purpose of exposition is to explain, to make something clear to a reader. Argumentative writing is more embattled, assuming an audience either undecided or hostile to the writer's views. An argumentative writer is primarily engaged in refuting opposing views and establishing his own, and his polemical stance usually carries with it temptations to emotional and intellectual excess.

He must guard against an intemperate, hectoring tone. Some writers assume an attitude of arrogant superiority and belittle their opponents' intelligence, morals, and competence to deal with the subject, behaving as if they were administering a verbal spanking instead of engaging in controversy. Extravagant abuse may amuse those who agree with the writer and infuriate those who oppose him, but it changes no one's mind. Invective in the hands of a literary master may be aesthetically brilliant, but it carries little weight in the serious evaluation of ideas.

The writer must also guard against the temptation to misrepresent opposing ideas by stating them in such a way that they sound weak or ridiculous. Before a serious audience, falsifying an opponent's position only brings contempt on the writer's own head. Full and fair statement of the opposition views is the only legitimate basis for a systematic criticism of their weaknesses. However, an opponent's views can be overthrown if it can be shown that inadmissible consequences follow from them. This means of argument, known as *reductio ad absurdum*, consists of showing that if a statement is pushed to its logical conclusion, it leads to results that even the author of the statement would be unwilling to grant. In the following quotation, Jason Epstein pushes an argument for abolition of the minimum wage into absurdity:

Roger Freeman, of the Hoover Institution, on the other hand, allows his disillusionment to carry him to extremes, such as his argument that if the minimum wage laws were revoked we would have less unemployment. Indeed, we might have none. But on this logic, we might also have slavery.

In refuting opposing views, the author must be aware of what part of the opponent's argument he is attacking, and what can be accomplished by the attack. If he shows that there is something invalid in the process of reasoning, he is revealing the logical flaws in a structure of argument, but reasoning may be invalid and the conclusion still be correct. He has not shown that the conclusion itself is false, but that it rests on a false logical structure. This destroys the validity of the opponent's argument, that is, shows that his explanation is inadequate, but leaves open the possibility that he has reached the right place by the wrong route.

To refute the main propositions themselves, the writer must uncover genuine self-contradiction. If two statements contradict one another, only one can be true. If a writer says in one place, "The graduated income tax is unconstitutional" and in another "The graduated income tax is no doubt justified by the fundamental law of the land," one of the assertions *has* to be false. But genuine self-contradiction is rare. The assertion, "Man's freedom lies in his complete submission to the will of God" may look self-contradictory, but Christian theology explains freedom in such a way that the contradiction disappears.

The argumentative writer is often tempted to seize on incompatible statements and behave as if they were contradictory; that is, he finds two propositions that do not dovetail with one another and treats them as if they met in head-on opposition. Thus, if he finds the statement "Americans are the best-fed people in the world" alongside the statement "At least thirty-million Americans are suffering from malnutrition," he may conclude that he has come upon a contradiction. But of course he has not. One statement does not preclude the other: both may be true, or both may be false. If most of the people in the world are ill-fed, Americans may be the best-fed of all and still have among them millions who are ill-fed.

Most argument is less concerned with logical consistency than with the adequacy of the evidence on which a conclusion rests. In most cases, argument is concerned with the question of whether the "inductive leap" from individual instances to generalization is justi-fied. Even the statement "The sun comes up every morning" involves an inductive leap from millions of past observations to an assumption about the future, but few would care to argue the point, since people seldom argue about what is regarded either as certain or as com-pletely unknowable. But the inductive leap that takes place in the sphere of the possible or the probable is often the subject of debate. Adequate support for a generalization involves a fair sampling of the available instances, a demonstration that the instances are typical ones, and an explanation of negative instances. A rigid generalization of the All X is Y type can be overthrown by a single instance of an X which is not Y. But the more usual kind of generalization is quali-fied by such expressions as "usually" and "in most cases," and can survive a good many exceptions. It cannot, however, survive a demon-stration that its instances are not typical, or that they do not represent a fair sampling of the available evidence. Nor can it survive a demon-stration that an alternative generalization covers more instances more accurately. A generalization can be overthrown if it can be shown that it is based on inadequate evidence, that it is not in concord with its own evidence, or that it is less comprehensive than an alternative generalization.

Acknowledged facts offered as evidence are not subject to debate, but authorities offered in evidence are. The pronouncements of a great physicist about his subject must always carry weight, but his pronouncements about politics or society need not be regarded as authoritative. An account of a historical event by an eye-witness carries the authority of first-hand experience, but that authority can be overthrown if the account can be shown to be biased or in discord with a mass of other evidence. The moral authority of saints, prophets, philosophers, and great artists exists only for those who already vener-ate them. The citation of an authority who is truly authoritative in the eyes of both the writer and his readers gives useful support to argument, but is not a substitute for it. A writer who assumes that every word written by, say, Plato represents fundamental truth, and who casts all his arguments in the form "It must be true because Plato said so," is not likely to change anyone's opinions—he is simply confirming the belief of the faithful.

Both in refuting opposing views and defending his own, the writer needs to keep the logical structure of his argument in mind and to beware of the logical pitfalls known as fallacies.

Logic and Writing

Classical logic is a means of testing the validity of statements—of showing whether or not they are consistent with one another. It does not test the truth of assertions, but determines whether they are in valid logical sequence. Its chief instrument is the syllogism. For example, "All men are mortal; Socrates is a man; therefore Socrates is mortal" is a pattern of syllogistic reasoning. It has a *major premise* that makes an assertion about all the members of the class "men," a *minor premise* that asserts that "Socrates" is a member of the class 'men." The syllogism asserts that an individual is a member of a class, and then concludes that the individual has the characteristic that distinguishes the class. Thus,

> Major premise: All men are mortal.   All A is B.
> Minor premise: Socrates is a man.   C is A.
> Conclusion: Socrates is mortal.   C is B.

Each statement has two terms, linked by *is* or *are*; there are three terms, each used twice. The relationship can be represented by a diagram:

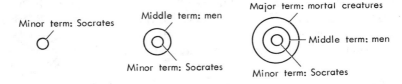

The smallest class (Socrates) is related to the largest class (mortals) through the middle-sized class (men).

Here are some of the commonest syllogistic patterns:

> All A is B.   All foods containing vitamins are nutritious foods.
> C is A.   Spinach is a food containing vitamins.
> C is B.   Spinach is a nutritious food.

> No A is B.   No cocker spaniel is a mongrel.
> C is A.   My dog is a cocker spaniel.
> C is not B.   My dog is not a mongrel.

All *A*'s are *B*'s.	All winners of Woodrow Wilson Fellowships are excellent students.
Some *C*'s are *A*'s.	Some members of the graduating class are winners of Woodrow Wilson Fellowships.
Some *C*'s are *B*'s.	Some members of the graduating class are excellent students.

Fully stated syllogisms seldom appear in normal prose; thus the substance of the three foregoing syllogisms might appear in this form:

Eat your spinach; it's full of vitamins.
My dog is *not* a mongrel! He's a cocker spaniel.
The graduating class must have some excellent students because four of them won Woodrow Wilson Fellowships this year.

Frequently in prose the major premise is taken for granted or only implied, and the minor premise and the conclusion may be presented in reverse order:

"As a strong advocate of civil rights (minor premise), Senator Doe will surely support the proposed legislation (conclusion)." (The major premise is unstated.)

Occasionally it is valuable to cast an argument into syllogistic form in order to make explicit its assumptions or to uncover a hidden flaw in the connection of one statement with another. If a writer senses that something is awry in a line of argument, a good way to test it is to find the conclusion and work backward toward the (perhaps unformulated) major premise. Suppose, for instance, that you have concluded that a certain neighborhood in your city should be torn down and rebuilt because most of its buildings are over a hundred years old. If you work backward from that conclusion to the assumption that buildings are bad simply because they are old, you may realize that the equation "old = bad" is a weak foundation for your argument; you may want to revise your line of argument to emphasize that the buildings are cramped, run-down, and rat-infested. Thus you have uncovered a false (or at least very shaky) assumption that needs to be changed.

In other cases, the premise may be correct but the conclusion false because of an invalid connection between the two. The following are two of the most common patterns of faulty reasoning:

All *A*'s are *B*. All socialists are opponents of laissez-faire economic policy.
All *C*'s are *B*. All communists are opponents of laissez-faire economic policy.
All *B*'s are *A*. All socialists are communists.

The flaw in the conclusion arises from the scrambling of the relations of the three terms. The only conclusion warranted by the premises can be represented in a diagram:

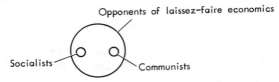

Opponents of laissez-faire economics

Socialists

Communists

There is no logical justification for taking the further step and concluding that the class "communist" overlaps with the class "socialist."

This invalid pattern of argument is also unfortunately widespread:

Some A's are B's.	Some politicians are corrupt.
All C's are A's.	All members of the City Council are politicians.
Some C's are B's.	Some members of the City Council are corrupt.

Fallacies

Fallacies are invalid forms of argument, and they are often so attractive, and apparently so natural to the human mind, that a writer must be constantly alert if he is to avoid them. A critical reader will almost certainly detect any fallacious argument, and besides rejecting it as unsound, may suspect the writer of being deliberately sophistical —that is, of arguing with a conscious intent to deceive. No one gets less attention or sympathy than an unmasked sophist.

In the following, the most common fallacies are defined and illustrated.

Taking the temporary to be permanent is the failure to consider the special circumstances of a particular period of time:

After the death of his wife, Mr. Smith had to spend a month in a sanitarium. His mental instability makes him unsuitable for a post on the Board of Directors,

or the failure to take the changeableness of things into sufficient account:

The popularity of straight, simple lines in women's clothes indicates a return to good sense and good taste in the American woman's attitude toward dress. (But next year's clothes may have flounces, ribbons, and bustles.)

Equivocation is an unacknowledged shifting of the sense in which a word is used during the course of an argument:

The *necessities* of life change with the times. Food, shelter, and clothing were sufficient for primitive man, but in the modern world education and rapid means of transportation and communication have become *necessities*. (Education, transportation, and communication are not necessities in the same sense that food, shelter, and clothing are.)

Ad hominem arguments attempt to discredit a view by casting aspersions on its source, ignoring the fact that statements must be judged on their own merits, not on the basis of who makes them. In the first example, there is an effort to discredit a view by saying that those who hold it do so for selfish reasons:

> Humanists always defend the study of the liberal arts. They have to. It's their livelihood.

In the following two examples, the implication is that no good ideas could possibly emerge from such disreputable sources:

> Let those who advocate the abolition of capital punishment remember that the autocratic police-state of Czarist Russia was the first to abolish capital punishment.

> Reform movements are always full of cranks, fanatics, disgruntled old maids, starry-eyed idealists, and hate-filled men who have failed in everything else.

Treating an abstraction as a real entity is a misuse of personification in which the idea personified is treated as if it had a life of its own independent of the facts on which it rests:

> If France disregards the dictates of her destiny and her historic mission as a bringer of light, she is lost.

> The more times the popular consciousness is made to buy a new car, the more moments of maximum pleasure the popular consciousness will enjoy, and the more money everyone will have circulating.

The *genetic fallacy* is the assumption that the present state of a thing reveals its origin, or that the origin of a thing is the key to its present state:

> Henry must have been a sickly child because as a man he is always weak and ailing.

> Since they are the descendants of the Spartans, the inhabitants of the Peloponnese must be a brave and hardy race.

Begging the question or arguing in a circle usually involves smuggling the conclusion of an argument into its initial assumptions, or treating the point at issue as if it had already been settled. In the following, Cardinal Newman points out the circularity of his opponents' arguments against miracles:

Unbelievers use the antecedent argument from the order of nature against our belief in miracles. Here, if they only mean that the fact of that system of laws, by which physical nature is governed, makes it antecedently improbable that an exception should occur in it, there is no objection to the argument; but if, as is not uncommon, they mean that the fact of an established order is absolutely fatal to the very notion of an exception, they are using a presumption as if it were a proof. They are saying, —What has happened 999 times one way cannot possibly happen the 1,000th time another way, *because* what has happened 999 times one way is likely to happen in the same way on the 1,000th. But unlikely things do happen sometimes. If, however, they mean that the existing order of nature constitutes a physical necessity, and that a law is an unalterable fact, this is to assume the very point in debate, and is much more than asserting its antecedent probability.

Arguing off the point is usually a maneuver to avoid confronting the central issue by focusing on secondary matters. During the agitation for women's suffrage, much of the debate centered on the "role of women," the ennobling influence of women on men, the sanctity of the home, and the impropriety of women's competing with men. A surprisingly small amount of the discussion was directed to the point of whether or not women had notably worse political judgment than men. In arguments about unequal treatment of minorities under the law, the main point—equity—is frequently ignored; instead, there are glowing accounts of the "progress of the Negro race" or assurances that "they are happier among themselves."

The *call for perfection* and the argument that *two wrongs make a right* are two sides of the same coin. The *call for perfection* assumes that because a proposal has serious drawbacks, it should be rejected. There is no effort to weigh advantages against disadvantages and then strike a balance. In both the following examples, the assumption is that there are no significant advantages to counter the disadvantages pointed out:

Urban renewal displaces thousands of people every year. Hundreds of small businessmen are forced out. Whole neighborhoods are disrupted or destroyed. We must call a halt to all current programs and declare a moratorium on building in our larger cities.

The study of foreign languages is very time-consuming, and even after years of study almost no students are able to speak the language as well as a native speaker. Students should not devote their time to a subject that takes up so much time and leads to such poor results.

The argument that *two wrongs make a right* usually takes a form like this: "Admittedly, X is bad, but no worse than Y or Z. Therefore X is not bad after all."

The United States certainly should not be too much blamed for its role in the Mexican War. Many nations have invaded their weaker neighbors with far less provocation.

Living conditions in the city prison are certainly no worse than they are in most of the city's slums.

Closely related to these two all-or-nothing modes of argument is the failure to recognize and state *differences of degree*. The assumption is that if two things are of the same kind, differences of degree between them make no difference:

Americans have become as cruel and debauched as the Romans of the late Empire. Our pornographic books and magazines, the frequency of divorce and adultery, our gladiatorial contests in football, our morbid interest in crime, all indicate a population as abandoned as the most debased Roman mob.

Football games are not quite equivalent to gladiatorial contests, and reading a murder mystery is not the same as enjoying the spectacle of public torture.

Analogy is useful and sometimes delightful in exposition, but it carries no weight in an argument. Most analogies can be picked to pieces by any determined opponent, or they can be cancelled out by the proposal of a counter-analogy, as in this passage from George Eliot:

Mr. Sterling concluded that Tom's brain, being peculiarly impervious to etymology and demonstration, was peculiarly in need of being ploughed and harrowed by these patent implements: it was his favorite metaphor, that the classics and geometry constituted that culture of the mind which prepared it for any subsequent crop. . . . It is astonishing what a different result one gets by changing the metaphor! Once call the brain an intellectual stomach, and one's ingenious conception of the classics and geometry as ploughs and harrows seems to settle nothing. But then it is open to some one else to follow great authorities, and call the mind a sheet of white paper or a mirror, in which case one's knowledge of the digestive process becomes quite irrelevant.

Post hoc, ergo propter hoc ("After that, therefore because of it") is the tendency to assume that when B follows A, then B is caused by A: a causal connection is inferred from a temporal sequence. But the mere fact that one event follows another in time is no guarantee of a causal relationship. If, in the mornings, a man always puts on his left shoe before putting on his right shoe, no one would want to say that putting on the left shoe is the *cause* of putting on the right shoe.

Even when there is good reason to assume a causal connection between events, there is a danger of fixing on a single cause at the expense of several cooperating causes. If a fuse blows out every time you plug in an electric heater, you are fairly safe in assuming that the overloading of the electrical system is caused by the heater. The overloading is the cause of the blowing of the fuse. But also, to give a full account of why the fuse blew, you would have to take into account the wiring of the building, the number of other appliances in use, and so on. If a man is drowned at sea, we can say that his death was caused by the storm, by the capsizing of his boat, by the loss of oxygen, by the fact that he was a poor swimmer. Most personal and historical happenings have so many aspects and so many antecedent circumstances that it is almost impossible to single out one cause and call it *the* cause of an event. Most things have a plurality of causes, and only in the laboratory, where all conditions can be controlled, is it possible to arrive at a full and precise account of all the causal factors that lead to a certain result.

The writer must be wary about assuming causal connections, and he must be willing to explore the alternative possibilities before he advances the theory that Cause A is the decisive cause in bringing about Result B.

22

FINISHING UP

THERE are as many ways to end an essay as to begin one, and among the best is stopping when you have come to the end of your material. Simply taking the paper out of the typewriter when you have had your say is often more effective than straining after some capping remark or overinsistent reinforcement of what has gone before. If a writer feels the need for some kind of formal conclusion, many devices effective in introductions are also effective in conclusions—a terse statement of the main point, an anecdote, an epigram, a final question. In addition, there are several special ways of ending that are illustrated below.

Conclusions

1. In formal essays that argue inductively from particularities to general statements, the final paragraph is a good place to enumerate the conclusions or results. Jacques Barzun states the results that follow from the practice of close reading:

Three things should follow. First, the student gains an idea of what *can* be done by applying one's mind and using others' ideas. He thus forms a standard for his own reading, based on what total comprehension might be. Second, he begins to discover the need for interpreting; the ways of testing a preference for one interpretation over another; and the desirability of checking doctrinaire inclinations in an uncertain world. Third, he comes to see that in the realm of mind as represented by great men, there is no such thing as separate, isolated "subjects." In Shakespeare's English are tags of Latin, allusions to medicine, elements of psychology, facts from history—and so on ad infinitum. Nor is this true of fiction alone. The great philosophers and scientists are—or were until recently—universal minds, not in the sense that they knew everything, but in the sense that they sought to unite all they knew into a mental vision of the universe.

A summary that briefly restates the main points may be useful if the argument is long or very complex. In a short essay, such recapitulation is usually superfluous, especially if the argument is a simple one. Inexperienced writers often summarize or enumerate results when there is no need to do so, but both methods of ending are useful if the writer bears in mind the needs of his reader and does not use them as mere mechanical tricks to round off discussion. The following summary is justified because it gives a comprehensive view of the mass of evidence presented in the body of the essay:

To sum up, we believe there are galaxies and clusters of galaxies that seem to be young because they evidently cannot last long in their present form, and because the natural forces acting in a rotating mass of gas always tend to produce order from disorder—symmetry from dis-symmetry. That young galaxies exist implies that galaxies may be forming even today. Yet although the steady-state cosmology predicts the continuous formation of galaxies, we still cannot go further and choose one cosmological model over another. [MARGARET AND GEOFFREY BURBIDGE]

2. Often in narrative—biography, history, and the personal essay —it is desirable to use the concluding section to tell the aftermath of the chain of events recounted in the body of the essay. George Orwell is telling what happened after he shot an elephant that had run amok:

Afterwards, of course, there were endless discussions about the shooting of the elephant. The owner was furious, but he was only an Indian and could do nothing. Besides, legally I had done the right thing, for a mad elephant has to be killed, like a mad dog, if its owner fails to control it. Among the Europeans opinion was divided. The older men said I was right, the younger men said it was a damn shame to shoot an elephant for killing a coolie, because an elephant was worth more than any damn Coringhee coolie. And afterwards I was very glad that the coolie had been killed; it put me legally in the right and it gave me a sufficient pretext for shooting the elephant. I often wondered whether any of the others grasped that I had done it solely to avoid looking a fool.

3. Sometimes a modest flight of imagination—an imaginary anecdote or a fully elaborated metaphor—can give effective climax to an ending, though the method is a dangerous one for beginning writers. Virginia Woolf has been writing about the pleasures of reading:

Yet who reads to bring about an end, however desirable? Are there not some pursuits that we practice because they are good in themselves, and some pleasures that are final? I have sometimes dreamt, at least, that when the Day of Judgment dawns and the great conquerors and lawyers and statesmen come to receive their rewards—their crowns, their laurels, their names carved indelibly upon imperishable marble—the Almighty will turn to Peter and will say, not without a certain envy when he sees us coming with our books under our arms, "Look, these need no reward. We have nothing to give them. They have loved reading.'

A conclusion may pick up and echo the introduction, giving the reader the feeling that the circle of discussion has been successfully closed:

Introduction: The American nightmare is the crime problem. It mocks the American Dream, so nearly translated into the Affluent Society. Statistics in superlatives assail our complacency each year, with many a gloomy moral drawn. We are accustomed to hearing a recurring dirge on criminality, ironically echoing our brighter accounts in economics, education, or population. Each year is a record year for crime; no American criminologist can complain of a lack of experience, raw material, or adequate data.

Conclusion: The nightmare will haunt us for a long while to come. Persistent good will and intelligence may yet transform its fearful events into closer correspondence with the American Dream. [JOHN P. CONRAD]

Numerous as the possibilities for effective conclusion are, they do not include everything. A conclusion should not be filled with concessions, hedging, admission of exceptions to the thesis advanced, or apologies for what has been said. Possible objections or weaknesses in argument should be dealt with in the introduction or body of the essay. Treating objections and exceptions at the end suggests that the writer is desperately trying to tidy up the discussion at the last minute. Apologies come too late after the reader has been through the whole essay, which the writer now tells him is probably not worth reading. A conclusion should strengthen the main effect of the essay, not undercut it.

Continuity: Transitions and Coherence

A reader is carried from the beginning to the end of an essay by a sense that all the sentences, paragraphs, and sections somehow form an interlocking chain. A very few works, such as La Rochefoucauld's *Maxims* or Neitzsche's *Beyond Good and Evil*, are made up of short individual assertions—epigrams, aphorisms, fragments of argument and reflection. But the great mass of all prose is *connected* discourse —connected both in the sense that it is so arranged that one idea leads naturally to another and in the sense that all the ideas focus on a common center. An essay has continuity when a reasonably attentive reader grasps easily the connection between an individual statement and the general idea of the paragraph in which it occurs; when he sees the connection between the idea of the paragraph and the idea of the whole essay; when he can see why sentence *B* follows from sentence *A* and precedes sentence *C*. Continuity is thus largely a result of good organization, but there are secondary means of strengthening this primary continuity which springs from the firm logical connection of ideas.

TRANSITIONS

Transitions are the verbal signposts that show the reader where the writer is taking him; they make the connection of parts explicit. The most commonly used transitional words are those that show relations in time or space (then, next, before, afterwards, meanwhile, when, above, below, further on, beyond); or show causal relationships (because, since, so that). Transition words also show logical relations (hence, thus, therefore) or show that a concession or change in direction is being made (still, yet while, nevertheless, however, on the other hand). Transitions can indicate that additional material of the sort that has gone before is to follow (moreover, in addition, also, further, and). When the method of organization is simple enumeration, the transitional device of "first," "second," "third," "fourth" is useful to mark divisions of the exposition.

In these two paragraphs, the transitional expressions are italicized. In the first paragraph, transitions are used primarily to keep a time sequence straight; in the second paragraph they are used primarily to show the connection of ideas:

John Charles Frémont was the illegitimate son of a Virginian lady, who had been married at seventeen to a sixty-year-old husband. She ran away with a French émigré, and *after* some years of wanderings in the South, *in the course of which* her lover died, she went to live in Charleston, South Carolina, where her son came to manhood in the duelling, drinking and racing society of the old South. He distinguished himself at Charleston College as an enthusiastic classical scholar: Greek especially, he *afterwards* wrote, "had a mysterious charm, as if behind the strange characters belonging to an ancient world I was to find things of wonderful interest"; but he *presently* fell in love with a beautiful Creole girl, with large dark eyes and blue-black hair, and *thereafter* so neglected his studies that he was dismissed from college. Of his escapades with Cecilia, *how-*

ever,. he was *afterwards* to write that "they were days of unreflecting life when I lived in the glow of a passion that now I know extended its refining influence over my whole life." He was handsome, and *at sixteen, already* exhibited what were *later* to prove his dominant characteristics: "ardor, imagination, ambition, quickness, endurance and reckless impetuosity." [EDMUND WILSON]

Whereas the countryside may be dull *because* it lacks novelty, *because* nothing happens, the city generates boredom by offering or imposing stimulation *so* relentlessly *that* people are numbed. *Both* absolute stillness *and* constant din tire our minds and spirits. *Further*, city dwellers become altogether accustomed to being entertained and diverted from the outside. *Thus* inner resources atrophy; cumulative and meaningful relations are discarded for the merely exciting and thrilling. Nothing, *in the end*, can be more monotonous. *So* many bells toll *so* deafeningly all the time *that* it is hard to participate in any of the services they are meant to announce. *Typically*, the city produces restless or agitated boredom, displayed in activity *as* meaningless *as* it is unceasing; *less frequently* it produces listless boredom, an apathetic withdrawal. *In either case*, there is an insatiable craving for excitement *as well as* an inability actually to get excited —to respond to anything. [JANE JACOBS]

Obviously, transitions must be used accurately. A "therefore" that connects two statements not in logical concord merely calls attention to the lapse. A writer who says "in the same manner" must be sure that what follows is in fact "in the same manner" or he will be calling attention to the injustice of his comparison. A "moreover" that introduces an entirely new point will misguide the reader.

Good transitions demand strict accuracy; they also require a certain tact and sense of proportion. An essay which omits necessary transitions leaves the reader puzzled as to where the writer is trying to lead him. An essay which uses too many transitions and insistently underlines every obvious connection of ideas is likely to sound simpleminded. Examples are the narrative in which every sentence is introduced by "then," "next," or "afterwards," and the show-of-logic essay in which *all* assertions are linked by "therefore," "thus," or "hence."

Since transitions are not part of the actual substance of an essay, since they are not lively or interesting in themselves, they should be unobtrusive. And the best way to make them unobtrusive is to make them short. Avoid such long-winded formulas as "The third point, which I am now going to take up, is . . ." In most situations, "Third" will suffice.

Effective transitions between paragraphs are even more important

than transitions between individual sentences. A paragraph indentation is a signal that a new point is being taken up, and transitions
show how that point is related to the preceding one. In addition to
the use of explicitly transitional phrases, one useful way to link paragraphs is to pick up a word or phrase from the last sentence of one
paragraph and repeat it in the first sentence of the next, as in this
discussion of Thackeray's *Vanity Fair.*

There has been no need of discursive analysis of motives: the *image* does
the work.
 Or—another instance of the work of the *image*—there is Joe, in his
obesity and his neckcloths and his gorgeous waistcoats. [DOROTHY VAN
GHENT]

Another is to use parallel syntax in successive topic sentences (see
p. 90):

Strange enough, no doubt, are the workings of the human mind.

Stranger still are the workings of the American mind.

Strangest of all are the workings of the mind of an old-fashioned New
Englander.

Pronouns can help carry over ideas from one paragraph to the next:

Rousseau always dreamed of retreating from society to some paradisal
country where all was innocence and pastoral bliss.
 These dreams of *his* were never to be realized. . . .

COHERENCE

These last three methods of transition are as much part of the
fabric of an essay as they are a kind of verbal stitching on its outside.
Transitions tie together parts of an essay in an external way, but
coherence arises from the unity and consistency of treatment of the
subject itself. The most important means of achieving coherence is
to keep the subject clearly at the center of discussion. The main way
of doing so is simple: make the person or thing you are writing about
the grammatical subject of most of the sentences in an essay. In the
following paragraph, the Emperor Alexander, or his mind, is the
subject of every clause but two:

Alexander had no very definite prejudices or desires in regard to the
future French dynasty. *His mind* flitted from one bright idea to the other.
He had no sympathy for the Bourbons, whom *he* regarded as outworn,

incompetent, and vastly conceited. At one moment *he* had favored the candidature of Bernadotte; at another *his mind* veered towards the nomination of the King of Rome with the title of Napoleon II, under the Regency of his mother, the Empress Marie Louise. The Duc d'Orléans also appealed to him as a possible candidate; *he* even thought of Eugène Beauharnais. In the face of Talleyrand's hints and suggestions, *he* avoided committing himself, alleging that *he* desired only to consult the wishes of the French people and these wishes were as yet obscure. [HAROLD NICHOLSON]

In the following paragraph, the author's subject is the problem of professional controversy among literary scholars; he keeps some aspect of the problem as the grammatical subject of all sentences but two, where the subject is, appropriately, the profession:

Our profession [literary scholarship] has no room for intemperate criticism of any kind, least of all in print. *Differences of opinion* there will always be, and scholarly competence not being a gift equally distributed among all practitioners, *lapses of judgment* and *imperfections of knowledge* will sometimes call for comment. Otherwise *literary study* would stagnate, complacent in its intellectual lethargy and spotted with uncorrected errors. But the *necessary process of debate and correction* can, and should, be conducted with dignity and courtesy. *Name-calling, personalities, aspersions on a man's professional ability*, and similar *below-the-belt tactics* are not to be condoned. *Controversial points* can be made, effectively and adequately, without betraying the ancient association of scholarship with gentlemanliness. [RICHARD D. ALTICK]

This simple and natural procedure of putting the dominant idea or person in the dominant grammatical position does more than any other single thing to strengthen continuity.

However, to achieve genuine coherence, the writer must apply all the principles of rhetoric. In style, the level of diction, tone, point of view, rhythm, and syntax must be consistent. In structure, the pattern of organization must be orderly and adequately developed. In thought, the ideas must be logical and sequential.

Rewriting and Revising

In a successfully completed first draft, the ideas are gotten out of the writer's head and onto paper, where they are arranged in some sort of order. There will be stretches here and there that convey the writer's meaning in reasonably finished form. Although the hardest part of the writer's task is over, he is far from done. To write well means to rewrite, and even the most experienced writers revise again and again before they relinquish their work to be judged by possibly hostile reviewers and the public. Only inexperienced writers imagine that a first draft is a finished piece of work.

If possible, the first draft should be put aside for a few days before the writer begins to revise. To most writers, what they have just finished writing looks perfectly splendid: they see no difference between the luminous idea in their minds and its dim, uncertain reflection on the written page. After a few days, the glow wears off and they can, by making an effort, look at what they have done with a critical eye. At the stage of revision, the writer should be more vigilant than his severest critic is likely to be.

Every writer ultimately devises his own methods of revision, and there is no neat sequence of stages which everyone should invariably follow. However, most writers find it useful to begin by looking at the largest units of what they have written and then work their way through the smaller units of paragraphs, sentences, and single words until they finally reach the scrutiny of single letters in proofreading. Moving from the paper as a whole to its smallest unit is the overall pattern of revision, but even on a first rereading the writer will probably spot and correct some misspelled words or tighten up the structure of a loose sentence here and there. Even at the stage of final proofreading, he may hit on the right word to substitute for one that has been bothering him ever since the first draft.

In the first revision, reread the whole manuscript at somewhat less than normal reading speed to get a sense of its total effect. Does the main thesis stand out clearly, or is it obscured by the proliferation of secondary matter? If the thesis is submerged, the writer needs to make sure that he has stuck to the point and made the connection between secondary points and the main thesis sufficiently explicit. At this stage, the writer sometimes recognizes that some of his matter is digressive and should be struck out. More often, he sees that he must be more emphatic in spelling out the connection of the part to the whole. Is the overall movement of the argument from the beginning to the end unmistakable? If not, the order of the paragraphs probably needs changing, and for this a pair of scissors is indispensable: the writer can cut up what he has written and rearrange it until he finds the sequence of paragraphs that reflects the sequence of ideas.

If the overall emphasis and pattern survive this initial scrutiny, the writer may next turn his attention to individual paragraphs, making sure that each one is unified around a single topic and is not a bundle of disjointed remarks. He will also look closely at the introduction and conclusion, on the assumption that they are probably both weak, and need to be completely rewritten in order to be made lively and relevant.

Next, the writer begins the laborious process of going through his work phrase by phrase and sentence by sentence. In dozens of places, both wording and structure will need changing—the vague word being replaced by an explicit one, the misplaced modifier moved to its proper place, the missing transition supplied, the superfluous detail eliminated, the short, choppy sentence reduced to a phrase, the long, rambling sentence broken up into more manageable units. At this point the writer needs to be particularly alert for verbal deadwood (see pp. 187), using his pencil ruthlessly to strike out the empty remark, the redundant adjective, the windy formula such as "It is interesting to note that. . . ." This detailed revision usually involves going through the paper two or three times, for nobody sees everything at once, and every trip through the manuscript will reveal new trouble spots that need attention. By the time this process is complete, the paper will almost certainly have to be retyped.

With the clean new copy comes the final task of revision—copyreading, in which the writer is no longer reading for meaning but for accuracy and mechanics. He looks at spelling, at punctuation, at paragraph indentation, at the form of footnotes, at capitalization. He checks to see if any words have been run together or if any words have been left out in transcribing. (An omitted *not* or *un-* can change the meaning of a whole argument.) If there are quotations, he compares them to the original text to ensure accuracy. Copyreading is drudge work, but it is necessary. An accumulation of small errors puts a barrier between the writer and the reader—who may be so distracted by misspelled words and misplaced commas that he is no longer able to attend to what the writer is saying.

After the copyreading is done, the only thing to do is to surrender the essay to the judgment of its readers.

APPENDIX ONE

GUIDE TO PUNCTUATION

Introduction

Punctuation is very far from being standardized; no one system is in general use. But even with considerable variation, there are a number of useful rules followed in practice by a good many writers and editors a good deal of the time. The guide to punctuation presented here, though plenty of exceptions to it will be found in the best edited prose, is traditional and acceptable everywhere. It is a system based chiefly on sentence structure.

Independent Clauses

If two independent clauses are joined by a coordinating conjunction, use a comma before the conjunction.

> Candy is dandy, but liquor is quicker.

In the absence of a coordinating conjunction, use a semicolon.

> Candy is dandy; liquor is quicker.
> Candy is dandy; however, liquor is quicker.

The conjunctive adverbs *however, moreover,* and *consequently,* are usually set off by commas wherever they appear in the second clause. *Nevertheless* and *therefore* are set off if they are meant to be read parenthetically. The other conjunctive adverbs need not be set off at the beginning of their clause but usually are elsewhere.

> Wyman was an alien; thus he could not hold office.
> Wyman was an alien; he could not, thus, hold office.

An independent clause used parenthetically is set off by dashes or parentheses.

> Wyman could not hold office (he was an alien), despite his popularity.
> Tweed—he was thought to be corrupt—was opposed by the reformers.

Subordinate Adjective Clauses

The idea of restrictiveness is important for punctuation. A restrictive clause or phrase is one that is used to *identify* the word it modifies.

> The man *who defeated Culbertson* was not well known.

> Culbertson, *who had been the unquestioned champion for years,* acknowledged defeat.

In the first sentence, the italicized adjective clause identifies which man is being spoken of; it is therefore restrictive and not punctuated. In the second sentence, the italicized adjective clause is *not* used to identify Culbertson; it is therefore nonrestrictive and set off by commas. Thus nonrestrictive constructions *are* set off by commas; restrictive constructions are *not*. Ordinarily the modifier of a proper (capitalized) noun is nonrestrictive, the assumption being that a name is sufficient identification. An exception arises when it is necessary to distinguish two persons or objects with the same name; then the word *the* or *that* usually precedes: "—the Mr. Smith who was here yesterday, not the Mr. Smith who was here today."

If the modified word has already been identified in context, its subsequent modifiers will be nonrestrictive.

A letter from Murphy lay on the desk. Jones did not look at the letter, *which he knew contained bad news.*

Compare the following sets alternating restrictive and nonrestrictive adjectival clauses:

1. In Lowry County there was only one doctor who lived in Coopertown.
2. In Lowry County there was only one doctor, who lived in Coopertown.
3. Men who are rational feel alien to animals.
4. Men, who are rational, feel alien to animals.
5. The natives who are prosperous eat well.
6. The natives, who are prosperous, eat well.

It is apparent that whether an adjective clause is restrictive or not can make a radical difference in meaning. Sentence (1) implies that although there might be more than one doctor in the county, only one lived in Coopertown, whereas (2) says definitely that there is only one doctor in the whole county. Sentence (3) suggests that there are some *irrational* men, whereas (4) implies that *all* men are rational. Sentence (5) leaves the impression that there are some natives who are not prosperous and who do not eat well, whereas (6) implies that all the natives are prosperous and all eat well. In the first sentence of each set, it is assumed that the modified word needs to be identified; the contrary assumption is made in the second sentence of each set.

Subordinate Adverbial Clauses

Any adverb clause at the beginning of a sentence may be set off by a comma. If it is elsewhere in the sentence, a similar but looser criterion of restrictiveness applies: if the adverb clause is necessary to the sense of the sentence, it is not punctuated; otherwise, it is set off by commas.

> Until the crown is located, they cannot continue.
> They cannot continue until the crown is located.
> Because he was ordered to go, he went.
> He went because he was ordered to.
> He went to the ball, only because he had to, and hated it.

Is the information conveyed by the adverb clause essential to the point of the sentence or not? If it is, then no punctuation should be used; if it is not essential, the clause should be set off by commas.

Subordinate Noun Clauses

If a noun clause is used as subject, object, or predicate nominative, it is not punctuated. If it is used as an appositive, the following rule applies: if the word to which the appositive is in apposition refers to something unique, the appositive is set off by commas; otherwise there is no punctuation.

> The only idea he ever cherished deeply, *that bears are really friendly*, cost him an arm.

> The idea *that bears are friendly* is an odd one.

Prepositional Phrases

Normally the prepositional phrase is not punctuated, but if it is out of normal word order or is meant to be parenthetical, it is set off by commas. What constitutes "normal" word order is not always easy to decide. The following sentences show prepositional phrases in what is certainly normal position:

> A carload *of campers* arrived *in the morning*.
> They were the bravest *of all the men who have tried to climb Everest*.
> Jackson saw a peaceful woods *across the river*.

We may regard the normal position of the prepositional phrase as following the word it modifies; in any other position, then, it should be set off by commas.

> *In the morning*, a carload of campers arrived.
> *Of all the men who have tried to climb Everest*, they were the bravest.

They were, *of all the men who have tried to climb Everest,* the bravest.
Jackson saw, *across the river,* a peaceful woods.

Some handbooks, out of a general wish to economize on punctuation,
frown on using a comma to set off a "short introductory" prepositional phrase, such as *In the morning.* General practice more than
adequately supports using the comma here, but it hardly matters one
way or another.

Participial Phrases

If the participial phrase comes immediately before the subject of a
clause (which should also be the implied subject of the participle),
it is set off by commas.

> *Crossing the river,* Jackson was mortally wounded.

If the participial phrase immediately follows, the adjective rule of
restriction applies:

> Jackson, *crossing the river,* was mortally wounded.
> The man *crossing the river* was General Jackson.

If it comes at the end of the sentence and there is no intervening
word that might be taken as the subject of the participle, no punctuation is required.

> Jackson was wounded *crossing the river.*

If the subject of the participle is an object, no punctuation is used.

> I watched him *dying slowly.*

Sometimes a comma is sufficient to distinguish the subject of a participial phrase:

> I watched him, *hoping for some change.*
> I watched him *hoping for some change.*

In the first sentence, it is clearly *I* hoping; in the second sentence, it
is clearly *he* hoping. Cases where punctuation can so clearly indicate
the subject are probably rather rare, however; it is usually better to
change the word order than to rely on punctuation.

Gerund Phrases

The gerund phrase is punctuated only when it functions as an appositive.

His one great ambition, *exploring the Arctic,* was finally realized.

Absolute Phrases

The absolute phrase is always set off by commas.

Her eyes dancing with pleasure, she told of her day at the zoo.
Mrs. Longbottom arrived, *her husband in tow,* and insulted the host.

Appositive Phrases

For the rule, see above, under noun clause.

The socialite *Mrs. Longbottom* was present.
Mrs. Longbottom, *the socialite,* was present.
Her son *Herman* was absent. (Implying that she has more than one son.)
Her son, *Herman,* was absent. (Implying that she has only one son.)

Series

Elements in series are set off by commas.

Snakes, weasels, and rats are all varmints.
They proceeded *slowly, cautiously, and painfully.*

A series connected by repeated coordinating conjunctions is not punctuated.

I don't like *snakes or weasels or rats.*
Platypuses and octopuses and hippopotamuses are all in the zoo.

If the elements in series have internal punctuation, semicolons may be used to make the proper divisions clearer.

Bounderby, the industrialist; his mother, now out of hiding; and the gaping townspeople all confronted one another.

A series in apposition is usually set off by a dash or dashes if it comes at the beginning or in the middle of a sentence.

The sectarians—artisans, laborers, shopkeepers—were in the lower strata of society.

Artisans, laborers, and shopkeepers—these were the members of the new movement.

If an appositional series follows a complete statement, it is introduced by a colon.

His followers were the poor and dispossessed: sharecroppers, migrant workers, unskilled laborers.

Coordinate Adjectives
Coordinate adjectives are separated by commas.

> On a *cold, windy* day they started out.

Both *cold* and *windy* modify *day* in the same way and are therefore said to be coordinate. In the phrase "a blue fountain pen," there is no punctuation because *blue* and *fountain* are not coordinate. A standard test to decide whether adjectives are coordinate is to try putting *and* between them or to reverse their order: if the result still sounds like English ("a cold and windy day," "a windy, cold day"), use a comma; if not ("a blue and fountain pen," "a fountain blue pen"), don't punctuate. If you can't tell from the test, then it probably doesn't matter which way you punctuate the construction.

Adjectives Heading Phrases or in Pairs
These may follow the rule of restriction.

> *Rational and moral* men naturally deplore war.
> *Rational and moral,* men naturally deplore war.

In the first sentence, the adjectives identify which men deplore war; the second sentence assumes that all men are rational and moral and deplore war. In this case, your ear is usually a dependable guide: if the pitch of your voice remains on the same level as you read "moral men," don't punctuate; if the pitch drops, insert a comma.

> Mrs. Wigger, *radiant as ever,* nodded to her host.
> He went down with the ship, *stubborn to the end.*
> *Hale and hearty at ninety-seven,* he still has his daily pint.

Parenthetical Remarks
Any unit in a sentence that you mean to be read as parenthetical, as an aside, should be set off by commas, dashes, or parentheses. The last two marks, pretty much equivalent, show a greater remoteness of the unit enclosed than do commas; they are also much less used than commas.

> Mr. Roche (*a former pugilist himself*) heads the new boxing commission.

There were, *one supposes,* many hardships.
He was president—*for a week*—of the society.
The Joneses (*of Greensborough*) will be present.
The singer—*if you can call her that*—gave a rendition of "Home, Sweet Home."

Similarly:

> I asked for pears, *not bears.*
> It was Jefferson, *not Franklin,* who wrote the Declaration.
> This is only the beginning, *not the end.*

Quotations

Direct quotations are put between double quotation marks—final periods and commas going before the closing quotation mark, colons and semicolons after, question marks and exclamation points before only if part of the original quotation. Omissions within the quotation are indicated by the marks of ellipsis(. . .). Quotations within quotations are enclosed by single quotation marks.

> Patrick Henry said, "Give me liberty, or give me death!"
> Who said, "Thy need is greater than mine"?
> "What," he asked, "is the reason for this?"
> The repairman said we need a new "capacitator," whatever that is.
> The candidate said, "What the Governor calls 'emoluments' I call graft"; Governor Stone did not comment.
> The Cavendish report says that "miners in Groton are . . . well paid."

Designations of Time and Place

When a string of word units is used to specify a particular place or time, the second and subsequent units are set off by commas.

> Hubbard, Iowa, U.S.A., was his birthplace.
> Mr. Campbell's unlikely summer address is The Bunch, Wotton-Underwood, Bucks, U.K.
> Book One, Chapter Four, Verse Twenty, . . .
> Nine o'clock A.M., Friday, May 15, 1964, . . .

Abbreviated titles are set off the same way.

> M. Wixman, B.A., M.A., . . .
> Viscount Portal of Hungerford, K.G., G.C.B., O.M., D.S.O., M.C., . . .

Footnotes

Footnotes can become very elaborate. For most nontechnical writing, a widely accepted form for references to books and periodicals is as follows:

[1] George Santayana, *Character and Opinion in the United States*, N.Y., 1920, pp. 4–5.
[2] Morton Bloomfield, "Symbolism in Medieval Literature," *Modern Philology*, LVI (1958), 73–81.

For more complicated references, an appropriate style sheet should be consulted.

APPENDIX TWO
EXERCISES

Grammatical Analysis (see pp. 14–16)

This pure flame of mind is nothing new, superadded, or alien in
America. It is notorious how metaphysical was the passion that drove
the Puritans to those shores; they went there in the hope of living more
perfectly in the spirit. And their pilgrim's progress was not finished
5   when they had founded their churches in the wilderness; an endless
migration of the mind was still before them, a flight from those new
idols and servitudes which prosperity involves, and the eternal lure of
spiritual freedom and truth. The moral world always contains undis-
covered or thinly peopled continents open to those who are more
10   attached to what might or should be than to what already is. Americans
are eminently prophets; they apply morals to public affairs; they are
impatient and enthusiastic. Their judgments have highly speculative
implications, which they often make explicit; they are men with principles, and fond of stating them. Moreover, they have an intense self-
15   reliance; to exercise private judgment is not only a habit with them
but a conscious duty. Not seldom personal conversions and mystical
experiences throw their ingrained faith into novel forms, which may
be very bold and radical. They are traditionally exercised about religion, and adrift on the subject more than any other people on earth;
20   and if religion is a dreaming philosophy, and philosophy a waking
religion, a people so wide awake and so religious as the old Yankees
ought certainly to have been rich in philosophers. [SANTAYANA]

A. Identify the parts of speech in this paragraph, giving in each
instance the reason for the identification. For example, *This* is an
adjective because it modifies the noun *flame; pure* is an adjective for
the same reason; *flame* is a noun, subject of the sentence; *of* is a
preposition joining *flame* and *mind; mind* is a noun, object of the
preposition *of;* etc. Continue until you feel quite confident of your
analysis.

B. Identify the phrases and indicate what part of speech they function as. For example, *of mind* (line 1) is a prepositional phrase used
as an adjective to modify *flame.*

C. Identify the subordinate clauses in the same way. For example,
*how metaphysical was the passion that drove the Puritans to those
shores* is a noun clause (see p. 37); *that drove the Puritans to those
shores* is an adjective clause modifying *passion.*

D. Identify the verbs and describe them as to type (linking, transitive, or intransitive) and voice (active or passive). For example *is* and
was (line 2) are forms of the verb *be,* a linking verb; *drove* (line 2)

is a transitive verb in the active voice; *went* (line 3) is intransitive; etc.

E. Identify the conjunctions and what constructions they join. For example, *or* (line 1) is a coordinating conjunction joining *alien* and *superadded*, parallel modifiers of *nothing*.

Pronoun Reference (see pp. 18–20)

Examine the pronouns in the following passages, and revise wherever the pronoun reference is misleading, vague, or clumsy.

1. Many investors are persuaded that the stock market will always continue to go up. Stockbrokers know this, and try to explain the workings of the market to their clients.
2. Senator Doe's speech was an attack on current tariff policy and international trade agreements, which astonished his supporters in his home state.
3. When I meet old friends these days, it reminds me of how much my life has changed in the last ten years.
4. Not long ago, a Rembrandt was bought by the Metropolitan Museum for about two million dollars, which demonstrates the immense prestige that his work enjoys today.
5. The examiners asked me to give an account of Goethe's early life and writings, which I could do only in a very sketchy fashion.
6. In London, they seem to have almost as many automobiles on the streets as we do here in Los Angeles.
7. It is often said that TV treatment of public affairs is trivial and perfunctory. But for several years now this has not been altogether true.
8. Determining the authorship of many Elizabethan plays presents problems whose solutions demand intelligence, patience, and luck. This is typical of most scholarly problems.
9. They seem to be very fond of hunting and fishing in western Canada.
10. Dr. Brown told Dr. Smith that he had very little confidence in his diagnosis.
11. Poetry does not sell as well as fiction, which is why there are more poets than novelists teaching in colleges and universities.
12. Wit, vigor, and grace characterize her novels. They are treasures not often found among the books of the last twenty or thirty years.
13. The City Council told the demonstrators that they were going to make sure that they were scrupulous in abiding by the letter of the law in all their efforts to solve the problem.
14. Never drink a Martini when it is hot and dry. It may make you ill.

15. If the cat refuses to eat the liver, try cutting it up in small pieces.

16. There are many people living busy and complicated lives amid the distractions of the great cities of America who yearn for the simple life.

17. It is dangerous to drive fast when it is raining; it makes the highways slippery and lowers visibility.

18. If you do not keep a careful record of expenses, it makes for difficulties in figuring income tax.

19. I enjoyed my French class very much and hope to be able to speak it a little when I go to Paris next summer.

20. Many people believe that you should feed a fever and starve a cold. This is not true.

21. In Jane Austen's *Pride and Prejudice* I found that the least sympathetic character of all was Mrs. Bennet, particularly in her treatment of her two eldest daughters. This was due to the way she constantly displayed her vulgarity and her inability to see the true worth of those around her. They are intelligent, beautifully mannered girls and always treat their mother with consideration, but this seems only to intensify Mrs. Bennet's preference for noisy, silly, ungovernable Lydia, which seems to be based on their similarity to one another. This makes Mrs. Bennet even more unattractive to the reader—she and Lydia set off one another's shallowness, and this reminds the reader of what a dreadful *young* woman she must once have been. Moreover, Mrs. Bennet does nothing during the entire novel but scheme to get her daughters married to wealthy husbands, which reveals her grasping, materialistic outlook. That is why Mrs. Bennet is the most repellent character in the book.

22. The social leader is also taking some of the glory from the star athlete. This is because many of the people look to the social leaders for advice and guidance. This is done mainly because the social leaders are the popular people around campus, and everyone has a desire to be popular.

Pronoun Case (see pp. 20–22 and 30)

Underline the correct form.

1. The Benson awards were given to Henry Jones, Arthur Smith and (I, me).

2. The Dean gave (we, us) girls to understand that there would be no monkey-business at Vassar.

3. Apathy and misunderstanding confronted (we, us) members of Local 604 (who, that) had been working for improvements in fringe benefits.

4. If I were (he, him), I would be annoyed too.

5. Everyone liked the new ballet except Julia and (she, her).

6. There is still some doubt about (who, whom) the new chairman of the board will be.

7. (Who, Whom) can be subjected to such shabby treatment and still make no complaint?

8. (Who, Whom) shall we give the credit for this discovery?

9. My roommate objected to (me, my) singing in bed.

10. The loan is just an informal arrangement between Dowson and (I, me).

11. (Who, Whom) would dare to defend the abuses that I have objected to?

12. This bungler is the efficiency expert (who, whom) Smith said would solve all our difficulties.

13. I advise you to give your car to (whoever, whomever) is willing to drive it away.

14. Hermione, unlike Jocelyn and (I, me), prefers the mountains to the seashore.

15. The other day I failed to recognize a man (who, whom) I have known for many years.

16. (Whoever, Whomever) Gregory trusted, he trusted completely.

17. I thought I saw Helen on the dance floor a moment ago. Is that (she, her) in the red dress?

18. The Planning Commission resented (us, our) criticizing their work on Operation Bogfill.

19. Considering the insults and humiliations involved, a rich man (who, that) is willing to endure a campaign for public office is a remarkable creature.

20. Henry Williams is the kind of man (whom, that) I have always had respect for.

21. The last person (that, whom) I expected to see was Henry.

22. The Dean said that he did not mind (us, our) contradicting him.

23. The Dean said that he enjoyed (us, our) singing.

24. (Whoever, Whomever) is chosen the Queen of the May may in turn choose (whoever, whomever) she likes for her retinue.

25. Uncle Henry left the summer cottage to me, (who, whom) he had ignored completely all his life.

Agreement: Pronoun and Antecedent, Subject and Verb (see pp. 22–23, 25–28)

Underline the correct form.

1. When one lives in a glass house, (he, they) must beware of people bearing stones.

2. Each of the club members (is, are) to be assessed an additional ten dollars this year.

3. Each of us (try, tries) to point out that the public does not really understand what (they are, it is) criticizing.

4. He is one of those painters who (spends, spend) years on a single canvas.

5. My favorite fruit (is, are) Malaga grapes.

6. Either of the two candidates (is, are) acceptable to us.

7. Mrs. Henderson, accompanied by four of her friends, (is, are) touring Greece and the Aegean.

8. In the museum there (is, are) a fine El Greco, several Vermeers, and eight Turner landscapes.

9. A public library that buys only current novels, how-to-do-it books, and standard reference works (is, are) failing to serve the public interest.

10. Everyone must send in (his, their) income tax return by April 15.

11. *Poole's Index* is only one of several reference works which (is, are) useful to the student.

12. Simone Weil's *The Iliad: The Poem of Force* is one of the most remarkable essays on Homer that (has, have) appeared in our time.

13. Behind the imposing façade of the building (is, are) floor upon floor of tiny, cramped apartments.

14. Not only the judge but also the district attorney (was, were) unprepared for the new turn of events.

15. Neither the members of the band nor the singer (is, are) very good.

16. Neither the singer nor the members of the band (is, are) very good.

17. All consumers agree that the price they pay for household appliances, automobiles, and television sets (is, are) too high.

18. High above the tropical valley and the forests of the lower slopes (is, are) the barren mountain peak.

19. Only one out of every ten applicants (is, are) accepted.

20. Each of us (has, have) (his, our) secret dreams of splendor and happiness.

21. Either Eileen or Mary (is, are) going to send out the invitations.

22. Each member of the staff will be given an opportunity to make (his, their) comments on new policy proposals.

23. There (is, are) fewer than a hundred registered voters in the entire village.

24. Everyone at some time or another will find (himself, themselves) confronted by apparently insoluble problems.

25. Languages, history, literature, and philosophy (is, are) the basis of a sound humanistic education.

Dangling and Misplaced Modifiers, Split Infinitives
(see pp. 30–33 and 40–41)

Correct any faulty sentences.

1. After driving ten hours a day for a week, the highway seemed nothing but an endless white blur of concrete.

2. Durkheim was the first writer to really study the causes of suicide.

3. Alarmed by the sharp pain in his side, the doctor was called in by Mr. Smythe.

4. Trevelyan tells the story of how William the Conqueror subdued England with his usual facility and humane wit.

5. After having served twenty years of his sentence, a pardon was finally given to Black Moe the Mole by Governor Milltown.

6. By playing the sedulous ape to his superiors year after year, a promotion was at last forthcoming to Smedley.

7. The enemy having retreated during the night, the town was occupied by Allied troops the next day.

8. Because of the increase of crime in the area, fire and theft insurance rates have doubled in the last ten years.

9. As the best known of all the horses in the race, my sister bet on Colonial King.

10. The Senate finally agreed to harshly censure the erring Senator.

11. Stoop-shouldered, gangling, and shy, my mother decided that the only solution was to send me to Miss Edison's dancing classes.

12. Having finished the newspaper and taken a nap, the rest of Sunday afternoon still faced me with a promise of dreary blankness.

13. To find tiny Ilix, the most detailed maps of the American Automobile Association have to be consulted.

14. Suffering from tired blood, recurrent hiccups, flying dandruff, palpitations, and chronic moral failure, the future sometimes seemed very black indeed to Mrs. Henderson.

15. The bandit only escaped because of the laxity of the security guard.

16. Margaret only agreed to the first of Henry's three proposals.

17. After studying Greek for two years, my interest unfortunately began to wane.

18. Judging from the evidence, the drug companies have consistently made a profit of several hundred per cent on many of their products.

19. Considering his age and eminence, Bertrand Russell is still a lively and invigoratingly disreputable figure on the contemporary scene.

20. Dazzled by his reputation for learning and intellectual power, Professor Smathers seemed to us as undergraduates almost superhuman.

21. Henry corrected many of the mistakes that he had made with the sage advice of his father.

22. Dr. Magid discussed the recent riots and civil-rights demonstrations at the weekly lunch of the Magnus Club.

23. Professor Munch has been able to conclusively show the errors of fact made in Gibbon's history with the help of six tireless research assistants.

24. The museum having been closed for repairs, we were unable to see the two Courbets we were so curious about.

25. Seeing the two black-coated figures coming toward me, my fear increased even more.

Predication, Patterns of Equivalency (see pp. 48–54, 64–66)

Using especially the principles of basic predication, rewrite the following sentences, all of which are structurally garbled or clumsy in one way or another.

1. The issues Brown supported were almost directly opposite from Nolan.

2. They used mass merchandising techniques in the campaign, consisting of Pavlov and his conditioned reflexes and Freud and his father image.

3. Nolan employed the father image in his campaigning; this is shown by big posters with a picture of himself and his family displayed in different sections of the state.

4. He was supposed to have great warmth, a sense of humor, and a good father and husband.

5. The father image was used in Nolan's campaign, which can be illustrated by a published letter from Mrs. Nolan, telling what a fine family man he was.

6. An image of the candidate is projected so that he seems a "fatherly type"; an example of this would be the last election.

7. The old story of being born with a silver spoon in the mouth seems like a terrible way to start life.

8. Their electric cars, caused by the depleting amount of gasoline, have to be charged every so often.

9. Our lives in this era of economic and political insecurity are in constant anxiety of what will happen. One's exerted efforts to advance in the field of education are readily acknowledged as a source of anxiety.

10. Our prodigious inventions are actually time-saving devices; but the advantage of these devices leads back to the idea of "rushing Americans."

11. The old man is not a typical part of the life Eliot describes J. Alfred Prufrock to be.

12. The description of Ahab includes a white scar on his face.

13. Therefore, unable to make a good living anymore, they would leave their farms, and go to work in a more profitable business, such as labor.

14. The central theme of the speech is the projection of the American woman from the obscuring years of the past to the position she occupies at present, that of the more perfected, protected, polished and far superior of the two sexes.

15. The Secretary calls for less federal intervention into the farming industry. He shows the real problem is one of surplus, and calls for support through the means of eliminating the surplus. He says it is the farmers' freedom to solve their own problem.

16. According to the usual definition, a comedy is when all the good characters are rewarded with happiness at the end.

17. The article points out that the reliability of public opinion polls, which are implicitly trusted by most Americans, is a mistake.

18. An urban renewal project always takes several years to complete because of the slow process of buying up or condemning land, finding sponsors for private developments, and relocating tenants cannot be artificially speeded up.

19. By proofreading every letter as well as every word is the best way to avoid errors in copy.

20. The earthquake has weakened hundreds of structures in the downtown area, and if not repaired at once, may collapse at any moment.

Periodic Sentences (see pp. 59–61)

Convert the following into periodic sentences by *suspending* the principal predication.

1. Emerson's affirmation of both physics and dialectic, of both science and myth, was of prime importance, for it justified the existence of the artist, the poet, the saint. [1] *

2. The cause of his death was poison; this had been a closely guarded secret for years until it was revealed by Glanov yesterday.

3. On that memorable day, Napoleon was crowned Emperor; he was the son of an illiterate Corsican peasant and had once been a lowly corporal in the French army.

4. No one knew his secret; his friends didn't know it, nor his children, not even his wife, with whom he shared every confidence.

5. The sponsor finally backed out; he had expended very large sums and got nothing in return but vague promises.

Convert the following into periodic sentences by *postponing* the principal predication.

6. The dominant note of the period was one of hope, despite the foreboding that every intelligent mind felt when it contemplated the barba-

---

* Numbers in brackets refer to "Notes to Exercises," beginning on p. 327.

rism of the industrial age, inimical to any culture except that which grew
out of its own inhuman absorption in abstract matter and abstract power.
[2]
    7. Pandolpho became premier on July 12th; he had been little known
to the rest of the world and never taken seriously even in his own country.
    8. The first controlled reaction was finally achieved after years of
preparation and months of concentrated effort by a team of the world's
best scientists; there had also been an outlay of millions of dollars.
    9. He continued to write his wonderful songs up to the end, though
he grew daily more ill and was constantly dunned by his creditors; moreover, his poverty was extreme and he had few friends.
    10. Miss Rutherford sat contemptuously at her ease while the women
were hoeing in the hot sun or milking the cows or feeding the chickens,
and while the men were laboring to build the new lodge.

Inversion (see pp. 61–63)

Invert word order in the following sentences to emphasize the italicized words.

    1. Hadrian retired frequently to his villa. He was able to meditate
there without distractions; no officious courtiers buzzed around him *there*.
He found *the peace of the countryside* ever more necessary.
    2. The Chancellor had become more important than the King. All
petitions were directed *to the Chancellor*. All state decisions were made
by him. All aspiration and finally much hatred were centered *on him*.
    3. They fought and died for *liberty*; they would always cherish *liberty*.
    4. Mr. Croque had an abundant supply *of ambition*, but he altogether
lacked *will power and perseverance*.
    5. The troops were well trained, but they had no experience *of actual
combat*. They were *disciplined*, however, and they proved to be *courageous*.

Subordination (see pp. 67–76)

In each exercise form one complex sentence (it may be a "compound-
complex" sentence) from the group of simple sentences. There will
be any number of ways to do this; the notes provide some possible
solutions. Remember that the most important ideas are best expressed
in the principal predication.

    1. Zanzibar was once a center of the Arab slave trade.
There were rich Islamic settlements along the East African coast.
Zanzibar was later a tributary of Portuguese rovers.
It was also a tributary of British empire builders.

It was a place of turbulence and mystery.
Then it was pacified by British rule.
It learned to live on its memories of the past.
It also lived on its exports of cloves.
These exports were declining. [3]

   2. On Sunday rebels overthrew the Sultanate.
The rebels were armed and were acting in the name of Zanzibar's black
   African majority.
The Sultanate was representative mainly of the island's minority elite.
This government had been in office since December 10.
At that time Zanzibar received its independence from Britain. [4]

   3. Augustine was suffering from a lung ailment.
This provided him with an excuse to retire from his professorship.
He wanted the excuse.
At Cassiciacum he endeavored to obtain a better understanding of the ·
   Christian religion.
This endeavor was made through reading and reflection and discussion
   with friends.
He used as an instrument concepts and themes taken from neo-Platonic
   philosophy.
His idea of Christianity was still very incomplete.
It was tinctured by neo-Platonism.
It was more tinctured then than it was to be later. [5]

   4. There is an alternative to the evolutionary theory of the universe.
It is that the creation of matter is taking place continuously.
Stars and galaxies evolve from this basic matter.
But the universe is in a steady state.
The theory considers the universe as a large-scale structure. [6]

   5. At length we ascended a high hill.
Our horses were treading upon pebbles of flint, agate, and rough jasper.
Then we gained the top.
We looked down on the wild bottoms of Laramie Creek.
The creek was far below.
It wound like a writhing snake from side to side of the narrow interval.
It wound amid a growth of shattered cotton-wood and ash trees. [7]

   6. A phase began in 1877.
It was inaugurated by the withdrawal of federal troops from the South.
At the same time the Negro was abandoned as a ward of the nation.
Also the attempt to guarantee the freedman his civil and political equality
   was given up.
The rest of the country acquiesced in the South's demand.
That demand was that the whole problem be left to the disposition of the
   dominant Southern white people. [8]

   7. We were bent double.

But our faces were raised.
We crept into the almost utter darkness.
Our pace grew slower with every step. [9]
    8. It is almost impossible to sum up Emerson's doctrine.
That is because he touched life on many sides.
And he touched it freshly, moreover.
He is a Platonist.
One will not find Plato's doctrines of Art in his essay on Art, however.
He was in a very derivative way a Kantian.
But one will not find Kant's principles at the bottom of his ethics. [10]
    9. Consumers anticipated possible shortages.
Immediately they began to protect themselves against a deprivation.
This deprivation they inevitably regarded as painful or even intolerable.
This was because of their peacetime persuasion. [11]
    10. The good novelist then is not the dupe of his subject-matter.
He has transformed his emotions into free emotions.
In the process of this discipline he cannot but have learned the importance and value of freedom. [12]

Grammatical Coordination

Underline the coordinating and correlative conjunctions in the following sentences and see whether they are correctly used according to the rules on pp. 77–82. Correct or improve those sentences in which the parallelism seems faulty.

    1. Ike was an orphan whose older cousin Cass took the place of a father and caring for him.
    2. As a boy he learned much about shooting and fishing and to train hunting dogs.
    3. He also learned about the great bear, the legendary lord of the forest but who had actually been seen by few men.
    4. The annual hunt for the bear was traditional, enthusiastic, and with many of the local people joining in.
    5. Both Ike and, with less passion, his cousin participated in the chase.
    6. When he was fourteen and with no gun or compass, he first sighted the bear.
    7. He was called Old Ben and though often but never mortally wounded had been hunted every year for many years.
    8. Either he was immortal, as some of the superstitious believed, or simply old and with an uncanny intelligence.
    9. Not only did Ike see him but at very close range.
    10. Ike stared at the bear and the bear at him.

11. For a long time, neither moved, nor was any sound to be heard in the forest.

12. Then slowly and with no indication of alarm, Old Ben moved off into the darkness of the trees.

13. Nor did Ike feel fright but rather simply awed by the bear's presence.

14. It was wonder, not terror, that stirred him.

15. Old Ben was enormous, very dark, and with one twisted paw.

16. He himself neither appeared often nor were his easily identifiable tracks often to be seen.

17. Ike knew that only because he had left behind his gun and by losing himself in the woods had he been permitted to see the bear.

18. In later years and when he had become intimately familiar with the forest, he saw Old Ben again.

19. Yet though he was armed and having a clear shot, neither he nor, even more unaccountably, his companion attempted to kill the bear or pursue him as he lumbered off.

20. In the end, it was not Ike, who had seemed destined to be the bear's killer, but, surprisingly, Boon and a hunting knife, not a rifle, that ended Old Ben's existence.

Rhetorical Coordination

Rewrite the following passages, using the principles of coordination discussed in Chapter 6. The footnotes offer useful comparisons, but are not to be considered the only possible revisions.

1. Our government, in which the people rule themselves, exists for the benefit of the same people. [13]

2. Although everyone complains about his memory, there is no one who expresses any dissatisfaction with his ability to make judgments. [14]

3. Great people are, almost by definition, often not very well understood. [15]

4. We have always known that heedless self-interest was bad morals, though only recently have we become aware of its unfortunate economic effects. [16]

5. The young man who has not wept is a savage; conversely, it is very foolish for old people never to laugh at anything. [17]

6. In skating over thin ice, it is the safest policy to go as fast as we can. [18]

7. It is men, not God, who have produced racks and whips. We build prisons; slavery is also our creation. Who made guns with bayonets? Men. We manufacture bombs and use them. You can't blame nature because we have poverty and people have to work too hard. Such things come about because of human avarice. Our stupidity is another factor. [19]

8. We once had a shortage of hospitals. That situation is not something anyone wants to go back to. The same is true as far as public health is concerned. The sweatshops there used to be in America are also a thing of the past that we are not going to revive. In the old days, children were working in factories, which was an undesirable condition. All these things are in the past, where they are going to remain. [20]

9. That men are, by nature and birth, of equal status is, in our view, a truism requiring no demonstration which entails a number of other rights which cannot be dissociated from mankind, among which may be cited those which permit the continuance of life itself while at the same time permitting the goals of personal felicity to be pursued without external impediment.

10. What lures the American student to the foreign university is the life of the boulevards, where there are cafes and bistros. The Latin Quarter is also attractive. Then, too, there is the opera, for the music lovers, and the ballet, whereas another's taste may be satisfied by the theatre and the experimental film. On every corner can be found a bookshop, while every city has a dozen newspapers. The student body, since it is mature, joins in the risks of life while at the same time educating itself formally, an active part being taken in literature as well as journalism, not to forget art and politics. [21]

11. While analogy provides clues, they may be false, thus providing light which may be a will-o'-the-wisp; so however pretty analogy may be and though it may be seductive, still, being only analogy, it never constitutes proof. [22]

Extended Series (see pp. 88–89)

The extended series of concrete examples can bring the following moribund sentences to life. Try developing the italicized generalities into more energetic series constructions.

1. She has a number of *unattractive characteristics*. [23]
2. We hear superstitious stories *everywhere*. [24]
3. In China I talked with *all sorts of people from many walks of life*. [25]
4. In the country there were *many nice smells*. [26]

Coordination—Subordination (see pp. 67–91)

Analyze the logic of coordination, subordination, and comparison in the following sentences; wherever desirable, change the constructions to reflect the relationship of the ideas.

1. Abelard came from a noble military family and decided to devote his life to the quiet pursuit of philosophy.

2. He abandoned, as he said, Mars for Minerva, his life turning out to be anything but peaceful.

3. He went to several schools, studied ardently, and surpassed his masters in a short time.

4. He was proud of his achievements and temperamental and soon became the most famous teacher in Europe.

5. Heedless of the consequences, he became involved in a scandalous affair with Heloise.

6. But it was not the romantic scandal, being unimportant compared to his heterodox theology, that led to his fall; the wagging of housewives' tongues was of no significance, whereas the wrath of Bernard was.

7. Bernard was a saint, Abbot of Clairvaux, and the most powerful ecclesiastic of his time.

8. His influence extended into more important places, including the Papacy itself, than Abelard's following, which was mostly students.

9. Though theoretically men of peace, in this conflict both assumed attitudes like a soldier.

10. Abelard's whole approach to theology and philosophy has been compared to a medieval knight errant, while Bernard looked upon him as virtually a pagan attack on the Church.

Voice (see pp. 92–96)

Convert the following sentences from active to passive:

1. Many people knew and admired Telemann's work in his own time.
2. Fewer people know it well now.
3. You might say the same of the philosophy of Boethius.
4. He influenced generations of thinkers, but one does not hear much of him today.
5. Time changes reputations.

Convert the following sentences from passive to active:

1. It was an extraordinary life that was lived by Lawrence.
2. Many bizarre adventures were undertaken in his short life, especially in Arabia.
3. Through his influence, many Arabs were roused to fight against the Turks.
4. Yet it was by the same man that a fine translation of Homer was produced.
5. For years the world has been fascinated by Lawrence.

Study the following passages, and see if they can be improved by changes of voice:

1. In studying the heavens, we are debarred from all senses except sight. The sun cannot be touched by us or traveled to; the moon cannot be walked around, nor a foot-rule applied to the Pleiades. Nevertheless, the geometry and physics which were found serviceable by astronomers on the surface of the earth, and which had been based upon touch and travel, have been unhesitatingly applied by them. In doing so, trouble has been brought down on their heads, which it was left for Einstein to clear up. It turned out that much of what had been learned by us from the sense of touch was unscientific prejudice, which must be rejected if a true picture of the world is to be had. [27]

2. Newton and his disciples thought light to be due to actual particles traveling from the source of light. But when subsequent investigators disproved this view of light and showed that light consisted of waves, some scientists revived the aether so that there should be something to undulate. The aether became still more respectable when they found it to play the same part in electromagnetic phenomena as in the propagation of light. Some people even hoped that atoms might turn out to be a mode of motion of the aether. At this stage, the atomic view of matter was, on the whole, getting the worst of it. [28]

3. Despite the foreboding that was felt by every intelligent mind, when the barbarism of the industrial age, inimical to any culture except that which grew out of its own inhuman absorption in abstract matter and abstract power, was contemplated, the dominant note of the period was one of hope. Before the Civil War the sense of achievement that came over the Eastern states was expanded by the promise of the Westward march; and the world was faced by men with a confidence that went beyond the complacent optimism of the British Utilitarians. [29]

4. At college a bud of interest in psychology was nipped by the chill of Professor Munsterburg's approach. In the middle of his second lecture I began looking for the nearest exit. Then psychology was put aside, and did not come up again until I began to wonder, after several years of research in biochemistry and physiology, why some of the men with whom I was associated at the Rockefeller Institute clung so tenaciously to diametrically opposing views about the simplest phenomena. [30]

5. At last he escaped with some companions and, after an adventurous crossing of the sea and much wandering on land, entered the monastery of Lérins. At least, so the story goes. Some years were spent there in religious practice, and then a visit to his relatives in Britain was marked one night by a vivid dream, which decided his future career. He returned to Gaul, and placed himself under Amator, Bishop of Auxerre, for the

training and other preparations necessary for a missionary to the Irish people. [31]

Point of View (see pp. 97–105)

1. Rewrite the passage by Eddington on pp. 99–100 giving it as impersonal a tone as you can.

2. Rewrite the passage by T. S. Eliot on pp. 121–22 in a more personal mode.

3. On the basis of the information and models in Chapter 8, pp. 97–105, and Chapter 19, pp. 252–56, write three paragraphs of description, one from a completely impersonal point of view, another from a personal point of view which does not involve the reader, and a third in which you try to draw the reader into the scene described.

Distinguishing Meanings

Distinguish the meanings of the following pairs and groups of words. Write sentences in which you illustrate the proper use of each word. Some of the word groups are almost identical in denotation, but differ in connotation or in the way they are used idiomatically. Write your sentences to bring out differences in connotation or idiom:

```
unique—unusual
latent—dormant
imply—infer
authoritarian—totalitarian
ambiguous—equivocal
fragments—segments
officious—official
depreciate—deprecate
continuous—continual
compose—comprise
irrational—unreasonable
compare—contrast
flammable, inflammable, nonflammable
healthy—healthful
less—fewer
personal—personnel
proof—evidence
plausible—feasible
raise—rise
```

sit—set
lay—lie
prone—supine
sensual—sensuous
affect—effect
practicable—practical
between—among
arduous—ardent
comparative—comparable
complement—compliment
emigrate—immigrate
excuse—pardon
human—humane
allusion—illusion
incredulous—incredible
acute—chronic
lightening—lightning
irony—sarcasm
seasonal—seasonable
sick—ill
toward—towards
amount—number
allude—refer
already—all ready
altogether—all together
idea—ideal
moral—ethical
genuine—authentic
real—actual
fancy—imagination
adorn, decorate, ornament, embellish, beautify, bedeck
advise, counsel, admonish, caution, warn
afraid, frightened, timid, terrified, timorous, fearful
alliance, league, coalition, confederation, union
alone, solitary, lonely, lonesome
quarrel, wrangle, altercation, squabble, spat
insanity, madness, psychosis, lunacy
origin, beginning, root, source, inception
base, mean, ignoble, abject, sordid, low, degrading
reward, prize, award, premium
smile, grin, simper, smirk
severe, stern, austere, ascetic
submission, yielding, acquiescence, compliance, nonresistance, obe-
dience, surrender, capitulation

instrument, tool, implement, machine, apparatus, appliance

elegance, refinement, distinction, gracefulness, felicity, propriety

completion, accomplishment, fulfillment, consummation, culmination, conclusion, upshot, denouement

thief, burglar, robber, pilferer, plagiarist, marauder, pirate, bandit, thug, racketeer

ridiculous, ludicrous, comic, droll, funny, laughable, farcical, whimsical

production, creation, construction, formation, fabrication, manufacture

contraction, reduction, diminution, decrease, shrinkage, attenuation, atrophy

discovery, invention, detection, disclosure, revelation

gulf, bay, inlet, estuary, fiord, lagoon

thought, reflection, consideration, meditation, study, speculation, deliberation

plan, scheme, design, project, proposal, proposition, suggestion

assumption, supposition, postulate, thesis, theorem, theory

desire, wish, want, need

small, minute, tiny, diminutive, miniature, microscopic, short, wee

exemption, exception, immunity, privilege

Levels of Usage (see pp. 165–78)

Rewrite the following passage, using a consistently formal level of diction. Pay particular attention to finding formal equivalents to the italicized colloquial or recently coined expressions. How is the passage changed by the changes in diction?

Some parents appreciate this *snob appeal* of Latin. At a recent educational conference I heard several guidance counselors talking over their problems and somebody soon brought up that *grand old headache*, Latin. The counselors seemed inclined to do away with it, but two circumstances daunted them: first, a strong and articulate body of parents in all their schools want it badly; second, where a good teacher offers Latin, the best students can usually be found taking it. The counselors scornfully implied that they just take it because it *has class*. The counselors are probably right, for these particular communities lie in a belt of suburbia and *exurbia* where *status hunger* is strong enough to awe Vance Packard. *Anyway*, their snobbery, not wholly unworthy and by no means unjustified, will enhance the standing of the field far better than the pedestrian pretexts of us latter-day Latinists. As an *inside tip*, let me add that many college admissions people, at least in the liberal-arts colleges, are snobs too, capable of being impressed by the sight of two or three, or better still, four years of Latin on a candidate's transcript. [RICHARD M. GUMMERE]

Translate the following passage taken from an Uncle Remus dialect story into general English. What happens as a result?

I can't skacely call to mine 'zackly w'at dey did do, but dey spoke speeches, en hollered, en cusst, en flung der langwidge 'round des like w'en yo' daddy was gwineter run fer de legislater en got lef'. Howsomever, de 'ranged der 'fairs, en splained der bizness. Bimeby, w'ile dey wuz 'sputin' longer one er nudder, de Elephent trompled on one er de Crawfishes. Co'se w'en dat creetur put his foot down, w'atsumever's under dar wuz boun' fer ter be squshed, en dey wa'n't nuff er dat Crawfish lef' fer ter tell dat he'd bin dar.

Dis make de udder Crawfishes mighty mad, en de sorter swarmed tergedder en draw'd up a kinder peramble wid some wharfo'es in it, en read her out in de 'sembly. But, bless grashus! sech a racket was gwine on dat nobody ain't hear it, 'ceepin may be de Mud Turkle en de Spring Lizzard, and dere enfloons wuz pow'ful lackin'. [JOEL CHANDLER HARRIS]

Rewrite the following quotation from the stately prose of Thomas Babington Macaulay, with a view to changing it to plain, un-bookish English. Pay particular attention to finding plainer equivalents to the italicized expressions. What is the result?

The Puritans were men whose minds had derived a *peculiar* character from the daily *contemplation* of *superior beings* and eternal interests. Not content with acknowledging, in general terms, an over-ruling Providence, they *habitually ascribed* every event to the will of the *Great Being*, for whose power nothing was too *vast*, for whose inspection nothing was too *minute*. To know him, to serve him, to *enjoy* him, was with them the great *end of existence*. They rejected with contempt the *ceremonious homage* which other sects substituted for the pure worship of the soul. Instead of catching occasional glimpses of the *Deity* through an *obscuring veil*, they *aspired to gaze* full on his *intolerable* brightness, and to commune with him face to face. Hence originated their contempt for *terrestrial distinctions*. The difference between the greatest and the meanest of mankind seemed to *vanish*, when compared with the *interval* which separated the whole race from him on whom their own eyes were constantly fixed. . . . If their steps were not accompanied by a *splendid train of menials, legions of ministering angels* had charge over them. Their palaces were houses not made with hands; their *diadems crowns of glory* which should never *fade away*. On the rich and the eloquent, on nobles and priests, they looked down with contempt: for they *esteemed* themselves rich in a more *precious treasure,* and eloquent in a more *sublime* language, nobles by right of an earlier creation, and priests by the *imposition* of a *mightier hand.*

Translate the following passage into a very formal style using complex sentence structure and formal diction:

By "criticism" I mean written commentary on and exposition of works of art. In this sense of the word no one claims criticism to be an end in itself. Art, too, may serve ends beyond itself, but need not be aware of them, and indeed performs its function much better if it is not. But criticism must always have its ends in view, which are, roughly, the elucidation of works of art and the correction of taste.[32]

Translate the following into the simple, terse style of Hemingway:

Burning with fever, Ann Rutledge lay in bed as the days passed. Though help arrived, it was to no avail, and she continued to moan in her fever for the one man to whom her thoughts ever turned. When he had been sent for, he rode out from New Salem to the Sand Ridge farm, where he was let in and they were left alone together a last hour in the log house, where slants of light from an open clapboard door shone on her face. After two days had passed, death came at last.[33]

Rewrite the "middle-style" passage by Trevelyan on p. 128 in the manner of Van Wyck Brooks (p. 126) and in the manner of Arnold (p. 123). Rewrite the passages by James and Hemingway (pp. 120–21) in the middle style (see pp. 128–29).

Suitability of Diction (see pp. 165–78)

Revise those of the following sentences in which the diction is unsuitable to the context:

1. Goethe hankered after the sunlit beauties of Italy and the splendor of the classical past.

2. After picking a loser three times in a row, Joe manfully redoubled his efforts to choose a winner in the fourth race.

3. If Dido and Aeneas had talked over their relationship and its problems, they might have been able to understand their incompatibility and arrange an amicable separation.

4. From a certain point of view, Berlioz and Chopin both look like squares.

5. Henry thought that he had made a viable plan for adding another room to his house.

6. After having himself crowned Emperor, Napoleon revealed himself as the fascist he really was.

7. Councilman Brown is incorrect in his assumption and dopey in his conclusions.

8. The Black Angels' rumble with the Spacemen never came off.

9. His Oedipal conflict nearly drove Hamlet crazy.

10. Most discussions of education in the daily press are pure fiddle-faddle.

11. Henry had failed to foresee the complexities of repairing the broken sink.

12. The grub in the hotel restaurant is only so-so.

13. The Kalikaks always dined on hominy grits.

14. The study group claims that it needs a fifty per cent increase in its budget.

15. Thomas Mann is among the jazziest of modern writers.

16. The crowd in the baseball stadium was most enthusiastic and gave vigorous support to the home team.

17. From the intemperate tone of these remarks, we must conclude that the Senator really had his dander up.

18. The Calvinist pitch never made much headway in Mediterranean countries.

19. That was a superlative hot dog, Mary.

20. If Joan wants to come with us, who is to say her nay?

Euphemism (see pp. 154–56)

Translate the following passages into plain English:

1. Many senior citizens who live on Social Security payments have dietary insufficiencies because they must spend so large a part of their income on medications.

2. The corporate family here at the Murky Vacuum Cleaner Company has selected our sales engineer, Mr. James Smith, to call at your home for a personal interview. We want you to have the opportunity to see some of the most advanced modern electronic devices at work in your own home. As part of our personalized service to our clients, Mr. Smith will be glad to explain to you our deferred payment plan.

3. Dear Mrs. Cross: It is with deep regret that the Office of the Dean must inform you that the personal conduct of your son Hubert has fallen below the expectations of the College. On last Saturday evening your son was one of the most vociferous participants in an unseemly disturbance that took place on the campus. He was apprehended as he was making his way from one of the women's residence halls with certain articles of feminine attire in his possession. It was apparent that he had partaken of intoxicants, and his language on this occasion was not that

of a gentleman. The College has reluctantly decided that Hubert must be requested to withdraw for the remainder of the semester. We hope that when he returns to us, he will have learned to govern himself by more mature values.

Borrowed Words (see pp. 158–61)

Indicate which of the following words are still printed in italics and treated as foreign words:

chauffeur	campagna
bête noire	bouquet
gloire	fiancée
valet	cappuccino
grande jete	graffiti
Zeitgeist	goyim
ersatz	Anschluss
viola da gamba	force de frappe
ergo	peripetea
non sequitur	differentia
cum grano salis	genre
pieds noirs	allegro
gestalt	andante

Triteness (see pp. 202–205)

Revise the following sentences to eliminate the jaded phrases:

1. Poker and fast women were Joe Smith's Achilles' heel.

2. In the twinkling of an eye, Mary Jane slipped into a chic little afternoon frock and was ready to go out on the town.

3. Last but not least, the rumor that Tsov had been arrested roused the mob to frenzy: the workers poured into the public square until they were packed in as tight as sardines.

4. Governor Green will bring to the helm of state a gift for golden oratory and a character of unimpeachable integrity.

5. The government has explored every avenue in an effort to break down the iron curtain of censorship that separates the two countries.

6. Since we had not even heard about their whirlwind courtship, the announcement of Jane's engagement to Jim came like a bolt from the blue.

7. In the full flush of victory, Jim held out the hand of friendship to his vanquished opponent and wanted to let bygones be bygones.

8. The Herculean task of building a just society can be undertaken only by men of vision and dedication.

9. Bottlenecks in production have skyrocketed the costs to the consumer.

10. All of Jean's pent-up emotion poured forth, and she threatened to leave Henry, bag and baggage.

11. Conciliatory language can cover a multitude of sins, but in this instance the fraud practiced on the public is as clear as daylight.

12. Precautionary measures will stand us in good stead in these perilous times.

13. The Senator's speech has triggered a chain reaction of adverse comment from informed sources.

14. With catlike grace, Desmond slipped past the gates and with one blow felled the guard like an ox.

15. There are no hard and fast rules that will enable you to pass an examination with flying colors.

Jargon and Abstract Language (see pp. 174–85)

Revise the following sentences, eliminating as much jargon and unnecessary abstraction as possible:

1. Interpersonal relationships are negatively influenced by disagreements about monetary matters.

2. Existential considerations give the character of necessity to the ingestion of nutriment.

3. The tension of ambiguity is of frequent occurrence in those of the electorate who are not uninfluenced by the opposing contentions of candidates.

4. Prudential considerations suggest that appropriate preventive action may require only one-ninth of the expenditure of time and energy required by action taken only after serious difficulties have arisen.

5. Failure to remit the specified amount promptly may result in termination of telephone service by the company.

6. Magisterial evaluation of the great monuments of the literature of Western culture is an intellectual privilege reserved to the humanistic thinker of sufficient moral and intellectual maturity to render such judgments authoritatively.

7. Overindulgence may lead to gastrointestinal disturbance.

8. The committee is of the opinion that the dispatch of business would be rendered palpably less complex if stenographic aid could be employed to record in full the transactions of the committee.

9. President Harding has well observed that it is a legitimate concern of Americans to pursue their commercial interests.

10. The criminal was apprehended as he attempted to disembark from the aircraft.

11. The continued intransigence of the right-deviationists has com-

pelled the Party to adopt coercive measures to liquidate counterrevolutionary intrigue and sabotage.

12. The temporal distribution of the events leading to the decline of the Roman Empire is such that objective evaluation of their respective significance is attended by all the difficulties that are encountered in fields of study that have complex variables as their subject matter.

13. The analysand has been severely traumatized by a preadolescent conflict with several significant authority figures.

14. The concatenation of events has made the committee realize that its policies have not normalized the situation, and thus the committee recognizes the need to reorient itself and to revitalize certain features of its program.

15. The audible dissent of the audience forced the speaker to terminate his address.

Paragraphs for Revision

These are primarily exercises in structural conciseness (Chapter 10, pp. 115–19) and in word choice (Chapter 14, pp. 187–96). Of the following passages, the first two are manufactured, the second two authentic; to turn any of them into readable English is no small challenge. Study them until you are certain of their content, then eliminate needless repetition, jargon, clichés, and empty verbiage; substitute meaningful vocabulary where necessary; and make the sentence structure as concise as you can. The problem is to communicate the content as directly, economically, and lucidly as possible. Do not be surprised if the last two examples are boiled away by this process to very little.

The general causes that rendered it exceedingly difficult for the English people and the American people to achieve an understanding with one another were at that particular time both very large in number and profound: many of these general causes of lack of understanding have been removed by the passage of the years, decades, and centuries, but at the present day differences of racial composition between England and America are much more pronounced than they were at the time of the American Revolution. English society at that time was still a society which was governed by aristocratic values, while the society of the American colonies was already governed by values of a democratic type. An ocean voyage of from six to seven weeks over a frequently disturbed or stormy ocean separated the capital of London from Boston, which was the leading city of the American colonies. For this reason, person-to-person contact was not very great, and emigration from the mother country of England had not been very considerable at all since the year

1640. In the mother country of England the world of political activity and the world of good society were not open to those who belonged to the Puritan sects, while Puritanism was a dominant factor in the colonies of New England and even extended its influence outward to others of the thirteen colonies; it was the Anglicanism of the Established Church of England that was not in fashion in the colony of Massachusetts. English society was of great antiquity; it was governed by a lot of elaborate social forms and usages; it had a great deal of artificialty; American society was of recent origin; its social forms were on the whole simple; much of its life had a quality of rawness.

But the peoples of the Southern States were far from fully united in their desire to break their ties with the Northern States and leave the Union. It is a matter of fact that in the states of Georgia, Alabama, Mississippi, and Louisiana there was a strong movement which was in opposition to secession from the Union; this opposition made its appearance in the large minority vote that was registered against secession. In addition to this opposition in four states that were in the Deep South, in the State of Virginia there were counties in the western region of that state that were so opposed to seceding from the North that they severed their ties with the Old Dominion and at a later period entered into partnership with the Union as the newly established state of West Virginia. Yet further opposition to secession is in evidence. In the part of North Carolina that lies to the west, there was a wide prevalence of loyalty to the Union. To the west and north of North Carolina, in the eastern parts of Kentucky and Tennessee, there were, it has been shown without a doubt, a majority of those who sympathized with the Union; thousands of men who lived in that region made evident that they were loyal to the Union by the fact that they volunteered for service in the army of the Federal Government. Further north, in the border states of Maryland and Kentucky, it is well known that there was a sharp division of loyalties, but, as it turned out, there was only a little force that was needed to ensure that those two states would remain within the boundaries of the Union. In somewhat less than twelve months after the first shot of the war had been discharged against the wall of Federal property (Fort Sumter), the optimistic hopes of those who adhered to the confederacy that the states which lay on the borders between the North and the South would decide to come to their assistance in the ensuing struggle for independence had been for once and all permanently dispelled.

One of the most noticeable factors in Frost's poetry is his emphasis on aloneness and the solitary individual. It appears that this emphasis is a distinctive facet of Frost's message to the world at large. It is the thesis of this paper that the recurrent theme of isolation in Frost's poetry is a significant factor in the understanding of Frost as a poet and as a man.

Of the examples of Frost's poetry which have been assigned there are several which can be seen to contribute directly to an understanding of isolation in Frost and his message. In order to deal with solitude in Frost's poetry it will be necessary to deal intensively with several of these poems in order to examine their individual contribution.

One of the most constantly recurring themes within which solitude appears in Frost's poetry is the storm theme in which the beings depicted by Frost are set in opposition to the elements of nature. In order to use the poems of Frost as an indication of the meaning of isolation it is necessary to understand that Frost employs natural phenomena as a sort of background from which he draws certain insights into the behavior of people.

Admittedly, the sum of all our knowledge about speech is still expressed by a small fraction. But in the fifty years or so since Speech began, once more, to be accepted as a possibly liberal study, the fraction has grown. At least mechanics and mysticism no longer govern most undergraduate instruction. The undergraduate may, once more, find in studying Speech some of his most fruitful opportunities to explore the relationships between the different natures of men and the different manners and modes of discourse.

It is scarcely possible today for anyone to explore his own speech behavior under sensible guidance from persons who know what is now knowable about speech without making significant, intimate discoveries about the nature of Man—his infirmities and his potentialities. For this reason properly conducted speech rehabilitation consultations, properly taught courses in general public speaking or argument or discussion or rhetorical literature, and properly directed dramatic rehearsals and productions become liberal education of a most meaningful sort. Only laboratory experience in science and in creative writing equal the speech clinic, the platform, and the stage in producing personalized understanding of the self and the realities of the external world. And in addition there are the commonly admitted values of accumulating factual knowledge about human speech and the literary remains of Man's significant speaking efforts.

But, "What is the *content* of Speech?" The central and unique "content" of Speech is the range and consequences of the choices Man may make in influencing others through speech. Speech explores the potentialities of a pervasive medium of human expression; its special peculiarity is that the "choices" and intentions of Man, when using this medium, are always in some degree more *social* than aesthetic.

Rhetorical Analysis

Following are two parallel passages, reproduced here for study, both written about the same time, both concerned with the social and economic condition of the southern Negro sharecropper in the 1930's. The first is part of a monumental sociological study bristling with notes, references, statistics, tables, and graphs, aiming for near scientific objectivity and addressed to a limited professional audience; its author is a disinterested Swedish economist. The second passage describes the same conditions from the point of view of those who have suffered under them. The author, a famous Negro novelist, was intimately familiar with these conditions; his audience is the general reading public, and his purpose frankly propagandistic. Together the two passages illustrate admirably how style is determined by the writer's purpose and by the audience he is writing for. They will repay close study.

Compare the two, and explain the rhetorical choices the authors have made. Why have they chosen very different points of view from which to present their descriptions? How successful is each point of view? Compare their use of figures: Myrdal tries to be exact, Wright does not. Compare their use of concrete, visual detail—what, for example, is "advanced" to the sharecropper according to each writer? Why are there these rhetorical differences? Why does Wright quote a folk rhyme while Myrdal refers to an economic study? What are the differences of word choice and what effects are achieved by vocabulary? Why, for example, does one writer say "landlords," the other "Lords of the Land"? Compare authorial commitment (pp. 97–103) particularly in the last paragraphs. Does Myrdal ever show the kind of personal involvement in his material that Wright does? What are the differences of sentence structure? Do coordinate structures, for example, prevail in one passage more than in the other? How does Wright achieve his rhythmic sonority of tone? What is its purpose?

As a difficult but very valuable exercise, try writing a pair of short essays on a similar subject, one from a dispassionate, objective point of view, the other from a more subjective, emotional point of view.

Wages are not fixed per week, per month, or per annum. Nor is the sharecropping agreement modeled after the ordinary piece-wage system. The cropper, rather, gets a share of the product. The quantity of the product depends not only on the efforts of the workers but on the conditions of the soil and on the hazards of wind and weather; and it is not the quantity of the output alone but also its price that determines the final reward for the toils of labor. . . .

Indeed, any study of the concrete details of the system will reveal that the sharecropper or share tenant usually has most of the disadvantages of being an independent entrepreneur without having hardly any of the rights that ordinarily go with such a position. Only in relatively few cases are his rights and obligations set down in a written contract. In most cases he does not sell even his own share in the cotton crop himself. According to the crop lien laws in most states, he has no right to dispose of it until he has paid to the landlord all the rent due and the advances he has received during the season. And since he cannot well do that until the crop has been sold and paid for, the landlord is legally entitled to handle all the marketing as he sees fit. Seldom is the tenant even consulted about how to sell and when.

Worse than that, however, is the general pattern of making all kinds of account-keeping a unilateral affair. The tenant usually has to take the landlord's word for what price has been obtained for the cotton, for what is the total amount of advances received from the landlord, and for what the interest on these advances is, and so on. . . .

In several conversations with white planters—as also with employers of Negro labor in cities, particularly of domestics—the writer has noticed the display of a sort of moral double standard. White people of the landowning class who give the impression of being upright and honest in all their other dealings take it for granted and sometimes brag about the fact that they cheat their Negroes. . . .

The "advancing" of food, clothing, and other necessities of life is a significant part of the system. Since the tenant is ordinarily without re-sources—otherwise he would not be a tenant—he cannot usually wait for his wages until the crop has been harvested and sold. He has, there-fore, to live on a credit basis at least during a large part of the year. For an average period of seven months, according to Woofter's sample study for 1934, the tenant receives credit from the landlord, often in a special store or commissary, where he can buy household supplies up to a certain amount a month. This amount varies according to the size of the family, the prospects for the crop, the market conditions, and so on. The average in Woofter's sample was $12.80 per month and $88 per year. . . . A flat rate of 10 per cent is usual but, since the duration of the credit is only a few months, the annual rate is several times higher.

According to Woofter's plantation study for the depression period 1930–1934, no less than 13–15 per cent of the tenants ended each crop year in debt to their landlords. This means that, in addition to their having to start the next crop year with a deficit, they have nothing to live on during the winter. The average debt for these tenants varied between $89 and $143. . . . . The practice of forcing an indebted tenant to stay on the plantation in order to work off his debt certainly became less prevalent during the period of relatively abundant agricultural labor which lasted from the beginning of the depression until the present war boom. We do not know whether the present shortage of farm labor has brought about any new increase in debt-peonage. What we do know is that the whole legal system previously gave the tenants but little protection against such abuses and that, so far, there has been no fundamental change in this legal system. . . .

It is our impression that the predominant feeling among most Negro tenants is that they can get more or less out of the landlord depending upon what kind of landlord he is, and how he is approached. But not often have they been taught to feel that they have definite rights and definite obligations, and that it is up to them to make good.

—Gunnar Myrdal, *An American Dilemma*, 1944

So, in the early spring, when the rains have ceased and the ground is ready for plowing, we present ourselves to the Lords of the Land and ask to make a crop. We sign a contract—usually our contracts are oral—which allows us to keep one-half of the harvest after all debts are paid. If we have worked upon these plantations before, we are legally bound to plant, tend, and harvest another crop. If we should escape to the city to avoid paying our mounting debts, white policemen track us down and ship us back to the plantation.

The Lords of the Land assign us ten or fifteen acres of soil already bled of its fertility through generations of abuse. They advance us one mule, one plow, seed, tools, fertilizer, clothing, and food, the main staples of which are fat hog meat, coarsely ground corn meal, and sorghum molasses. If we have been lucky the year before, maybe we have saved a few dollars to tide us through the fall months, but spring finds us begging an "advance"—credit—from the Lords of the Land. . . .

Most of the flogging and lynchings occur at harvest time, when fruit hangs heavy and ripe, when the leaves are red and gold, when nuts fall from the trees, when the earth offers its best. The thought of harvest steals upon us with a sense of inescapable judgment. It is time now to settle accounts with the Lords of the Land, to divide the crops and pay old debts, and we are afraid. We have never grown used to confronting the Lords of the Land when the last of the cotton is ginned and baled, for we know beforehand that we have lost yet another race with time, that we are deeper in debt. When word reaches us that the Lords of the Land are bent over the big books down at the plantation commissary, we lower our eyes, shake our heads, and mutter:

> A *naught's a naught,*
> *Five's a figger;*
> *All for the white man,*
> *None for the nigger.* . . .

And after we have divided the crops we are still entangled as deeply as ever in this hateful web of cotton culture. We are older; our bodies are weaker; our families are larger; our clothes are in rags; we are still in debt; and, worst of all, we face another year that holds even less hope than the one we have just endured. We know that this is not right, and dark thoughts take possession of our minds. We know that to tread this mill is to walk in days of slow death. When alone, we stand and look out over the green, rolling fields and wonder why it is that living here is so hard. Everything seems to whisper of the possibility of happiness, of satisfying experiences; but somehow happiness and satisfaction never come into our lives. The land upon which we live holds a promise, but the promise fades with the passing seasons. . . .

In the main we are different from other folks in that, when an impulse moves us, when we are caught in the throes of inspiration, when we are moved to better our lot, we do not ask ourselves: "Can we do it?" but: "Will they let us do it?" Before we black folk can move, we must first look into the white man's mind to see what he is thinking, and the white man's mind is a mind that is always changing.

—RICHARD WRIGHT, *12 Million Black Voices,* 1941

Selections for Praxis

The following extracts are all from famous writers who have highly distinctive mannerisms of style. Study each of these passages until you are aware of its characteristic diction, sentence structure, and rhythm. Then try writing a paragraph of your own in the same style. The point of this exercise is not to get you into the habit of writing like Pater or Henry James, but to enlarge your sense of the possibilities of style:

Sir Francis Bacon, *Essays,* from "Of Studies"

Studies serve for delight, for ornament, and for ability. Their chief use for delight, is in privateness and retiring; for ornament, is in discourse; and for ability, is in the judgment and disposition of business; for expert men can execute, and perhaps judge of particulars, one by one: but the general counsels, and the plots and marshalling of affairs come best from those that are learned. To spend too much time in studies, is sloth; to use them too much for ornament, is affectation; to make judgment wholly by their rules, is the humour of a scholar: they perfect nature, and are perfected by experience: for natural abilities are like natural plants, that need pruning by study; and studies themselves do give forth directions too much at large, except they be bounded in by experience. Crafty men contemn studies, simple men admire them, and wise men use them; for they teach not their own use; but that is a wisdom without them and above them, won by observation. Read not to contradict and confute, nor to believe and take for granted, nor to find talk and discourse, but to weigh and consider. Some books are to be tasted, others to be swallowed, and some few to be chewed and digested; that is, some books are to be read only in parts; others to be read but not curiously; and some few to be read wholly, and with diligence and attention.

Lord Chesterfield, from *Letters to His Son*

Women have, in general, but one object, which is their beauty; upon which scarce any flattery is too gross for them to follow. Nature has hardly formed a woman ugly enough to be insensible to flattery upon her person; if her face is so shocking that she must, in some degree, be conscious of it, her figure and air, she trusts, make ample amends for it. If her figure is deformed, her face, she thinks, counterbalances it. If they are both bad, she comforts herself that she has graces, a certain manner, a *je ne sais quoi* still more engaging than beauty. This truth is evident from the studied and elaborate dress of the ugliest woman in the world. An undoubted, uncontested, conscious beauty is, of all women, the least sensible of flattery upon that head; she knows it is her due, and is therefore obliged to nobody for giving it her. She must be flattered upon her understanding; which, though she may possibly not doubt of herself, yet she suspects that men may distrust.

Do not mistake me, and think that I mean to recommend to you abject and criminal flattery: no; flatter nobody's vices or crimes: on the contrary, abhor and discourage them. But there is no living in the world without a complaisant indulgence for people's weaknesses, and innocent, though ridiculous vanities. If a man has a mind to be thought wiser, and a woman handsomer, than they really are, their error is a comfortable one to themselves, and an innocent one with regard to other people; and I would rather make them my friends by indulging them in it, than my enemies by endeavouring (and that to no purpose) to undeceive them.

Samuel Johnson, from *Preface to Shakespeare*

But the admirers of this great poet have never less reason to indulge their hopes of supreme excellence, than when he seems fully resolved to sink them in dejection, and mollify them with tender emotions by the fall of greatness, the danger of innocence, or the crosses of love. He is not

long soft and pathetic without some idle conceit, or contemptible equivocation. He no sooner begins to move, than he counteracts himself; and
terror and pity, as they are rising in the mind, are checked and blasted by
sudden frigidity.

A quibble is to *Shakespeare*, what luminous vapours are to the traveller;
he follows it at all adventures, it is sure to lead him out of his way, and
sure to engulf him in the mire. It has some malignant power over his
mind, and its fascinations are irresistible. Whatever be the dignity or
profundity of his disquisition, whether he be enlarging knowledge or
exalting affection, whether he be amusing attention with incidents, or
enchaining it in suspense, let but a quibble spring up before him, and he
leaves his work unfinished. A quibble is the golden apple for which he
will always turn aside from his career, or stoop from his elevation. A
quibble, poor and barren as it is, gave him such delight, that he was content to purchase it, by the sacrifice of reason, propriety and truth.
A quibble was to him the fatal *Cleopatra* for which he lost the world,
and was content to lose it.

Thomas Carlyle, from *Past and Present*

Blessed is he who has found his work; let him ask no other blessedness.
He has a work, a life-purpose; he has found it, and will follow it! How, as
a free-flowing channel, dug and torn by noble force through the sour
mud-swamp of one's existence, like an ever-deepening river there, it runs
and flows;—draining-off the sour festering water, gradually from the root
of the remotest grass-blade; making, instead of pestilential swamp, a green
fruitful meadow with its clear-flowing stream. How blessed for the
meadow itself, let the stream and *its* value be great or small! Labor is Life:
from the inmost heart of the Worker rises his god-given Force, the sacred
celestial Life-essence breathed into him by Almighty God; from his inmost heart awakens him to all nobleness,—to all knowledge, "self-knowl-
edge" and much else, so soon as Work fitly begins. Knowledge? The
knowledge that will hold good in working, cleave thou to that; for Nature
herself accredits that, says Yea to that. Properly thou hast no other knowledge but what thou hast got by working: the rest is yet all a hypothesis
of knowledge; a thing to be argued of in schools, a thing floating in the
clouds, in endless logic-vortices, till we try it and fix it. "Doubt, of whatever kind, can be ended by Action alone."

Walter Pater, from "Conclusion" to *Studies in the History of the Renaissance*

To burn always with this hard, gemlike flame, to maintain this ecstasy,
is success in life. In a sense it might even be said that our failure is to
form habits: for, after all, habit is relative to a stereotyped world, and

meantime it is only the roughness of the eye that makes any two persons, things, situations, seem alike. While all melts under our feet, we may well grasp at any exquisite passion, or any contribution to knowledge that seems by a lifted horizon to set the spirit free for a moment, or any stirring of the senses, strange dyes, strange colours, and curious odours, or work of the artist's hands, or the face of one's friend. Not to discriminate every moment some passionate attitude in those about us, and in the very brilliancy of their gifts some tragic dividing of forces on their ways, is, on this short day of frost and sun, to sleep before evening. With this sense of the splendour of our experience and its awful brevity, gathering all we are into one desperate effort to see and touch, we shall hardly have time to make theories about the things we see and touch. What we have to do is to be for ever curiously testing new opinions and courting new impressions, never acquiescing in a facile orthodoxy of Comte, or of Hegel, or of our own. Philosophical theories or ideas, as points of view, instruments of criticism, may help us to gather up what might otherwise pass unregarded by us. 'Philosophy is the microscope of thought.' The theory or idea or system which requires of us the sacrifice of any part of this experience, in consideration of some interest into which we cannot enter, or some abstract theory we have not identified with ourselves, or of what is only conventional, has no real claim upon us.

Henry James, from the Preface to *The Princess Casamassima*

This in fact I have ever found rather terribly the point—that the figures in any picture, the agents in any drama, are interesting only in proportion as they feel their respective situations; since the consciousness, on their part, of the complication exhibited forms for us their link of connection with it. But there are degrees of feeling—the muffled, the faint, the just sufficient, the barely intelligent, as we may say; and the acute, the intense, the complete, in a word—the power to be finely aware and richly responsible. It is those moved in this latter fashion who "get most" out of all that happens to them and who in so doing enable us, as readers of their record, as participators by a fond attention, also to get most. Their being finely aware—as Hamlet and Lear, say, are finely aware—*makes* absolutely the intensity of their adventure, gives the maximum of sense to what befalls them. We care, our curiosity and our sympathy care, comparatively little for what happens to the stupid, the coarse, and the blind; care for it, and for the effects of it, at the most as helping to precipitate what happens to the more deeply wondering, to the really sentient. Hamlet and Lear are surrounded, amid their complications, by the stupid and the blind, who minister in all sorts of ways to their recorded fate. Persons of markedly limited sense would, on such a principle as that, play a part in the career of my tormented youth; but he wouldn't be of markedly limited sense himself—he would note as many things and vibrate to as many occasions as I might make him.

Punctuation (see pp. 283–90)

I. COMPOUND SENTENCES
Correct the punctuation where necessary:

1. William Marcy Tweed started his political career in 1848 as a volunteer fireman, by 1870 he had risen to a position of great power and notoriety.

2. He practiced graft and patronage and bribery and by such means became the political boss of New York.

3. For a while Tweed was a Representative in Congress but soon returned to New York, where the political pickings were easier.

4. In 1868 he bribed several judges to create 60,000 new citizens from among recent immigrants, some of them swearing allegiance on a French grammar book.

5. The new voters elected one of Tweed's henchmen mayor, now he owned the key men in New York from the governor to the county sheriff.

6. Opportunities for graft were now nearly unlimited and the Tweed Ring were finally stealing eighty-five per cent of the money collected by the city.

7. A million dollars a month were being stolen but no one protested, Tweed had put fifty-nine opposition leaders on his payroll.

8. He was exposed by the *Times* in 1871 and fled to Cuba.

9. The escape a failure, he was apprehended and returned to New York, there he was kept in jail until his death in 1878.

10. But he remained unregenerate, he felt his corrupt methods were the only practical means of governing New York.

II. RESTRICTIVE AND NONRESTRICTIVE MODIFIERS
Supply the correct punctuation in the following sentences:

1. Miss Jones who is the reference librarian is always very helpful.
2. The Miss Jones who is reference librarian is always very helpful.
3. Please stop by my office whenever you have a free moment.
4. The airplane which was invented by the Wright Brothers took off from Kitty Hawk in 1903.
5. A supply train carrying much-needed food and medicine was sent out early the next day.
6. This train which also carried ammunition was ambushed and wrecked.

7. In May of 1864 General Grant who was in charge of all the Northern armies took direct command of the Virginia campaign.

8. The general who was finally chosen to take command of all the Northern armies was Ulysses S. Grant.

9. Be sure to lower the heat as soon as the mixture begins to boil.

10. The little schooner set out across the channel although the seas were choppy and the sky threatening.

11. For a long time after its passage in 1890 the Sherman Antitrust Law which was directed against the monopolies was seldom enforced.

12. The head man of the village carrying a sheaf of wheat stood before the sacred tree.

13. The villagers carrying the first fruits of the harvest gathered in a circle around the sacred tree; the villagers carrying sacrifices to placate the dead gathered about the funeral mounds.

14. The numbers three and seven are often thought to have magical properties.

15. Only two numbers three and seven are widely considered to have magical properties.

16. We came out of the building just as the snow began to fall.

17. Our flight for Washington which was finally allowed to take off was an hour late.

18. Our flight for Washington was finally allowed to take off after the fog had lifted slightly.

19. The literary critic usually judges a literary work aesthetically while a scholar usually judges it historically.

20. Be sure to spend a day at the National Gallery of Art while you are staying in Washington.

III. GENERAL EXERCISES

Supply the necessary punctuation in the following passage:

After a sketchy grammar-school education Carry Moore attended the Missouri State Normal School where she received a teaching certificate. In 1867 she married Charles Gloyd a physician and Union Army veteran but he proved to be an alcoholic and they soon separated. When he later died from alcoholism Carry was left with an infant daughter who became insane. Carry subsequently met and married David Nation he was a minister and educator. In 1901 after twenty-four years of marriage they were divorced in Medicine Lodge Kansas Nation charging her with desertion. She had recently organized a local branch of the Woman's Christian Temperance Union and begun her anti-saloon campaign. With a hatchet which was to become her permanent symbol she descended on Wichita Kansas in 1900 and wrecked a number of saloons. Later dressed in black and armed with the ever present hatchet she invaded Topeka's Senate Bar a raid that brought her national attention leaving a wake of broken bottles smashed furniture and pools of whiskey. Saloon raids destruction arrests lecture tours to pay her fines more raids such was the pattern of Carry Nation's later career. Sometimes earning as much as $300 a week which was a great deal in those days she never became wealthy for she contributed heavily to such charities as a home for drunkards' wives. Many temperance societies received her support but most of the leading reformers embarrassed by her extraordinary methods were reluctant to give her their endorsement though they shared her goals the closing of all saloons and the prohibition of intoxicating liquor.

Correct the punctuation in the following:

P. T. Barnum often called the "prince of showmen" dedicated himself to fooling all of the people all the time and making them like it, this forerunner of the modern ad man, soon realized that the American public was both curious, and gullible. His first discovery: a woman named Joice Heth who claimed to be 161 years old, was a great success. After she had been seen by thousands, Barnum claimed she was, actually, a dummy, thousands trooped back even though they had already seen her to find out if they had been cheated before. They didn't find out and Barnum was twice as rich; his gift for showmanship now thoroughly established. His most notorious fraud the Feejee Mermaid: a monstrosity stitched together from the body of a monkey and the tail of a fish—was exhibited in the American Museum which he opened in 1841. He was often quoted as saying—The American people love to be humbugged. Not all of his enterprises were frauds however, Jenny Lind and Jumbo the great elephant were among his most celebrated stars, and he himself was a temperance lecturer. But, an adman to the end he had a New York paper print his obituary, four days before his death in 1891; so that he could enjoy this last publicity stunt.

Notes to Exercises

1. COMPARE: "Emerson's affirmation of both physics and dialectic, of both science and myth, an affirmation which justified the existence of the artist, the poet, the saint, was of prime importance." [LEWIS MUMFORD]

2. COMPARE: "Despite the foreboding that every intelligent mind felt when it contemplated the barbarism of the industrial age, inimical to any culture except that which grew out of its own inhuman absorption in abstract matter and abstract power, the dominant note of the period was hope." [MUMFORD]

3. COMPARE: "A center once of the Arab slave trade and rich Islamic settlements along the East African coast, a tributary later of Portuguese rovers and British empire builders, Zanzibar was a place of turbulence and mystery until, pacified by British rule, it learned to live on its memories of the past and its declining exports of cloves." [NEW YORK *Times*]

4. COMPARE: "On Sunday armed rebels acting in the name of Zanzibar's Black African majority overthrew a Sultanate representative mainly of the island's Arab minority élite—a government in office only since Dec. 10, when Zanzibar received its independence from Britain." [NEW YORK *Times*]

5. COMPARE: "A lung ailment from which he was suffering gave Augustine the excuse he wanted to retire from his professorship, and at Cassiciacum, through reading and reflection and discussions with friends, he endeavoured to obtain a better understanding of the Christian religion, using as an instrument concepts and themes taken from neo-Platonic philosophy, his idea of Christianity being still very incomplete and tinctured, more than it was to be later, by neo-Platonism." [F. COPLESTON]

6. COMPARE: "The alternative to this theory is that creation of matter is taking place continually and that although stars and galaxies evolve from this basic material, the universe, when considered as a large-scale structure, is in a steady state." [A. C. B. LOVELL]

7. See p. 74.

8. COMPARE: "The phase that began in 1877 was inaugurated by the withdrawal of federal troops from the South, the abandonment of the Negro as a ward of the nation, the giving up of the attempt to guarantee the freedman his civil and political equality, and the acquiescence of the rest of the country in the South's demand that the whole problem be left to the disposition of the dominant Southern white people." [C. VANN WOODWARD]

9. COMPARE: "Bent double, but with faces raised, we crept into the almost utter darkness at a pace that grew slower with every step." [GEORGE ORWELL]

10. COMPARE: "It is almost impossible to sum up Emerson's doctrine, for he touched life on many sides, and what is more, he touched it freshly, so though he is a Platonist, one will not find Plato's doctrines of Art in his essay on Art; and though he was in a very derivative way a Kantian, one will not find Kant's principles at the bottom of his ethics." [MUMFORD]

11. COMPARE: "Consumers, anticipating possible shortages, immediately began to protect themselves against a deprivation which, in light of their peacetime persuasion, they inevitably regarded as painful or even intolerable." [J. K. GALBRAITH]

12. COMPARE: "The good novelist then, the one who is not the dupe of his subject-matter, who has transformed his emotions into free emotions, cannot but in the process of this discipline have learnt the importance and value of freedom." [IRIS MURDOCH]

13. COMPARE: "government of the people, by the people, for the people." [LINCOLN]

14. COMPARE: "Everyone complains of his memory, and no one complains of his judgment." [ROCHEFOUCAULD]

15. COMPARE: "To be great is to be misunderstood." [EMERSON]

16. COMPARE: "We have always known that heedless self-interest was bad morals; we know now that it is bad economics." [F. D. ROOSEVELT]

17. COMPARE: "The young man who has not wept is a savage; the old man who will not laugh is a fool." [SANTAYANA]

18. COMPARE: "In skating over thin ice, our safety is our speed." [EMERSON]

19. COMPARE: "It is men, not God, who have produced racks, whips, prisons, slavery, guns, bayonets, and bombs; it is by human avarice or human stupidity, not by the churlishness of nature, that we have poverty and overwork." [C. S. LEWIS]

20. See p. 91.

21. COMPARE: "What lures the American student is the life of the boulevards, the cafes, the bistros; it is the Latin Quarter; it is the opera and the ballet, the theatre and the experimental film; it is the bookshop on every corner, the dozen newspapers in every city; it is the mature student body, educating itself, joining in the risks of life, taking an active part in literature, journalism, art, and politics." [HENRY STEELE COMMAGER]

22. COMPARE: "Analogy thus provides clues, but they may easily be false clues; it provides light, but the light may be a will-o'-the-wisp. However pretty, however seductive, analogy remains analogy and never constitutes proof." [JULIAN HUXLEY]

23. See p. 89.

24. COMPARE: ". . . in news, stories, in table talk, in radio and television interviews, from pulpit, press, rostrum, forum, microphone, street corner, classroom, bar and parlor, these stories descend on us in an uninterrupted stream." [BERGEN EVANS]

25. COMPARE: "And I talked with soldiers, peasants, workers, intellectuals, students, composers, teachers, doctors, lawyers, scientists, journalists, actors, pediatricians, nurses, gardeners, ex-capitalists, lumbermen, nomads, prisoners, priests, cadres, ex-landlords, research workers, jailers, ballerinas, union leaders, housewives, movie stars, poets, inventors, acupuncturists, engineers, V.D. specialists, state planners, cancer specialists, former acquaintances, harp makers, gentlemen in the park, Mongols, Tibetans, Miaos, Lisus, Mohammedans, assorted foreign diplomats and one ex-emperor." [EDGAR SNOW]

26. COMPARE: "To the boy Henry Adams, summer was drunken. Among senses smell was the strongest—smell of hot pine-woods and sweet-fern in the scorching summer noon; of new-mown hay; of ploughed earth; of box hedges; of peaches, lilacs, syringas; of stables, barns, cow-yards; of salt water and low tide on the marshes; nothing came amiss." [HENRY ADAMS]

27. COMPARE: "In studying the heavens, we are debarred from all senses

except sight. We cannot touch the sun, or travel to it; we cannot walk around the moon, or apply a foot-rule to the Pleiades. Nevertheless, astronomers have unhesitatingly applied the geometry and physics which they found serviceable on the surface of the earth, and which they had based upon touch and travel. In doing so, they brought down trouble on their heads, which it was left for Einstein to clear up. It turned out that much of what we learned from the sense of touch was unscientific prejudice, which must be rejected if we are to have a true picture of the world." [BERTRAND RUSSELL]

28. COMPARE: ". . . light was thought by Newton and his disciples to be due to actual particles travelling from the source of the light. But when this view of light was disproved, and it was shown that light consisted of waves, the aether was revived so that there should be something to undulate. The aether became still more respectable when it was found to play the same part in electromagnetic phenomena as in the propagation of light. It was even hoped that atoms might turn out to be a mode of motion of aether. At this stage, the atomic view of matter was, on the whole, getting the worst of it." [RUSSELL]

29. See note 2, p. 327.
30. H. A. Murray.
31. E. Duckett.
32. See pp. 121–22.
33. See pp. 257–58.

INDEX OF AUTHORS
AND SOURCES

SUBJECT INDEX

Absolute phrase, 40, 73, 109
Abstractions, adding to active vocabulary, 137; elusive, 141–42; definitions of, 142; giving tangibility to, 179–82, 238; in generalizations, 232–34; as topic sentences, 234–37; exercise, 314
Active voice, 24, 92–96
Adjectives, 16, 33; appositional, 33; predicate, 24, 33; with adverbial modifier, 34; clausal and phrasal equivalents, 67–69
Adjectives and adverbs of intensification, 188
Adverbs, 16, 34–35; clausal and phrasal equivalents, 69–73
Aggravate, 140
Agreement, of pronoun and antecedent, 22–23; of subject and verb, 25–28; exercises, 295–96
Alliteration, 110
Allusion, 152–54; in specialized prose, 152–53; in general prose, 153; clichés in, 153; appropriate use of, 153–54
Ambiguity, 185–87
Analogy, in definitions, 147; as metaphor, 200–201; in expository writing, 247–48; as a fallacy in argument, 271
Analysis as a means of organization, 246
Antecedent of pronoun, 18–19, 22–23, 26
Any, 27
Appositive, 17
Archaisms, 157–58
Argumentative writing, 263–72
Aspect, 192
Assonance, 110
Awful, 140

Beginning an essay, 215–16
Borrowed words, 158–61; changes of form in, 159; changes of meaning in, 159–60; appropriate use of, 160–61; exercise, 313
Briticisms, 158

Causes and effects in exposition, 241–42

Clause, defined, 16; subordinate, 16, 37–39; independent, 16, 39, 69; elliptical, 16, 30–31
Clichés, 202–205; exercise, 313–14
Coherence, 278–79
Collective nouns, 27
Colloquial language, 165–66
Comparison and contrast in exposition, 242–45
Comparison, grammatical, 84–86
Complement, 48
Compound subject, 25
Conciseness, 115–19, 187–90; exercise, 315–17
Conclusions, 90–91, 273–75
Concrete words, 179–82; adding to active vocabulary, 137
Conjunctions, 16, 35–36, 78–79; correlative, 25, 36, 79–80; coordinating, 35–36, 79; subordinating, 36, 69–73; conjunctive adverb, 36; in series constructions, 87–88; exercise, 302–303
Connotation, 148–52; private associations in, 150; divergence among groups, 151; exercise in distinguishing meanings, 307–309
Continuity, 275–79; and word order, 62; and voice of verb, 95–96, 278–79; and subordination, 73–75; and suspended predication, 60–61
Contradictory statements, 264
Coordination, 77–91; faulty, 40–41, 81; ironic, 82–83; as a transitional device (parallelism), 278; exercises, 302–305
Criticism, 141

Dangling modifiers, 30–32, 184–85; exercise, 297–98
Definition, and predication, 66; formal, 137–38, 144; of abstractions, 142; when needed, 142–43; length and complexity of, 143–44; stipulative, 144–45; functional, 145–46; stressing purpose, 146; negative, 146; analytic, 146; by example, 146–47; by analogy,

333